MW00997771

THE LIMITS OF LOYALTY

We prize loyalty in our friends, lovers, and colleagues, but loyalty raises difficult questions. What is the point of loyalty? Should we be loyal to country, just as we are loyal to friends and family? Can the requirements of loyalty conflict with the requirements of morality? In this book Simon Keller explores the varieties of loyalty and their psychological and ethical differences, and concludes that loyalty is an essential but fallible part of human life. He argues that grown children can be obliged to be loyal to their parents, that good friendship can sometimes conflict with moral and epistemic standards, and that patriotism is intimately linked with certain dangers and delusions. He goes on to build an approach to the ethics of loyalty that differs from standard communitarian and universalist accounts. His book will interest a wide range of readers in ethics and political philosophy.

SIMON KELLER is Research Fellow at the Centre for Applied Philosophy and Public Ethics at the University of Melbourne, and Adjunct Professor in the Department of Philosophy at Boston University.

THE LIMITS OF LOYALTY

SIMON KELLER

CAMBRIDGE
UNIVERSITY PRESS

CAMBRIDGE UNIVERSITY PRESS

Cambridge, New York, Melbourne, Madrid, Cape Town, Singapore, São Paulo

Cambridge University Press
The Edinburgh Building, Cambridge CB2 8RU, UK

Published in the United States of America by Cambridge University Press, New York

www.cambridge.org
Information on this title: www.cambridge.org/9780521874618

© Simon Keller 2007

First published 2007

Printed in the United Kingdom at the University Press, Cambridge

A catalogue record for this publication is available from the British Library

ISBN 978-0-521-87461-8 hardback

Contents

Preface

We all have loyalties; think of some of yours. Probably, many of your loyalties are to other people: your friends, for example, and perhaps your colleagues, parents, children or romantic partner. You might also be loyal to certain institutions, like a university or a political party; or to your favorite brands or shops or restaurants; or to your pets, your country or your profession. Some of your loyalties, probably, are very important to you, playing a major role in your life and your self-conception; examples might be your loyalties to your spouse and children. Others, while having their place, probably do not seem quite so important: your loyalty to a local coffee shop, say, or your loyalty to your favorite football team.

If you are loyal to something, then you probably favor it, in one way or another, in your actions. You might promote its interests, treat it with respect or veneration, follow its orders, or act as its advocate. But loyalty is not just a matter of how you act; it is also a matter of how you think, and how you are motivated. If you are loyal to something, then thoughts of it may inflame your passions, it may be something towards which you feel warmth and affection, and you may be saddened by thoughts of its suffering or demise. You may think of it as *yours* – your country, your friend; in any case, you probably think of it as something with which you have a special connection, perhaps by virtue of a shared history or commitment. You may also form judgments about it in distinctive ways; you might give it the benefit of the doubt, or trust it implicitly, or you might, as someone who has a stake in its performance, judge it with an especially harsh and critical eye. And it may play a special role in your imagination; you may imagine it to meet a certain ideal, and you may imagine yourself as its special champion or guardian.

This book is about the nature of loyalty, and the ethical issues that loyalty raises. I am particularly interested in three questions. First, what is involved in different forms of loyalty? For example, what exactly is patriotism, and how does it differ from other kinds of loyalty? Second, how should different forms of loyalty be regarded from an ethical point of view? For example, are we obliged to show certain sorts of loyalty to our parents, and is it always good to be a good friend? Third, what is the ethical status of loyalty as a general proposition? For example, is loyalty a virtue, and is it, as some suggest, the phenomenon on which healthy moral thinking is founded?

We need to pay a great deal of attention to the first question before we can make much progress with the other two. There are many ways in which loyalties differ, in kind as well as in object. A loyal patriot, for example, does not treat her country in the same way that a loyal friend treats her friends, or that a loyal parent treats her child, or that a loyal fan treats her favorite football team. The differences between loyalties are ethically significant. Just because we say that one kind of loyalty is good, dangerous, permissible, obligatory, or whatever, does not mean that we should say the same about other kinds of loyalty. Investigating loyalty and its ethical significance begins, then, with questions in moral psychology. We should start by looking carefully at different kinds of loyalty, and the kinds of action and thinking that they involve, and only then look to questions about loyalty in general.

In taking this approach, I set myself apart from most philosophical writing on loyalty. The literature on loyalty can be divided into two major strands. The first and most prominent is the discussion of the problem that loyalty poses for universalist morality.[1] Universalist

---

[1] The literature is vast. For some examples, see Godwin, *An Enquiry Concerning Political Justice*, Book II Chapter 2; Stocker, "The Schizophrenia of Modern Ethical Theories"; Williams, "Persons, Character and Morality"; Baron, "Impartiality and Friendship"; Railton, "Alienation, Consequentialism, and the Demands of

moral theories say that individuals are valuable by virtue of properties that they possess inherently, like rationality or sentience, and that our moral principles should therefore be impartial principles; they should not pay attention to how others happen to be connected to us. Loyalty is a problem for universalist morality because loyalty involves partiality (if you are loyal to your daughter, then you favor her over other children, just because she is your daughter); and it seems obvious that loyalty is sometimes desirable (it would be wrong *not* to pay special attention to the interests of your own daughter). Yet universalist theories, like utilitarianism and Kantianism, seem to imply that we should be impartial (your daughter is no more valuable than anyone else simply because she is your daughter). Should we then reject universalist morality, or disapprove of loyalty? Or can loyalty be satisfactorily accounted for after all, provided our universalism is sufficiently sophisticated?

The second strand of philosophical writing about loyalty is more constructive, sometimes aggressively so. It is a strand followed in the two major English-language books about loyalty, Josiah Royce's *The Philosophy of Loyalty* and George P. Fletcher's *Loyalty*, as well as in much communitarian writing. Its central claim is that loyalty is a central human need and, indeed, the foundation of moral agency. You need to be loyal, runs the suggestion, in order to understand or construct your very identity, and in order to have a plan for a moral life and the motivation to live it. The moral life is, or at least grows out of, the loyal life.

Both strands of the literature on loyalty have features that tend to obscure the questions I am most interested in. First, they involve top-down approaches to the ethics of loyalty. We start with a high-level moral theory, then we see if we can find and cope with potential counter-examples; or, we set out with the ambition of showing how loyalty can serve as the foundation of morality, then try to make individual loyalties fit into that project. Secondly,

Morality"; Cocking and Oakley, "Indirect Consequentialism, Friendship, and the Problem of Alienation"; Velleman, "Love as a Moral Emotion"; and the articles referred to in the discussion of universalism and communitarianism in Chapter 3.

neither approach has much use for subtle distinctions between loyalties. For the literature on loyalty and universalism, what matters, for the most part, is that loyalty involves partiality. For the project of grounding morality in loyalty, there is pressure to make loyalty look like a single, unified phenomenon – a basic element in whose terms more complex moral phenomena can be explained.

This book takes a "bottom-up" approach to the ethics of loyalty. I begin by looking at some particular kinds of loyalty and some of the ethical issues they raise, then move on to consider loyalty as a more general phenomenon. As far as possible, I proceed independently of any agenda in higher-level theory. The first part of the book examines different kinds of loyalty, focusing on friendship, patriotism and filial loyalty. The second part of the book turns to questions about the place that loyalty should take in our thinking about morality. I argue that there is no such value or virtue as loyalty, and that the notion of loyalty is not suited to any foundational theoretical role. Here is a summary of the chapters.

Chapter 1 offers and defends a definition of loyalty, arguing that the concept of loyalty is fairly thin – there are many very different things that all count as forms of loyalty – and that it is not deeply evaluative; there is no conceptual reason to think that just because something counts as a loyalty, there is something good about it.

Chapter 2 is about friendship; I argue that good friendship can involve being prepared to form beliefs independently of the evidence, and that there are sometimes good (epistemic) reasons not to conduct yourself as a good friend. Chapters 3 and 4 are about patriotism; again my concern is with dispositions of belief. I try to show that patriotism involves a tendency towards self-deception, of a certain unattractive sort, and that this is a reason to think that patriotism is a vice. Chapters 5 and 6 discuss filial loyalty, by way of filial duty. I begin with the conviction that we have special duties to our parents, defend a particular account of how those duties arise, and end with the claim that filial loyalty – in the fully fledged psychological sense – can be a duty.

The remainder of the book focuses upon the moral role of loyalty, considered as a general notion. Chapter 7 argues that loyalty is not a value or a virtue. Chapter 8 considers and tries to defuse some well-known arguments for the claim that loyalty has some kind of central ethical importance. Chapter 9 looks closely at the system developed in Royce's *The Philosophy of Loyalty*. I argue that the development of Royce's thought reveals some formidable obstacles to the project of replacing universalist morality with an "ethics of loyalty," as well as some problems for a certain broad kind of communitarianism. Chapter 10 is about disloyalty, and the question of whether a view like mine, according to which loyalty is not a virtue, can explain why disloyalty seems so clearly to be a vice. The Conclusion states the overall view of loyalty and its value to which the arguments of the book lead.

It will already be clear that I have something to say about the view that loyalty could be the foundation of morality; I think that it is mistaken. I do not address the literature on loyalty and universalism directly in the main body of the book, though I touch upon it at several points. In the Postscript, though, I try to bring together the various claims that are relevant to that debate, and make some tentative suggestions.

Beyond advocating views about friendship, patriotism, filial duty and the ethical status of loyalty and disloyalty, I hope to advance a programmatic suggestion too. The psychology of loyalty is complicated, and often problematic. Loyalties affect the way we behave, the way we think about ourselves, and the way we form beliefs, among other things. The psychology of loyalty constitutes an important area of ethical enquiry. I hope to show that the right way to engage in that enquiry is to start with careful distinctions between different kinds of loyalty, and also that much of the enquiry can be carried out in isolation from commitments to higher-level moral and political ideologies.

Acknowledgements

Many people have contributed to the writing of this book, through conversations about the material and in other ways. I have the space (and memory) to mention only some of them.

Much of the book was written while I was a fellow at the Center for Ethics at Harvard University. I am grateful to the Center and the Boston University Humanities Foundation for funding my time there, and to Arthur Applbaum and my group of fellows for helpful discussions about my work. I owe special thanks to Deborah Hellman and Catherine Lu, who gave comments on drafts of several chapters.

I have talked through almost all of the material in the book, at one time or another, with Casey O'Callaghan, Aaron Garrett, David Lyons, Amelie Rorty and Caspar Hare. My thoughts about patriotism owe much to conversations with Igor Primoratz and Marcia Baron. I have benefited from the input of several audiences at talks and conferences; I received especially helpful feedback during vigorous conversations about friendship at the University of Manitoba in Winnipeg, about filial duty at Monash University, and about Royce at the "Royce and Community" conference in Oklahoma City. My chair, Charles Griswold, has been very supportive of my research and my requests for time to focus on it.

Two of my reviewers for Cambridge University Press, I now know, were Jimmy Altham and John Doris. I learned a great deal from their careful and generous reports, and also from that of a third reviewer, who remains anonymous. Nick Zangwill provided helpful feedback and suggested the book's title. While preparing the final manuscript, I received very extensive and insightful comments from

Alice MacLachlan; these led to many changes in the text and in my thinking, and made me aware of just how far I am from having said the last word.

Most of all, I am grateful for the support and encouragement of my wife, Maree Henwood. I fear that it would send the wrong message to dedicate a book called *The Limits of Loyalty*, so let me just say that she is the one who makes it all possible and worthwhile.

Some of the material in the book has been previously published, in the following articles.

"Friendship and Belief," *Philosophical Papers* 33:3 (2004): 329–351.

"Patriotism as Bad Faith," *Ethics* 115:3 (2005): 563–592.

"Four Theories of Filial Duty," *Philosophical Quarterly* 56:223 (2006): 254–274.

"Royce and Communitarianism," *The Pluralist* 2:2 (2007): 16–30.

CHAPTER I

What is loyalty?

THE QUESTION

There are different things to which you can be loyal and different ways in which you can be loyal. The way you feel and act towards your spouse, for example, is probably quite different from the way you feel and act towards your favorite football team, even though both are manifestations of loyalty.

This chapter begins to formulate a definition of loyalty, looking at what it is that all loyalties have in common, and how loyalties can differ in object and type while still counting as loyalties.

As far as possible, I want to answer these questions without prejudging or second-guessing our everyday uses of the concept. In telling a story about the nature of loyalty, there is a temptation to try to guarantee that anything that *really* counts as a loyalty will be something valuable, or something that deserves our approval. But I do not think that we should begin from the assumption that loyalty is, or ought to be made to look like, something that answers to certain independent evaluative standards. The first goal is to reach a better understanding not of true or good or sensible or rationally defensible loyalty, but just of loyalty.

Loyalty is sometimes spoken of as a character trait, as when we say that a particular person is, as well as being brave and clever, loyal. We can also speak of loyalty as a principle or ideal. Behind all these ways of thinking about loyalty, though, is the idea of a certain kind of relationship between individuals and the things to which they are loyal. There is the subject who is loyal, and there is the object to which she is loyal (which I will sometimes, unimaginatively, call X).

I start by making some important, but often overlooked, observations and distinctions. Then, I examine some of the things that philosophers say or presuppose about loyalty's nature. All of this in hand, I offer and defend my own suggestion about what makes something a loyalty.

LOYALTY AND CONSCIENTIOUSNESS

Imagine a person who has thought through the arguments and decided that classical utilitarianism is correct, and who, as a result, always endeavors to maximize happiness and minimize suffering. It is natural to say that she is committed to the cause of maximizing utility, and, if she follows the utilitarian principle in her everyday life, that she is principled and conscientious. (If you doubt that a utilitarian can really be principled or conscientious, then imagine a conscientious Kantian, or a conscientious follower of some other ethical theory.) It would be forced, though, to say that she is *loyal* to utilitarianism. What drives her is not loyalty to the utilitarian principle, but rather her considered conviction that that principle is true.

The point here is not that abstract moral principles are not the sorts of things to which a person can be loyal. Perhaps they are. Imagine a different person who also follows the utilitarian principle as best he can, but does so not because he thinks that the principle is true, exactly, but rather because he identifies with it; perhaps he has been brought up in a community of utilitarians, has developed a fondness for the utilitarian principle, and thinks of it as one to which he, by virtue of his unusual history, has a special connection. He follows the utilitarian principle because he thinks of it as *his* principle. It seems fair enough to say that this character is loyal to utilitarianism, and that that is why he acts as he does.

I take this to show that there is a difference between loyalty and conscientiousness. Just because someone deliberately follows a principled pattern of behavior, or is committed – perhaps fiercely – to a cause, does not mean that she is loyal.

The point is related to a further one, which is that the facts about how a person acts are not in themselves enough to tell us whether, or to what, she is loyal. If I reliably keep my promises to you, then that might be because you are someone to whom I am loyal. Or, it might be because I believe that people should always keep their promises, or because I want to think of myself as the kind of person who always keeps promises, or because I promised your father that if I made you any promises I would keep them. In these later cases, it appears that the loyalties that drive me to act, if any, are to things other than you. The fact that you act towards something in the way that you would if you were loyal to it does not establish that you really are loyal to it. Whether or not you are loyal to something depends not only on what you do, but on how you are motivated.

EXPRESSIONS OF LOYALTY

There are several broad ways in which loyalty might be expressed. I want to focus attention on five. I will call them "loyalty in concern," "loyalty in advocacy," "loyalty in ritual," "loyalty in identification," and "loyalty in belief." I do not mean the list to be exhaustive. There may well be other ways of manifesting loyalty. And, I do not mean to suggest that every expression of loyalty falls neatly into just one of these categories; the boundaries between types of loyalty can be blurred.

Loyalty in concern

You might express your loyalty to X by prioritizing X's interests, or welfare, over the interests of comparable others. To prioritize X's interests is to care more about X's interests than about the interests of others, and to be motivated to do more to advance them. If you prioritize X's interests, and if you do it out of loyalty to X, then you are displaying loyalty in concern.

A parent's loyalty to her child, for example, typically includes loyalty in concern. A loyal parent is prepared to do things for her own child that she would not do for just any child.

Loyalty in advocacy

Imagine that you feel an allegiance to Al Gore. Perhaps you have always liked and admired him, perhaps he did something kind for you many years ago, or perhaps you are from the same town. At a dinner party, your companions start to talk about what a hopeless presidential candidate Gore was, and how incompetent he must have been to lose that election. You disagree, but if they were talking about anyone else you would play along or just stay silent. But this is Al Gore, so you feel compelled to say something in his defense. It is natural to think that in doing so you are acting out of loyalty to Gore. It may certainly seem that way to you; given the way that you feel about Gore, it may seem to you that you would be letting him down or doing the wrong thing by him if you did not stick up for him in this hostile environment. Your loyalty is expressed here as something other than a preparedness to do what advances its object's best interests. You are not trying to advance Al Gore's interests by defending him at the dinner party. (Perhaps there is a respect in which Gore is better off if he has a vocal sympathizer at a distant dinner party, but it is far-fetched to think that *that* consideration is what drives you to take your stand.) Rather, you are expressing your loyalty to Gore by being his advocate, by standing by him or sticking up for him.[1] That is loyalty in advocacy.

Loyalty in ritual

Loyalty is sometimes expressed through the performance of or participation in rituals, or more generally in practices that are understood to symbolize or express loyalty.[2] This is obviously the case with regard to patriotism; when a person expresses her patriotism

---

[1] Stroud gives a similar case, in which you are present when someone makes a mean joke about your friend: "it is *disloyal* to join in the joke". "Epistemic Partiality in Friendship," p. 503.

[2] See the discussion in chapter 4 of Fletcher's *Loyalty*.

by reciting a pledge of allegiance, saluting the flag or standing to attention during the national anthem, she is participating in a structured, conventional ritual that carries meaning as an expression of loyal commitment to country. For another case, think of someone who does not especially enjoy or value attending church for its own sake, but nevertheless feels loyal to her religious heritage and goes to church every week for that reason. It would be distorting things to say that she is trying to advance the interests of her religious heritage, or that she is acting as its advocate. Rather, through the ritual of attending church she honors and affirms her loyal commitment to the way of life in which she was raised.

There are many other cases in which loyalty is expressed in the same basic way – cases in which loyalty is manifested through the engagement in rites or practices or customs that are conventionally associated with loyalty – even though the word "ritual" is probably not the one we would first choose to describe the behavior involved. In wearing a wedding ring, or staying to the very end of your team's game even though it is losing badly and the weather is miserable, you are doing something similar to the patriot in saluting the flag. It is less a matter of trying to benefit the object of your loyalty, or advocating its cause, than doing what you do if you really are a loyal romantic partner or fan.

George P. Fletcher suggests that the point of engaging in a ritual of loyalty is to demonstrate loyalty, by which he means that the point is to communicate loyalty, to make it public and visible; through rituals, he says, communal loyalties are established and deepened.[3] I think that the more fundamental unifying feature of rituals of loyalty is that those who perform them see them as ways of honoring and respecting the objects of their loyalties. A patriot who salutes the flag in private is not communicating her loyalty to anyone, but she is still expressing her patriotism. The person who attends church out of loyalty to her religious heritage, or who wears a concealed token of her love for her romantic partner, may well do so not in order to announce her loyalty, but just as its

---

[3] See *Loyalty*, chapter 4, especially p. 62.

expression. She is venerating the thing to which she is loyal, whether her veneration is communicated to anyone or not.

Loyalty in identification

One way in which someone's loyalty might be expressed is through a tendency to identify herself with the object of her loyalty. Such a loyal person to some extent treats the thing to which she is loyal as though it was her, feeling as she would feel and acting as she would act if certain things that are true of it were true of her. If your loyalty to your favorite sporting team is expressed in such a way, then you may feel like a success yourself when your team is doing well, and like a failure when your team is doing badly. You may feel pride when your team does something good – when it wins a tough game or raises money for charity – and you may feel shame when your team does something bad – when it gives an insipid performance or mistreats its players. Such reactions exist beyond any tendencies to want to advance the interests of the object of your loyalty, to serve as its advocate, or to venerate it through involvement in appropriate rituals.

Loyalty in belief

The last kind of loyalty that I want to discuss has its primary expression not in particular emotions, desires or actions, but rather in the tendency to form or resist certain beliefs. As someone's loyal friend, you may be especially inclined to believe that she is not guilty of the crimes of which she is accused. As a loyal parent, you may be especially inclined to believe that your child has special virtues and talents. As a loyal fan of a football team, you may be especially inclined to believe that it was someone from the other team who started the fight.

Your loyalty to X is expressed as loyalty in belief if being loyal to X inclines you to hold or resist certain beliefs, independently of the evidence. One way of seeing whether you are displaying loyalty in belief is to ask whether you would have the beliefs that you have about X if it were not X but some other comparable thing (to which you are not loyal) that was involved, and if you had just the same evidence with regard to this alternative thing as you actually have with regard to X. So, a father might be displaying loyalty in belief if he believes, having watched his daughter play in a soccer game, that she was one of the best players on the field, but would not believe the same about another girl if he saw her do on the field exactly what was done by his daughter. Later chapters show that loyalty in belief is a common and often problematic part of some familiar manifestations of loyalty.

LOYALTY AND SELF-AWARENESS

A curious feature of loyalty in belief is that it is difficult to see how someone could display it with full awareness of what she is doing. It is difficult to see how someone could form a belief in conscious response to a consideration that she knows not to bear upon its truth.[4] (There is something very odd about someone who believes P, while happily admitting that her reasons for believing P do not bear upon the question of whether P is true or false.) Rather than being a problem for the idea that loyalty could be expressed as loyalty in belief, this observation illustrates something that there is good independent reason to believe: it is possible to be loyal to something, and to have your loyalty influence your actions, without knowing it.

Suppose that you are on a hiring committee, and a good friend of yours is an applicant for the job. You make a special effort to consider your friend's application on its merits and without bias, and believe that your effort is successful. After considering all the applicants, you come to the conclusion that your friend really is the best person for the job, and so he gets your vote. Some years later, perhaps after your friend has been hired and the appointment has not worked out well, you look back at the hiring process and realize that really, all along, you were influenced by your loyalty to

[4] See Williams, "Deciding to Believe."

your friend. You thought at the time that you were not acting out of loyalty, but, looking back, you realize that you were.

Along similar lines, people can be imagined who insist that they are not loyal to something, when it is clear to others that they are. I might insist, and really believe, that I feel no love or loyalty towards my father, and that when I do things for him I am really just acting out of self-interest – trying to secure my inheritance or keep him off my back – when it is obvious to those around me that I am wrong about my motivations, that I am in denial about the deeply felt connection with my father which really leads me to act as I do, even as I do my best to rationalize it away.

There is, by the way, a quite different argument that could show that those who are loyal need not be aware of it: some nonhuman animals can be loyal. Some birds are loyal to their mates, and a dog, or a breed of dog, can be informatively described as more loyal than another. But loyal birds and dogs presumably are not aware of being loyal, because they have no idea what loyalty is. (The same might be said of young children.) I suppose that when we talk about loyalty in animals we might just be getting it wrong – perhaps animals are not really *loyal* at all – and it is possible that loyalty in animals, though it exists, is utterly different from loyalty in humans. My own view is that animals really can be loyal and that some kinds of loyalty in animals are not so different from some kinds of loyalty in humans. I am, for this reason, motivated to provide an account of loyalty that is less intellectualized than some.[5] But my arguments for the account will not depend upon the claim about animals.

LOYALTY AS PRIORITIZING INTERESTS

The next two sections describe and criticize some claims about the nature of loyalty that appear in the philosophical literature. Philosophers who write about loyalty sometimes take it for granted that to be loyal to something is to have a special concern with its

[5] For a different view, see Fletcher, *Loyalty*, pp. 9–10.

interests. Philip Pettit, for example, says that "to be loyal is to be dedicated to a particular individual's welfare"; and R. E. Ewin suggests that loyalty is, at least in part, "the binding of oneself preferentially to the interests of a certain group or individual," and, later, that loyalty is a willingness to "take the interests of others as one's own."[6]

The philosophers who work with this conception of loyalty tend to be those who are dealing with the question of whether a universalistic moral theory can make room for partiality. The problem here is essentially a structural one: if a moral theory says that the value of individuals has nothing to do with their particular connections to other individuals, can it nevertheless allow us to favor some individuals in virtue of the connections that they happen to hold to us? To motivate the discussion, all that is needed is an idea of someone who acts well, even while acting partially. This partiality is, in such discussions, called "loyalty."

I have suggested that there are ways of expressing loyalty that do not come down to prioritizing the interests of the loyalty's object; there are expressions of loyalty other than loyalty in concern. That might be consistent with the conception of loyalty under discussion, though, if it turns out that prioritizing something's welfare is always a way of being loyal to it, and if loyalty, whatever else it involves, always includes loyalty in concern. But that is not the way things are; prioritizing X's interests is neither sufficient nor necessary for loyalty to X.

You can prioritize something's interests without being loyal to it. I might prioritize your interests because I was ordered to do so by my commanding officer, or as a way of expressing my loyalty to your father, or because I decided for my own eccentric reasons to prioritize for the rest of my life the interests of the next person to walk through that door, who happened to be you. In all these cases, I am prioritizing your interests without feeling any special regard for you. They all count as cases in which I

[6] Pettit, "The Paradox of Loyalty," p. 163. Ewin, "Loyalty and Virtues," pp. 406, 419.

prioritize your interests, even though you are not someone to whom I am loyal.

Further, you can be loyal to something without prioritizing its interests. A university professor works at an institution whose president is very unpopular among the faculty. This professor, like his colleagues, has no affection for the president; he dislikes and disapproves of him, and thinks it would be a very good thing if he were replaced. Still, the professor will not, on principle, criticize the president, or sign petitions calling for his removal. The reason he will not speak out against the president is that the president played a large part in bringing this professor to the university, and the professor feels that he owes the president his job. To that extent, he feels a special connection to the president, and feels that it would be disloyal – that he would be failing to honor this special connection – if he were to turn around and speak badly of the president.

This does not change the fact that the professor really does not care for the president. The professor's belief is not that speaking out against the president would cause him harm – the professor may well judge that his involvement will make no difference to anything – but rather that it is inappropriate, or unedifying, for one who owes his job to the president to then take a stand against him. There is certainly no generalized concern for the president's welfare; the professor would not make special sacrifices in order to secure any of the president's best interests, and would not be upset to learn that the president had fallen under a bus. His loyalty, which is, in its own way, deeply felt, is expressed purely through a refusal to criticize the president in public. He is recognizably loyal to the president, but does not prioritize his interests.

There is really nothing odd about this case. Cases in which loyalty to X does not involve a heightened level of concern for X's interests are quite common. Let me give one more example. If I am loyal to a brand of running shoes, then I have a kind of emotional attachment to the brand and go out of my way to buy and wear shoes of this brand rather than others. Perhaps it is in the interests of the brand to have a customer like me, but I certainly do not buy and wear the shoes with that in mind. I am not motivated to benefit the brand; I am loyal to it, but only in so far as I am motivated to wear its shoes. Whether I would do anything to make it better off – whether I would be motivated to help save the brand from bankruptcy or help it expand into a new market – is another matter entirely.

LOYALTY AND THE SELF

A different claim about the essential nature of loyalty is often made by those whose initial interest in loyalty comes from a desire to embrace it, or to show what a deep, rich and important notion it is; this is the second strand in the literature on loyalty, referred to in the preface. The claim is that for you really to be loyal to something, it, or your being loyal to it, must have some intimate connection with your identity. Different authors construe that connection differently – actually, its nature is usually left obscure – but here are two pertinent cases in which it is invoked.

Fletcher gives perhaps the most thoroughly worked-out story about the connection between loyalty and personal identity, through his notion of "the historical self." The historical self, for Fletcher, is constituted by the distinctive features of an individual's history, with an emphasis upon those that cannot be chosen, like the individual's being of a certain family, nation and religious heritage. Liberal conceptions of the self, Fletcher says, take the self as fully formed prior to any particular relationships with others, and in this they go wrong; the "ethics of loyalty," which Fletcher defends, "takes relationships as logically prior to the individual."[7] The historical self, then, is taken to be in a sense the true self, and it is in the historical self that the ground of loyalty, for Fletcher, is to be found. The historical self is the source of loyalties – it "generates duties of loyalty toward the families, groups, and nations that enter into our self-definition" – and it is the *only* source of loyalties – "as the historical self inculcates a sense of loyalty, loyalties, especially to

[7] p. 15.

nations, derive exclusively from the historical self."[8] For Fletcher, being loyal is hence fundamentally a matter of personal identity. In acting loyally, "one recognizes who one is."[9]

A slightly different story is told by Richard Rorty. He says that the self is "a centre of narrative identity," and that it is at least partially constituted by memberships of particular communities.[10] Moral dilemmas, says Rorty, arise when a person's loyalty to one group conflicts with her loyalty to another group; if you are deciding whether to look after your sick mother or go away to fight fascism, for example, then your loyalty to your family conflicts with your loyalty to your country. When deciding what to do in such cases, Rorty says, you are deciding which loyalty to privilege, hence with which community you are most fundamentally aligned, hence which community is most fundamental to the narrative with which you identify. In deciding to which things we are loyal, then, we are choosing "between alternative selves."[11]

In all this talk about the connection between loyalty and personal identity, it can be difficult to see exactly what claim is being made, and what is meant literally and what is supposed to be taken as rhetorical flourish. I suspect that those who say that your loyalties make you who you are often mean merely to say that loyalty really matters, that the facts about a person's loyalties are very interesting and important facts about that person. Nevertheless, the suggestion that a person is made who she is by her loyalties arises so often that we ought to try to see whether it is, taken literally, true – and, if not, whether there is any less-than-literal sense in which it is both plausible and interesting.

Let me start with a problem case for the thesis. You are a loyal fan of a football team. As a loyal fan, you follow and care about the team's fortunes, you go to a game every now and then, you own

---

[8] pp. 16, 17. It may be that Fletcher is hedging his bets when he makes the perplexing suggestion that loyalties to nations derive *especially* exclusively from the historical self.

[9] p. 25.   [10] "Justice as a Larger Loyalty," p. 141.

[11] "Justice as a Larger Loyalty," p. 141.

some team paraphernalia, you stick with the team through good times and bad, and you resist temptations – perhaps social or geographic – to move your support to some different team. But you are by no means a fanatic. You have plenty of other interests that are far more important to you than football, and there are many people who know you well but have no idea that you are a fan of that particular team. You are not one of those people whose mood seems to be tied almost exclusively to the fortunes of your team; supporting this team is in your eyes a valued but relatively insignificant part of your life.

It would be very far-fetched, in such a case, to suppose that your supporting this football team is partially constitutive of your deepest identity. If you supported a different team, or no team at all, you would still be the same person. Others do not need to know about your interest in football in order to understand who you really are. It is simply not that important. Yet, there is no need to deny that you are in fact loyal to your favorite football team; of course you are. What we have here, then, is a case in which a person is genuinely loyal to something, without that loyalty having anything much to do with her identity, or the essential nature of her self. It is easy to come up with other cases. You can be loyal to your boss, a not-especially-close friend, your pets, or your corner store, without imagining that the loyalties involved are essential to your identity.

Now, when authors like Fletcher and Rorty talk about connections between loyalty and identity, they are probably not thinking of the kinds of loyalties whose role in a person's life is peripheral. They are thinking of loyalties that are passionate and consuming, and saying that *those* loyalties structure the very identities of those who have them. Even this claim, however, in so far as it is supposed to tell us something interesting about the nature of loyalty, is overstated.

If taken literally, the claim is that if you are (deeply and passionately) loyal to something, then your being you depends upon your having that loyalty; it is impossible to imagine *you* without the loyalty; if you ceased to have that loyalty – well, if you ceased to have that loyalty, then you would cease to exist. That strong claim is false. People do, sometimes, betray or otherwise lose their deep and passionate loyalties – patriots go over to the other side, and devoted husbands leave their wives – and when that happens, we have a story of a person who changes in an important respect, not of a person who ceases to exist and is replaced by someone else. People cannot lose their deep and passionate loyalties without changing, but they can do so without changing into other people.

But perhaps there is still something to the basic idea. We certainly often think in ways that are friendly to the suggestion. When you have a strong loyalty to something, you may feel as though in losing that loyalty you would be giving up something that makes you the person you are. You may think that to betray a dear friend, for example, would be to betray not just your friend but also your true self. Do such thoughts not reflect something real about our identities as persons?

They do, I think, but not in a way that reveals anything about the nature of loyalty. There are two points to make. First, it is not the case that all loyalties, even all passionate and consuming loyalties, play this role. Sometimes, your having a particular loyalty may actually inhibit your ability to be, in the sense in question, your true self. A woman who is deeply loyal to an abusive husband, for example, may feel that it is only in purging herself of that loyalty that she will be able to find her authentic identity.

Second, the sense in which your loyalties help constitute your identity is a sense in which virtually anything that counts as an important fact about you can be presented as a fact about "who you really are." It can also be a part of your identity, in this sense, that you want to write a novel, have red hair, or love motor sports. Asked to give up your Saturdays at the raceway, for example, you might feel that to do so would be to abandon something at the heart of your very identity, that your interest in motor sports is so much a part of you that you owe it to yourself not to leave it behind. What you are saying is not that you could not exist without being a motor sports enthusiast, but rather that that interest is a valued part of your distinctive history and something that you want to maintain.

The idea that loyalties are intimately connected to the identities of those who have them ultimately reflects nothing more than the obvious truth that, sometimes, we care very deeply about being and remaining loyal to certain things. In my opinion, the popularity of the idea is largely due to an illegitimate move from the claim that a person's identity is constituted partly by her *membership* of particular communities to the claim that a person's identity is constituted partly by her *loyalties* to those communities; I say more about this in Chapter 8.

WHAT IT IS LIKE TO BE LOYAL

In providing my own account of the nature of loyalty, I want to start by thinking about what it feels like – what seems to be going on within you – when you do something out of loyalty, and know that you are doing it out of loyalty. Here is the case that I will use as an example. You are approached by a superior at the firm where you are employed, and asked to take part in a process that will eventually lead to the outsourcing of several of the firm's jobs, including those of the members of the team with which you currently work. Your task would be to decide which of several agencies would be the best one to whom to contract out the work; once the decision has been made, you will be promoted and your present colleagues will all be fired. After considering your options, you decide, out of loyalty to your colleagues, to turn down the role. If it really is loyalty to your colleagues that motivates your choice – loyalty as opposed to, for example, enlightened self-interest, political ideology, or simple commitment to a principle – then what must be going on in your mind?

First, I think, you will feel an attachment to your colleagues that is in part emotional. There must be something drawing you to turn down the role that is not fully answerable to your rational or considered judgment. Even as you try to think through your options dispassionately, even as you perhaps start to come around to the opinion that it might really be best, all things considered, to accept the role, you will have a strong, emotionally-driven desire to stand by your colleagues, and perhaps a feeling of revulsion at the thought of failing to do so.

Second, what drives you to act as you do will be, in part, consideration for your colleagues. You will be moved by the awareness that the people who stand to lose their jobs are *Joan*, and *Karen*, and *Bob*. Your concern is not with the mere fact that some people will be fired, but with the fact that these particular people will be fired. These people, with the characteristics that set them apart as individuals, will somehow be present in your deliberations and motives.

Third, in acting out of loyalty to your colleagues you will be motivated in part by thoughts of your particular connection to or relationship with them. You are colleagues; you have worked closely together in the past; you have faced the same struggles and enjoyed the same benefits; you know about each other's lives; you have worked and socialized together. These are connections that you do not share with most people, and that most people do not share with your colleagues, and they are connections whose force you will feel as you decide what to do. What motivates you to do the right thing by your colleagues is not just an awareness of their value or interests as such, but an awareness of their special relationship to you.[12]

THE MOTIVE OF LOYALTY

All displays of loyalty, I want to suggest, contain the three elements that I identified in the case just described. Whenever you are loyal to X, you are emotionally drawn, perhaps despite yourself, to regard and treat X in a certain way; your motive is focused upon X itself, recognized as a distinct individual; and your motive depends upon or makes essential reference to a special relationship in which you and X stand. I will take these three phenomena one by one, and say something more about each of them.

---

[12] See Ladd's *Encyclopedia* entry on loyalty, end of p. 97 and beginning of p. 98.

The emotional pull

An emotional attachment is found whenever we look closely at our own displays of loyalty. Part of what makes me a loyal supporter of the Geelong Football Club is the fact that I have passions that draw me towards caring about the club, even when I have decided that there are very good reasons why I should not. When thinking of your loyalty to a dear friend, you will find not just a judgment that you should conduct yourself as a loyal friend would, but also an emotional response that moves you towards such conduct independently of your judgment. Part of what it is to be a patriot is to have an emotional connection to your country, an impulse to serve and take pride in it, regardless of whether or not you think, on reflection, that your patriotism is justified.

Responding to X itself

When you display loyalty to your colleagues, you are aware of them as particular individuals. It would be different if what drove you to stand by your colleagues was something other than loyalty to them. If you were motivated just by your adherence to the principle that people should stand by their colleagues, then your colleagues themselves, as individuals, would not necessarily loom large in your thoughts; you need only know that they, whoever they are, are your colleagues. If you were motivated by loyalty to your father, whom you remember always standing by his colleagues and whom you know would be disappointed in you if you failed to do the same, then it would be consideration of your father that would play the relevant role in your thinking; you will not do what would disappoint your father, because it is *him*.

When I talk about responding to the object of loyalty itself, I am not suggesting that you are responding only to its essential properties, or to its bare haecceity. The point is rather that you are conscious of and drawn towards the thing as a particular distinctive entity, not just by virtue of its falling under some generic description. What I am trying to get at is the difference between having your passions aroused by the thought of "my country, whichever that is," or "the children that happen to be mine," or "whichever baseball team I'm contracted to this year," and having your passions aroused by the thought of Australia, or of Daniel and Steven, or of the Red Sox. Think of a young, as-yet childless couple, who make the odd claim that they are putting money into a college fund out of loyalty to their future children; their claim is odd because they do not yet know who their future children *are*.

The specialness of the relationship

To be loyal to something, I suggest, you must be drawn to it by virtue of a special connection that the two of you share. If you are loyal to your colleagues, then your motivation depends not just upon their being decent people who do not deserve to lose their jobs, but also upon their being your colleagues. If you are an Australian patriot, then you are motivated not just by Australia's being a great country, but also by its being *your* country. If you keep a promise out of loyalty to Bob, then what motivates you is not just the general principle that promises should be kept, nor the thought that it is in general a bad thing for a person to suffer the disappointment of a broken promise; you are motivated by the thought that Bob is a person to whom you made a promise. To put it another way, you are essentially motivated *as a colleague*, or *as an Australian*, or as *a person who made a promise to Bob*.

   The best way to put this is to say that an individual who is loyal to X must have a motive whose nature depends upon, or makes essential reference to, a special relationship that that individual takes herself and X to share. When you are loyal to X, what is presented within your motivation, so to speak, is not only X, but X as something to which you are connected in a special way. There is a distinctive kind of motive that includes this sort of reference to a special relationship. There is a difference between being motivated to look after Joan, on the one hand, and being motivated *as someone who has a special relationship to Joan* to look after Joan, on the other – and this is part of the difference between simply being motivated to look after Joan, and being motivated to look after Joan out of loyalty to Joan.

Fletcher speaks of the "contingency" of the connections that underlie loyalties. To be loyal to X, on Fletcher's account, you must have some connection to X that you might have failed to have to X; you might have had that connection to something apart from X, or to nothing at all.[13] This, however, is not quite the right way of putting it, because we should not rule out the possibility of your being loyal to something on the basis of a connection that you have to it essentially, not accidentally. Philosophers sometimes speak, for example, about loyalty to the human race, so that you are loyal to humanity because it is your species – but this is quite consistent with the claim that you are not just contingently human.[14]

For this reason, I think it better to emphasize not the contingency but the *specialness* of an individual's connection to the object of her loyalty. What matters is that you have, or think that you have, a connection to X that you do not have to just anything (in some relevant comparison class) and that not everyone (in some relevant comparison class) has to X.

A final point to emphasize about the special connections that underlie loyalty is that they really are present in the loyal individual's motives, as opposed to only (if at all) being part of a causal story that explains how the individual came to have those motives. Suppose that you care deeply about Christianity, and are motivated to spread Christian values throughout the world. Suppose that what caused you to value Christian values is your having been brought up in a Christian family; had you not been brought up Christian, you would not be so attached to Christianity. But suppose also that what grounds your commitment to Christianity is your conviction that Christian beliefs are true and Christian values are the greatest values. So far as your motivations are concerned, the fact that you were brought up a Christian is neither here nor there. In this case,

---

[13] p. 9. Note that Fletcher's suggestion here sits uncomfortably with his claims about the *essentially* relational character of the historical self.

[14] See R. Rorty, "Justice as a Larger Loyalty"; and Oldenquist, "Loyalties."

there is a special connection between you and Christianity that explains why you are a Christian, but it is not a connection that makes itself felt in your motives. For that reason – because your commitment to Christianity is not essentially the commitment of someone who has a Christian heritage – I think that it would be a mistake to say that you are loyal to Christianity. It is not *loyalty* that makes you want to spread Christian values throughout the world. It would be different if Christianity presented itself in your motives as importantly *your* religion and *your* heritage; then, perhaps, we would have loyalty.

WHAT IS LOYALTY?

I have had much to say about the kind of motivation that is involved in loyalty. But at what is that motivation directed? What does the motivation of loyalty lead you to do?

One way to see the need for an answer to this question is to see that an individual's motivations can have the features I have identified in the motives of the loyal person, without being of the sort that leads to loyal conduct. Consider the motives that might be had by someone who hates the Yankees. His relevant motives may be emotionally driven, so that he cannot expunge his feelings about the Yankees simply by deciding that he would be better off without them; his motives may be in direct response to Yankees team itself, so that the mere thought of *the Yankees* is enough to get his pulse racing; and his motives may make essential reference to a particular relationship that he and the Yankees share, so that he feels this way about the Yankees by virtue of the special enmity between the Yankees and his own team. In these structural respects, our Yankee-hater's feelings are similar to those of the loyal individual, but of course he is not loyal to the Yankees.

Remember the different expressions of loyalty discussed in the section "Expressions of loyalty." Any of these expressions of loyalty can be ushered in by the motive of loyalty. Moved by loyalty to X, an individual might show a special level of concern for X's interests, become X's advocate, perform rituals that manifest a commitment to X, identify with X, or form or resist certain beliefs pertaining to X. The best way to draw these expressions of loyalty together, I think, is to say that loyal conduct always involves *taking the side* of the object of your loyalty. There are many different ways in which you might take something's side; taking X's side may mean identifying with X, or treating X with concern, respect, veneration, reverence or love, or having any of a number of other attitudes of positive regard toward X. (Attitudes of negative regard would then be such things as hatred, disdain and contempt.) To take something's side is to treat it with an attitude of positive regard.

Pulling all of this together, I think that the following definition of loyalty, and some other concepts in the vicinity, gets things right.

Loyalty is the attitude and associated pattern of conduct that is constituted by an individual's taking something's side, and doing so with a certain sort of motive: namely, a motive that is partly emotional in nature, involves a response to the thing itself, and makes essential reference to a special relationship that the individual takes to exist between herself and the thing to which she is loyal. To be loyal to something is to have loyalty towards it. To act out of loyalty to something is to be driven to action by the motive just described.

None of this is pithy, exactly, but I hope that it is clear enough. The next section fleshes things out by exploring some of the consequences of this account.

SOME CONSEQUENCES OF THE ACCOUNT

First, if my account is correct, then loyalty is a fairly thin concept. The information that a person is loyal to something does not tell you as much as you might expect about how he is disposed to think and behave. There are many different ways of being loyal; a particular loyalty may involve any of several kinds of motive, so long as they have a certain basic structure, and it may involve any of several quite different ways of acting. Your loyalty may or may not involve a tendency to act out of concern for its object's welfare, to form and resist particular beliefs, to engage in particular rituals, and so on.

Second, loyalty is not an intrinsically evaluative concept. Without some substantive argument, there is no guarantee that if something counts as a loyalty then it counts as something good, or something that merits our approval or encouragement. Presumably, the Nazi Party has, for some people in history, been an object of the kinds of motivation and conduct described in my account; there could be a loyal Nazi.

Third, the class of things to which you can be loyal is very large indeed. You can be loyal to anything that arrests your attention and influences your conduct in the right sort of way; if you are emotionally drawn to the thing itself, and if your motive to take its side makes essential reference to a special relationship that you take the two of you to share, then you are loyal to it. Usually, I think, the things to which we are drawn, in the relevant way, are such things as other people or animals, countries and clubs, but an individual could quite conceivably have the same sort of response to a principle, an ideal, a tie that binds him to another (as opposed to the other herself), and so on. All it takes is the requisite kind of psychology, and people have all sorts of strange psychologies.

Fourth, it is possible to bring under the core concept of loyalty loyalties to businesses and brands; these loyalties are discussed frequently in business textbooks, but almost never by philosophers. If you are loyal to Bob's Socks, for example, then you are drawn to buy Bob's Socks rather than some competing brand because it is *Bob's Socks*, and because you feel yourself to be related to Bob's Socks in a special way – you feel that Bob's Socks is your brand, that you are a Bob's Socks customer or a Bob's Socks person – and that motivation exerts some force upon you even when you have decided that in this particular case there are good reasons to choose a different brand. Your feelings about Bob's Socks may of course be related to a history in which you have found buying Bob's Socks to be in your best interests, usually yielding a better price and better quality than you have received elsewhere, but they consist of something more than a simple judgment that it is in your best interests to choose Bob's Socks. That something more, I think, is what is indicated in my account of the nature of loyalty, and is also quite plausibly the thing that businesspeople and advertisers have in mind when they try to generate brand or business loyalty.

Fifth, there is a straightforward reason, on my account, why it is possible to be loyal without knowing it, and that is that it is possible to be mistaken or otherwise lack knowledge about your own motivations. You may fail to realize that you are emotionally drawn towards something; you may fail to realize that you are driven by consideration of the thing itself, as opposed to some other consideration; and you may be unaware of the essential role that your special connection to something is playing in your motivations. These are the sorts of awareness lacked by the characters described earlier, in the section on loyalty and self-awareness.

Sixth, it seems to me that differences between different kinds of loyalty – between *kinds* of loyalty, not just objects of loyalty – are, potentially, of great ethical interest. If so, then there might not be much sense in the questions, "Is loyalty a good thing or a bad thing?," and "What is it that makes loyalty so important?" The sensible questions will, rather, be about the ways in which loyalties differ, and the different ethical treatments that they should be given. The rest of the book demonstrates that the approach that such questions entail – an approach that involves distinguishing between loyalties, emphasizing their differences, assessing them one by one, and doubting that there is such a thing as a general value or virtue of loyalty – is well-founded and productive.

CHAPTER 2

Friendship and belief

LOYALTY IN BELIEF

An incident from the sitcom *Friends*:

Joey and Chandler are driving from New York to Las Vegas, where Joey has landed an acting job that he hopes will be his big break into show business. They are playing a game, which involves Joey asking questions and Chandler giving immediate, unreflective replies. (Example: "Whom would you rather sleep with, Rachel or Monica?") One of Joey's questions is, "Is this job going to be my big break?," and Chandler, before he can catch himself, answers "No." A crisis in the friendship ensues; Joey feels betrayed, and Chandler feels like a betrayer. Joey expels the remorseful Chandler from the car, and drives to Las Vegas alone.

Why should Chandler's admission throw the friendship into question? Not, it seems, because Chandler chooses to *tell* Joey that he does not believe that his big break is imminent. The whole point of the game is to reveal things of which Chandler is only subconsciously aware and would not normally say aloud. There is a crisis in the friendship because Chandler does not believe that this acting job will be Joey's big break. If he were really a good friend, Chandler would have more optimistic beliefs about Joey's prospects – whether the evidence supported those beliefs or not.

Whatever the quality of my *Friends* exegesis, the incident as related certainly connects with some familiar platitudes about friendship. Good friends believe in each other; they give each other the benefit of the doubt; they see each other in the best possible light. The suggestion contained in these platitudes, and in the incident from *Friends*, is that when good friends form beliefs about each other, they sometimes respond to considerations that have to do with the needs and interests of their friends, not with aiming at the truth. That is part of what makes them good friends.

I believe that this suggestion is correct, and hence that good friendship can involve (what I called in the first chapter) loyalty in belief; it can involve the tendency to form certain beliefs and resist others, independently of the evidence. It follows, I will argue, that sometimes, being a good friend can mean failing to be good in another important respect; it can mean failing to be a good believer. Sometimes, to be a good friend, you need to compromise your epistemic integrity.[1]

Later in the book, I will argue that patriotism, too, involves loyalty in belief, and that it, like friendship, comes into conflict with certain standards of good epistemic conduct. The consequences for the ethics of patriotism, though, are quite different from the consequences for the ethics of friendship. So far as our ordinary conduct as friends is concerned, the fact that good friendship is not always compatible with responsible believing is far less surprising, and far less threatening, than it may at first appear. The interesting implications have less to do with how we should behave as friends than with the ways in which philosophers have thought about friendship, both intrinsically and with regard to its place in the ethical life. When it comes to patriotism, I try to make a more damning case – but that is a topic for later chapters.

This chapter concerns friendship; my basic claim is that there can be conflicts between two norms: norms of friendship on the one hand, and epistemic norms on the other. A norm of friendship is a truth about what you should do, in so far as you are a particular

---

[1] The view that friendship involves partiality in belief is also defended in Sarah Stroud's "Epistemic Partiality in Friendship," which appeared at about the same time as the paper of which this chapter is a descendant. Stroud's argument has much in common with the one I offer in this chapter, though there are important respects in which they diverge. Most importantly, Stroud shows more sympathy for (though does not commit herself to) the suggestion that prevailing views about the standards of good believing should be revised so as to accommodate the bias of good friends.

person's good friend. If you and I share a close friendship, then there may be norms of friendship telling me to keep in touch, to come and pick you up when your car breaks down, and to let you know if people are saying horrible things about you behind your back. These are all things that I would not do for just anyone, but they are things that a good friend would do for you. An epistemic norm is a truth about what you should do, in so far as you are an agent who forms and holds beliefs, and who is answerable to reasons for forming and holding beliefs. One epistemic norm might be that you should believe things for which you admit there to be overwhelming evidence; another might be that you should not bring yourself to believe something just because you think that believing it will get you tenure.

When I say that the two norms can conflict, all I should be taken to mean, initially, is that there are cases in which an agent cannot meet both the highest standards of friendship and the highest standards of epistemic responsibility. Later in the chapter, I will turn to questions about which of the two norms is more important, about what it is possible and desirable to do when they conflict, and about what all this says about the relationship between friendship and morality.

TWO OBSERVATIONS

In getting started, two mundane truths are worth noting. First, the fact that a person is someone's friend can sometimes explain why that person is inclined to believe certain sorts of falsehoods. Suppose that someone tells you that her friend was the best player on the football field today, or that her friend would make a perfect employee, or that her friend could not possibly have committed the crime of which she is accused, or that her friend will likely be president within twenty years. You may well doubt that such reports are reliable. This might be because you suspect that your informant is exaggerating, but it might be because you suspect that your informant's beliefs, though truly reported, are biased. Similarly, when discussing a friend of yours with others – when, for example, recommending your friend for a job – you may feel the need to let your audience know that the person under discussion is your friend, not because that is a reason to think that you are lying, but because it ought to be taken into account by those who need to form judgments about the accuracy of your beliefs.

Second, it can sometimes *feel* as though loyalty to a friend pulls you in an opposite direction from your better epistemic judgment. Suppose that your friend is denying an accusation, and that the evidence against her is strong but not conclusive. You might find yourself believing your friend's story, while being uncomfortably aware that, did she not happen to be your friend, the evidence against her would be enough to make you reject her denials outright. Or, you might find yourself beginning to doubt your friend's denials, and feeling a little guilty about it; even if you keep your doubts to yourself, you might feel that in having them you are letting your friend down, just when she needs you most. And, if you maintain your belief in your friend's innocence when others do not, she may praise you for being such a good friend, or tell you that she is learning who her real friends are; if you secretly doubt that her story is true, then her saying such things may make you feel all the guiltier.

The thesis that the norms of friendship can clash with epistemic norms offers one explanation of these observations. With the goal of showing that it is the right explanation, let me offer a more detailed variant of the case from *Friends*.

A FRIENDLY HEARING

Rebecca is scheduled to give a poetry reading at a café. She is nervous about reading her poetry in public, but has decided to do it on this occasion because she knows that a certain literary agent will be present and she hopes that her work might catch his attention. She lets her good friend Eric know that she will be giving the reading, and asks whether he would mind coming along to be in the audience.

Eric, as it happens, is a regular visitor to the café, and has over time accumulated strong evidence for his belief that poetry read there is almost always mediocre, and that it is very unlikely that anything read there would make any literary agent take notice. He had not known that Rebecca fancies herself as a poet, and has no familiarity with her work. But he is her friend, and he makes sure that he is there for the reading.

Think first about Eric's attitudes before hearing Rebecca read. If some stranger were about to give the reading, then Eric would believe that the poetry he is about to hear will probably be pretty awful, not of the type that is likely to impress a literary agent – and he would have good evidence for his belief. Seeing as he is Rebecca's good friend, though, and because he is there to offer her support, he ought not, before she takes the stage, have those beliefs about her. He ought not be expecting that the poetry about to come out of Rebecca's mouth will be awful. Yet, the fact that Rebecca is Eric's friend, rather than a stranger, does not make it any less likely that her poetry will be awful, and there is no need to imagine that Eric, as a friend, should think that it does.

Next, think about the way in which Eric might listen to Rebecca's poetry. If it were a stranger giving the reading, and if Eric were setting out to make an accurate judgment about the poetry's quality and likelihood of impressing an agent, then he would listen attentively and with an open mind, and then form critical and dispassionate judgments, informed by such things as a hard-headed comparison of this work with others and a set of realistic expectations about the average literary agent's psychology.

Rebecca, however, is a friend, and that seems to be a reason for Eric to listen with a more sympathetic ear. In listening as a friend, he will allow the poetry to strike him in the best possible light; he will actively seek out its strengths and play down its weaknesses; he will be disposed to interpret it in ways that make it look like a stronger piece of work. A particular technique might strike Eric as a piece of mindless repetition when used in a stranger's poem, but as a piece of astute dramatic emphasis when employed by his friend.[2] As Rebecca's friend, he should listen to her poetry in a way that makes him more likely to emerge with the belief that it is good poetry, and hence more likely to emerge with the belief that it might well make a favorable impression upon a literary agent. He should put himself into a situation under which it is more likely that he will form certain beliefs, but his reason for putting himself into that situation is not one that bears upon the likelihood that those beliefs are true.

Finally, and related to the two previous points, think about Eric's beliefs after Rebecca's performance has concluded. If her poetry really is brilliant, then he will probably believe that it is. If her poetry is truly awful, then he will probably notice. If Eric behaves as a good friend would, however, then there will be possible situations under which Eric will believe that Rebecca's poetry was pretty good, and that there is a decent chance that the literary agent will show some interest in publishing it, even though he would not have those beliefs about the work of a stranger who read exactly the same poem in exactly the same way.

Now, it is very plausible to think that there is an epistemic norm telling us that our beliefs should, in standard cases at least, be responsive only to the evidence, or to what we take to be the evidence, for or against their truth. And it is plausible to think that there is an epistemic norm telling us not to put ourselves into situations from which we are likely to emerge with beliefs that are not in the right ways responsive to the evidence. (It is epistemically irresponsible to decide to pay attention only to the arguments for one side of an issue, or to make an appointment with a hypnotist who specializes in making his patients believe that they are Napoleon, because to do so is to make yourself more likely to form a belief for reasons other than its being true.) If what has been said in this section is correct, then Eric will violate these norms if he acts as a good friend would. So, this is a case in which the requirements

---

[2] For more on the importance of interpretation in forming judgments about the qualities of others, and on the way in which friendly bias can influence such interpretation, see Stroud, "Epistemic Partiality in Friendship," pp. 506–507.

of good friendship conflict with the requirements of good epistemic judgment.

Much more needs to be said in defense of my presentation of the case. I will clarify my claim, and then consider some objections.

CLARIFICATIONS

The strength of the case does not depend upon its being representative of *all* good friendships. I do not mean to suggest that *any* friend, when placed in a situation similar to Eric's, will come under pressure to listen to her friend's poetry with an especially sympathetic ear, to expect that her friend's poetry will be better than the usual, and so on. It may well be that some of the best and strongest friendships are grounded in the friends regarding each other with an uncompromising lack of bias. To show that the norms of friendship can conflict with epistemic norms, it is enough to show that Eric and Rebecca's friendship *could* give rise to the kinds of norms identified in my presentation of the case, without thereby being a worse friendship than it would otherwise be.

Note also that my rendering of the case is not premised upon the claim that good friends provide each other with slavish, unconditional affirmation. That, of course, is false. A good friend is not a sycophant or cheerleader; he will sometimes tell you truths that are difficult to hear. One of the things to hope for in a good friend is a preparedness to notice, and let you know, when you are pursuing a project at which you have no realistic chance of succeeding, or when you think yourself to have talents that you in fact lack. But this is consistent with my story about Eric and Rebecca.

A sympathetic interpretation need not be ultimately favorable. Even if Eric listens sympathetically to Rebecca's poetry, even if he sees and interprets it in the best possible light, it is possible that he will end up believing that her poetry is no good, and that she does not have a realistic chance of getting it published. And if that is what he concludes, then it is likely that he should, in so far as he is Rebecca's good friend, believe (and tell her) that this project of hers is best left behind. The thought behind my presentation of the example, then, is just that good friendship can require that you make a special effort – effort that you need not make with regard to just anyone – to see value in your friends' projects before you decide (and say) that you think them misguided. (And this seems right. Think about the conditions under which *you* would accept such criticism as an act of good friendship.)

OBJECTIONS

In saying that the norms of friendship can clash with epistemic norms, I am neither saying that such conflicts are pervasive, nor assuming that good friends will only ever have nice things to say about each other. I will shortly mention some deeper truths about friendship that I take to lie behind the posited conflicts, but before that I want to consider some ways of resisting the message that I draw from the case of Rebecca and Eric.

First, it could be suspected that I have read too much into the actions, as opposed to the thoughts, that good friendship requires. The norms of friendship might demand that we act differently towards our friends than towards others, without making any demands upon our beliefs. Perhaps Eric should nod encouragingly and chuckle appreciatively while listening to the reading, and perhaps he should tell Rebecca afterwards that he thought it went well, but he can do all this regardless of whether he believes that the poetry is any good.

This kind of pretend approval, however, is not what we really want in a good friend. It is not likely to be what Rebecca wants when she looks for a supportive person in the audience. You want a friend who is on your side, not one who is good at faking it.

Second, the example performs as advertised only if Rebecca's being Eric's friend does not give him evidence that she will write decent poetry. That assertion can be contested. We do not make friends at random; we make friends with people whom we take to have certain qualities. In particular, we are likely to make friends with people we respect and admire, so it is hardly surprising, it might be said, that we are inclined to expect our friends to display excellence. If Eric really is Rebecca's friend, we might say, then he will have perfectly good reasons to expect that her poetry will be better than average.

There is an important point here. If I say, "That Steven, he certainly isn't a selfish lying scoundrel," and you say, "You only believe that because you are his friend," then you are probably getting things the wrong way around. I am friends with Steven partly *because* I do not think that he is a selfish lying scoundrel. It would be going too far, however, to think that whenever a norm of friendship requires a certain disposition to believe, evidence for that disposition will be found in the prerequisites of the friendship. Friendships need not be predicated upon anything that makes the friends especially likely to be talented poets, and we did not need to stipulate that Eric's friendship with Rebecca has such a basis in order for the example to make sense. The requirement that you be disposed to think well of your friends can extend beyond the cases in which you already have good reason to do so.

Third, it can be granted that good friendship requires the posited tendencies to form beliefs, but doubted that these tendencies conflict with any important epistemic norms. Who says that our beliefs should respond only to evidence? Why not think that Eric's being Rebecca's friend constitutes an unimpeachably solid reason, consistent with all epistemic norms, for him to assume that she is a capable poet with a decent chance of attracting a literary agent's attention?

Well, it seems obvious enough that we are, in standard cases, under some normative pressure to have beliefs that are sensitive to considerations that bear upon their truth and falsity, and to respond to such considerations in reasonably consistent ways. To believe something is to take it to be true, and there is something odd going on when someone forms a belief based on considerations that do not, even on her own considered judgment, have anything to do with the belief's truth. Eric is not in the type of situation described in James's "The Will to Believe," considering a proposition in the absence of strong evidence either way. Eric *does* have relevant evidence. Were it not Rebecca whose poetry is in question, Eric would form beliefs different from those that he is under pressure to form about Rebecca, and would take himself to have perfectly good evidence for those beliefs.

Certainly, if Eric's beliefs were responsive to the pressures that friendship places upon them, and if Eric were willing to bet upon his beliefs, then it would be very easy to take his money; whenever a friend of his gets up to read some poetry, we would just offer Eric a bet on whether or not the literary agent will show any interest. That is one indication that things for Eric are going epistemically astray.[3]

Fourth, does the example really uncover a norm of friendship, or merely something friendship often accompanies? Of course, we might say, friends tend to disregard or go beyond the evidence in their assessments of each other (that is one reason why we do not let them sit on each other's juries), but that is not to say that, in so far as they are friends, they should. Eric's readiness to believe the best of Rebecca may be evidence that he is really her friend, without making him a *better* friend.

It seems to me, though, that the tendency to treat us sympathetically is not only one that we think likely to be manifested in our friends, but one that we can want them to manifest. They can be better friends for having it. We can imagine Rebecca feeling pleased and comforted to think that there is at least one person in the audience who will give her poetry a sympathetic hearing. One of the distinctive goods of friendship is the knowledge that someone is on your side.

I want to say more in defense of the claim that the tendency to have certain sorts of beliefs is the source of a distinctive good in friendship, and hence that we are really dealing with a norm of friendship here. I will start with an intuitive argument, and then try

---

[3] But see the option outlined (though not endorsed) in Stroud, "Epistemic Partiality in Friendship," pp. 522–523. The suggestion there is that epistemic rationality is a more practical matter than is commonly acknowledged, and that this may leave room for a more forgiving attitude to beliefs like Eric's.

to show that the claim fits well with some independently compelling claims about the nature of friendship.[4]

SOME THINGS THAT FRIENDS ARE FOR

I said earlier that not all friendships give rise to norms that conflict with epistemic norms. You are probably unlikely to be convinced of my claim that there can be a distinctive good in having a friend who is inclined to believe certain things independently of the evidence, if what you are thinking of is a friendship between two competent, self-assured philosophers. In a philosophical colleague, there is obvious reason to want someone whose belief-forming mechanisms, when she is dealing with you and dealing with philosophy, aim unflinchingly at the truth. As a way of thinking of a different sort of friendship, think of a relationship that you might have with a coach.

If you are working towards a goal, like increasing your fitness or performing well on an exam, you might benefit from having a coach who does not just teach you skills and give you information, but provides motivation and encouragement. It can be helpful in such a coach to have someone who believes that you really are capable of achieving what you want to achieve, who takes your failures to be temporary and anomalous and your successes to indicate greater things to come, who thinks that the obstacles in your way can be surmounted, and so forth. The reason why it can be helpful to have such a coach is not that those beliefs are probably true, and so a coach with lesser expectations would just be getting it wrong, but that associating with such a coach can make you more positive about your prospects, more likely to work hard and hence more likely to improve. It can also make life more pleasant. This is true, perhaps especially true, even if the coach is overestimating your abilities somewhat, and you can never get quite as far as she thinks you can. And it is true even if an impartial observer would

---

[4] Stroud offers a different (though compatible) story about how good friendship leads naturally to bias in belief, on pp. 510–512 of "Epistemic Partiality in Friendship."

give you a less optimistic assessment; what you will benefit from in a coach is not a hard-headed critic but someone who thinks the best of you.[5]

If you are friends with the people with whom you play in a lunchtime basketball league, with whom you regularly go running, or with whom you are learning a foreign language, then a significant part of your friendship may involve your playing for each other the role of a coach. As a philosopher, you may hope that your friend will notice if your latest idea is misguided, but as an ageing player on the lunchtime basketball team, you may benefit from having people around you who believe, perhaps in spite of the evidence, that you are a capable player who with full fitness will be a potent offensive weapon. When you are battling with injuries, losses of motivation and the pressures of life, you can benefit from having some friends and teammates who are strongly disinclined to think that you made a fool of yourself on the court, or that you were the weak link that caused them to lose. This can be the case even if you know that your friends' beliefs on the relevant matter are biased. Even if you are pretty sure that you *were* the weak link that caused the loss, there is comfort in having friends who will not believe it.

Once noticed, the point can be extended to many cases beyond those in which it is natural to think of the friend as playing the role of a coach. It is encouraging, motivating and reassuring to have friends who are inclined to believe that things for you are improving, that your business venture will work out, that you will surely get published eventually, that you look good in your new outfit, and so on, even as you realize that their beliefs are less than fully reliable. It is one of the good things about having friends.

---

[5] There can also, of course, be dangers in having a coach with an inflated view of your capabilities. Good coaches and motivators are people who, among other things, are optimistic about the prospects of those whom they are coaching, without this leading to their setting expectations or training regimes whose eventual effect will be to harm performance.

OPENNESS, RESPONSIVENESS AND BELIEF

A number of philosophers have developed versions of the idea that good friendship, along with other kinds of love, essentially involves two people's in certain ways opening themselves to each other's influence. Dean Cocking and Jeanette Kennett, more of whose work we will soon encounter in a different context, flesh out this idea by saying that good friends characteristically engage in mutual directing and interpreting.[6] If you are open to being directed by your friend, then you are willing to make decisions, develop new interests and explore new activities, just because your friend leads you towards them; you might, to give one of Cocking and Kennett's examples, happily accept a friend's invitation to the ballet, and go along with an open mind, even though you have never felt any inclination to attend the ballet before.[7] If you are open to being interpreted by your friend, then your views about what you are like are responsive to your friend's views about what you are like; in your interactions with your friend, you come to notice, and perhaps to change or nurture, the characteristics that she sees in you. Through the process of mutual direction and interpretation, runs the view, the self in friendship is altered, not just revealed or reflected.

I doubt that Cocking and Kennett's conditions of mutual directing and interpreting are sufficient for friendship, because I can imagine pairs of people who are open to each other's direction and interpretation, but are not friends.[8] Mogul-one may be utterly obsessed with his rival, Mogul-two, so much so that he allows himself to be directed by all of Mogul-two's interests and activities; if Mogul-two gets a new car, a blond wife or a ballet subscription, then Mogul-one

[6] "Friendship and the Self." See also A O Rorty, "The Historicity of Psychological Attitudes: Love Is Not Love Which Alters Not When It Alteration Finds"; Delaney, "Romantic Love and Loving Commitment: Articulating a Modern Ideal"; and my "How Do I Love Thee? Let Me Count the Properties."
[7] "Friendship and the Self," p. 504.
[8] In defending themselves against the case of the two psychiatrists on p. 523 of "Friendship and the Self," Cocking and Kennett appear to accept that their view is intended to identify necessary and sufficient conditions for good friendship.

has to have one too. Mogul-one may grudgingly concede that his rival is the one person who truly understands him, and his self-conception may be sharply responsive to the snide psychoanalyses offered by Mogul-two in the press. Mogul-two may regard Mogul-one in just the same way. While open to each other's direction and interpretation, the two Moguls may nevertheless despise each other. You can be led by love to be open to another's direction and interpretation, but you can also be led there by obsessive loathing.

That said, Cocking and Kennett identify a necessary condition of good friendship. It seems right to say that two people who are not responsive to each other's direction and interpretation could hardly be good friends. To be someone's good friend is, in part, to expose yourself to the influence of his interests, likes, habits and opinions, and to his ways of thinking about you.

It would be mistaken to say that openness towards a good friend must be predicated upon the independent judgment that this is a person whose interests are likely to interest you, and whose impression of you is likely to influence your self-development positively. Usually, that is not how things work; you do not open yourself up to your friend's influence in response to a judgment that his influence is likely to bring about desirable results. Of course, the kinds of influence that you allow your friend to wield will sometimes depend upon such judgments; you may learn that it is for the best to allow a particular friend to direct you towards attending concerts, but not political events. But there is, without wanting to overstate things, a kind of risk, or facing of the unknown, that arises as you form a close friendship. You are, in a sense, responding to the person himself, not (or not only) to judgments about his tendencies to direct and interpret you in ways that you find attractive – but, to the extent that you become his good friend, these are tendencies to which you are exposed.

Different sorts of openness, or openness to different sorts of things, will be important to different friendships, and in some perfectly good friendships, I want to suggest, the friends will be open to being directed by each other's beliefs. The fact that one friend believes something, or sees the world in a certain way, will sometimes be

taken by the other as a reason to adopt or entertain that same
perspective. I do not take this to constitute an optional extra, a way
of regarding your friend that is merely additional to those already
discussed, but rather to be entangled with the same basic attitude of
openness that gives rise to the phenomena discussed by Cocking and
Kennett. Put it this way: when your friend invites you to come with
her to a rap concert, and you agree to go along, her reason for
wanting to go may not be just that she enjoys the music, but that she
takes it to be an important art form, expressing something meaningful about the reality of contemporary urban life. Her interest in
the concert is associated with her holding certain beliefs, so it is
difficult to see how you could allow yourself to be directed by her
interest without being open to those beliefs – without making some
effort to hear the music as she hears it.

Part of the reason why it is plausible to characterize friendship as
involving such openness and responsiveness is that such attitudes
are closely linked to some of the important goods that friendship
characteristically provides. I am not going to try to offer a com-
prehensive account of why it is good to have friends, or to suggest
that such an account would deal only in the provision of goods to
individuals. But a full story about the value of friendship would
surely mention the goods of sharing and support.

Materially and psychologically, a life shared with friends is less
precarious. To share your thoughts and interests with a friend, and
to take an active interest in hers, is to escape a little from your
individuality, to reduce the intensity of being you; that, in part, is
why it is good to share. To have a supportive friend is, or can be,
to have someone who sees value in your projects and commitments,
even when you – weary or self-doubting – do not. Robert Nozick
says that loving relationships ideally place a floor under your well-
being.[9] One way that they can do so is by mitigating the fickleness
that you sometimes show towards your own priorities.

Sharing and support are two of the goods of friendship, and it is
easy to see why they are more likely to be manifested within a

---

[9] *The Examined Life*, p. 71.

relationship in which each friend is prepared to be guided by the other's interests, and is in the right ways responsive to the other's ways of thinking. Friends who are open to each other's direction and interpretation put themselves into a position from which it is easier to provide wholehearted support.

It is perhaps worth noting that the goods to which I have tried to give expression do not, on the surface, have much to do with the good of being kept on the epistemic straight and narrow. Thinking, indeed, about what motivates us to have friends – what we look for in friendship, and why it is frightening to contemplate a life without it – well, the reinforcement of our epistemic integrity simply does not seem to have much to do with it. Why should there be any guarantee that a really good friend will never depart from epistemic norms? If epistemic norms always were consistent with the norms of friendship, would that not be a surprise?

Anyway, here is what I think is going on in the case of Eric and Rebecca. It is obvious to Eric that Rebecca's poetry is important to her, and that it is important to her because she sees it as having certain qualities and prospects. As a sharing and supportive friend, Eric has a general openness to Rebecca's perspective, especially when it comes to things that matter to her, and in the case under discussion the way to be open to Rebecca's perspective is to be open to the beliefs that are required in order to see her poetry in the way that she sees it. Eric will not be open to Rebecca's way of seeing things, in the relevant sense, if he antecedently expects that her poetry will not be any good, or if he fails to hear it with a special degree of sympathy; and this, for reasons discussed earlier, would put him into conflict with epistemic norms.

WEIGHING UP THE CONFLICTING NORMS

That is all that I am going to say in defense of the claim that epistemic norms can conflict with the norms of friendship. I now want to consider some questions about the claim's significance. I will begin by asking how we should decide which kind of norms to favor in the cases in which they clash, and then move towards some more theoretical considerations.

It is important to distinguish two perspectives from which the question of which norms to favor can be approached. First, we can take the perspective of an observer, asking of a certain person, "Ought his beliefs in this instance conform to the norms of friendship or to epistemic norms?" or asking more generally, "Ought it be the case that people follow epistemic norms or the norms of friendship in these kinds of cases?" Second, we can take the perspective of the believer, asking what kinds of thought processes an agent should go through and what kinds of actions he should choose to take in response to the conflicting pressures of the different norms. It is especially important to distinguish the two kinds of questions because there are well-known difficulties with the idea of an agent consciously forming a belief in response to considerations that she does not take to bear upon its truth. There is something very odd about an agent who has such thoughts as, "I realize that the balance of evidence suggests that this proposition is true, but there are other considerations that I need to take into account before deciding whether to believe it."[10] We might conclude that it is desirable or permissible for an agent's beliefs to be influenced by certain considerations, while accepting that they are not considerations to whose influence the agent can consciously be susceptible.

When different norms conflict, it can be difficult to find a plausible theoretical perspective from which to weigh the competing claims against each other.[11] I am certainly unable to offer a meta-normative theory that would tell us how to choose in any given case between epistemic norms and the norms of friendship. It is still possible, though, to say something about the relative importance of friendship and epistemic integrity, at least with regard to particular sorts of cases.

On the one hand, it seems that epistemic norms always give rise to reasons to believe. If considerations of epistemic responsibility

---

[10] See Williams, "Deciding to Believe."
[11] Wolf, "Moral Saints"; see the last section, especially.

would have you believe something, then there is a reason to believe it; the reason might be defeasible, but it counts for something. To put it another way, there is always a loss, always something to regret, in a failure to follow epistemic norms. Suppose you know that God will destroy the world if you do not believe by next Saturday that grass is pink. It seems obvious that it would be a very good thing for you to believe by next Saturday that grass is pink, and that you ought to visit whichever hypnotists or brain surgeons might help that to be the case. Nevertheless, it is unfortunate that you have to do so. All the epistemic considerations – considerations that have to do with your status as a believer – count against your altering your beliefs in this way, and so a non-trivial sacrifice – a sacrifice of your epistemic integrity – is being made. Even though it is defeated, there is a reason not to save the world through an act of epistemic irresponsibility. Epistemic norms always offer reasons, and it follows from this and the main argument of the chapter that there are sometimes reasons not to be a perfectly good friend.

On the other hand, friendship is a source of many important goods, and some of those goods are dependent upon certain dispositions of friends that involve their forming beliefs in ways inconsistent with full epistemic responsibility. In a world in which everyone always formed beliefs only in the ways dictated by epistemic norms, some of the things that we value about friendship would be missing. So long as the lapses in epistemic responsibility required for the sake of friendship are not too egregious, and so long as they do not have undesirable results in other respects, we can be pleased that ours is not the world of uncompromised epistemic integrity. Observing a person whose failure always to meet epistemic norms is linked to his being a very good friend, we may be pleased that he is as he is, and that he and his friends enjoy certain kinds of sharing and support. Observing a person who always forms his beliefs only on the best epistemic grounds, we may wish that he were a little more susceptible to other sorts of influences upon his beliefs, because he would be a better friend if he were.

My view, then, is that there are reasons to wish for epistemic responsibility and reasons to wish for the kinds of beliefs that produce the distinctive goods of friendship. In some situations where the two conflict, it will make sense to favor the norms of friendship, and in others it will make sense to favor epistemic norms.

Some fairly fine-grained details of the particular cases will matter here, including the facts about how much the believer values having true beliefs about the subject matter at hand. For example, suppose that a friend of yours decides to write a book defending a controversial view about the building of the Egyptian pyramids. If you have no strong antecedent beliefs about or interest in the question of how the pyramids were built, then it might be desirable for you to be especially open to your friend's side of the story, to entertain his theory without making yourself fully aware of its competitors, and hence to be able to offer a kind of support that he will find helpful; the norms of friendship may win out. If, however, you know quite a bit about ancient Egyptian history and have a strong interest in knowing the truth about how the pyramids were built, then the fact that it is your friend who is defending this thesis should not make you any more likely to entertain it sympathetically; epistemic norms turn out to be more important, and there is a kind of friendly support for which your friend, if he needs it, should look elsewhere.

FRIENDSHIP AND BELIEF-MANAGEMENT

While there can be reasons to think that it would be good if the beliefs of a person, perhaps yourself, were sometimes influenced by factors that do not bear upon their truth, this fact cannot enter straightforwardly into the believer's deliberations. You cannot decide to believe something as a conscious response to a consideration that you know to have no bearing on its truth; we do not have that kind of direct control over our beliefs. In indirect ways, though, we can affect our beliefs, by doing such things as making true the thing we want to believe, making decisions about which sources of evidence to consult, surrounding ourselves with people who have a particular point of view, or, at the extremes, visiting hypnotists or neurosurgeons.

There is one way of indirectly managing our own beliefs that is quite commonly used in response to the norms of friendship. The beliefs that go along with good friendship tend to come to us naturally, as a result of the ways in which we regard our friends and the kinds of activity that our friendships involve; usually, we just find ourselves with the relevant kinds of bias towards our friends. When considering a particular belief, you may be unable to admit to yourself that you hold it partly because you are someone's friend, and that your friendship does not make the belief any more likely to be true, without thereby throwing the belief into question. You can, however, be aware of your tendency to form certain sorts of beliefs where your friends are concerned, and if you think that this tendency is harmless or positively desirable, then you can choose not to think too hard about the individual beliefs on which it has influence. You can decide not to make the effort to assume a more objective stance – not to make the effort to critically investigate all sources of evidence – when it comes to your beliefs about your friends. This, I think, is in effect the policy that many of us follow.

The awareness that our beliefs about our friends may be biased can be called into play when what we believe about our friends takes on an increased level of importance. You might genuinely believe, for example, that your friend is an excellent candidate who will surely do very well in the job market. But would you give this friend a job working for you, if you had the power to do so, without hesitating first? You might genuinely believe that your friend is a decent businessperson whose latest project will probably work out for the best. But would you be prepared to invest your own money? Would Eric, after complimenting Rebecca's poetry, smoothly agree to provide the funds for her self-publishing venture? Most of us, when confronted with such decisions, will have a little warning light come on. We are less likely to base important decisions of certain sorts upon beliefs about our friends than upon beliefs about others. It is as though our beliefs about our friends are marked, or quarantined. It is not that we do not really have those beliefs, it is just that we know that the people in question are our friends, and so we are aware that the beliefs might not have been formed for reasons that really bear upon their truth. That is why it is risky to use them, at least without taking a more critical perspective first, when making significant decisions.

Epistemic norms and the norms of friendship, then, each have their own importance. It is not possible consciously to weigh them against each other when forming particular beliefs of your own, but there is an attainable and familiar strategy of belief management that takes the importance of both norms into account.

THEORETICAL APPROACHES TO FRIENDSHIP AND MORALITY

A great deal has been written recently about how the perspective that we take as lovers and friends relates to the perspective that we take as moral agents. Michael Stocker and Bernard Williams, among others, have argued that the ways in which people are regarded from the standpoint of deontological and consequentialist moral theory are very different from the ways in which we regard our friends and loved ones, and the ways in which we hope that they regard us.[12] Here is a brief taxonomy, with commentary, of the philosophical responses to such arguments.

One response is to say that we should bring together the perspectives of love and morality by abandoning the idea that the perspective of morality is essentially impartial. We should, on this view, let go of the consequentialist and rights-based theories that have dominated the recent history of ethics, and instead adopt a partialist, or particularist, or virtue-oriented, or – sometimes – communitarian approach, one that is often taken to be broadly Aristotelian in inspiration.[13] A second response, nicely articulated by

---

[12] Stocker, "The Schizophrenia of Modern Ethical Theories"; Williams, "Persons, Character and Morality."

[13] See, for example, Stocker, "How Emotions Reveal Value and Help Cure the Schizophrenia of Modern Ethical Theories"; Blum, *Friendship, Altruism and Morality*, especially chapters 3–4. For further discussion, see Thomas, *Living Morally: A Psychology of Moral Character*, especially chapters 4–5.

J David Velleman, seeks to reconcile the perspectives of love and morality in a different way. Working within a Kantian framework, Velleman argues that the perspective of love and friendship, like the perspective of morality, is, in a certain important sense, impartial.[14]

Common to each of these views is the thought that if you act as a good friend, or act out of true love, then you cannot really go wrong. The considerations that appear to be important from the perspective of friendship, whether we take that to be partial or impartial, do not clash with the considerations that appear to be important from the moral perspective. Especially among those writing about friendship from a virtue-oriented point of view, there can be found in both substance and tone a commitment to the idea that people are at their absolute best when they are acting out of true friendship. On these views, friendship fits seamlessly into the moral life; there is no good reason not to be a good friend.

A third response, defended by Peter Railton, is a little different.[15] Taking consequentialist moral theory as his background, Railton accepts that the perspectives of friendship and morality are different – that morality is impartial and friendship is not – but argues that this does not require that friendship or morality be too greatly compromised. From the impartial perspective of morality, says Railton, we can see good reasons to often adopt the partial perspective of the lover and friend, and we can move between these perspectives as needed without doing any serious harm to our psychological health or the integrity of our evaluative outlook. Railton seeks on the whole to legitimate friendship in moral terms, but he does say, as his consequentialism seems to force him to say, that sometimes acts of good friendship or true love will be morally wrong (even if we should be thankful that people perform such acts rather than failing to love at all). So responses in Railton's style do not accept the claim that there is never a good reason to fail to be a good friend.

A fourth way of seeing things is defended by Cocking and Kennett in "Friendship and Moral Danger." Against what they call

---

[14] "Love as a Moral Emotion."
[15] "Alienation, Consequentialism, and the Demands of Morality."

"moralized" accounts of friendship, Cocking and Kennett argue that we sometimes have to choose between acting out of friendship and doing what is morally right. Their central case is of a man who lies and helps move a body in order to keep a friend out of trouble. He does the morally wrong thing, say Cocking and Kennett, yet he acts as a good friend would.

Cocking and Kennett do not draw the moral that friendship is of only conditional value; they do not say that we ought to abandon friendship whenever morality calls. They instead respond to conflicts between friendship and morality by saying, in effect, "so much the worse for morality." Moral reasons, they say, are not the only reasons there are, and they can sometimes be outweighed by other reasons – in particular, by reasons of friendship. Here, there is an appeal to Susan Wolf's influential argument that we do not really want to be, or to be around, people whose governing motivation is to be morally virtuous; other things are important too.[16] So while Cocking and Kennett reject moralized accounts of friendship, they end up with a position that shares something of the spirit of such accounts. They do not say that being a good friend will never lead you morally astray, but they do seem to suggest that there is a non-moral sense in which we ought, or may, always act as good friendship requires. Just because there is sometimes moral reason to fail to be a good friend does not mean that there is ever reason on the whole to fail to be a good friend.

CONFLICTS WITH EPISTEMIC NORMS AND CONFLICTS WITH MORALITY

There are two ways in which the claim of this chapter – that the norms of friendship can conflict with epistemic norms – bears upon the debate just described. First, if our goal is to show that there are important norms with which the requirements of friendship can conflict, then there is an advantage in focusing upon clashes between friendship and epistemic responsibility, rather than friendship and morality. When we offer a case like that of the man who lies and

---

[16] "Moral Saints."

moves a body to help a friend, people often respond by saying that any normative conflict here is within morality, not between morality and something else. On this view, the man is morally obliged to help out his friend, and his obligation just happens to be unusual among moral duties in requiring him to tell lies and conceal a dead body. Once this response is offered, the debate turns into a demarcation dispute over the scope of the moral, and such disputes are very difficult to resolve.

The analogous move with regard to epistemic norms is much less appealing. If you agree that there are conflicting demands upon Eric in my case, or upon Chandler in the case from *Friends*, then I think that you will agree that the conflicting considerations are very different in type. It is not remotely plausible to say that Chandler's reason for believing that Joey is about to have his big break is an epistemic reason, or that his reason to believe the opposite is one that arises from his friendship. It might not be too implausible to think that the norms of friendship can be brought under the umbrella of morality, but it is very implausible to think that there is no distinction of type between the requirements of friendship and the requirements of epistemic responsibility.

Second, I think that the "so much the worse for morality" style of response, which Cocking and Kennett seem to endorse with regard to their own cases, is harder to pull off when epistemic norms are in question. Oddly, but truly, it is easier to say "so much the worse for morality" than to say "so much the worse for epistemic responsibility" – "so much the worse for forming beliefs on the basis of the evidence" or "so much the worse for the idea that you should avoid situations from which you are likely to emerge with false beliefs." It is easier to think that moral norms are not all that powerful when it comes to friendship than to think that epistemic norms are not all that powerful when it comes to forming beliefs. In showing that you sometimes need to sacrifice your epistemic integrity if you are to be a good friend, we have not just found one more interesting way in which friendship has its costs; we have shown that there can be very good reasons not to be a good friend. We have shown that friendship is not something to be unreservedly embraced.

FRIENDSHIP AND ALIENATION

Perhaps epistemic norms are moral norms. If that is what you believe, and if you agree with what I have said so far, then you will quickly deduce that moralized accounts of friendship – those that say that acting out of good friendship cannot lead you morally astray – are false. Even assuming that epistemic norms are not moral norms, though, the claim they can clash with the norms of friendship indirectly gives us a reason to doubt that any moralized account of friendship could be correct.

One way of putting this is to say that the result with regard to epistemic norms makes it easier to believe that the norms of friendship could conflict with moral norms too. There are cases that support that claim; Cocking and Kennett's is one, and another is of friendships between mafiosi, who, according to the stories, will do the most horrific things in order to honor their friendships. It is easy to see that these are not good people, harder to see why they are not good friends. Why not just accept that friendships between mafiosi and the rest can be good friendships, while being very bad in other ways?

There is another way in which moralized accounts of friendship are undermined when we show that friendly and epistemic norms are not always mutually consistent. It is often said that our lives are structured and given meaning, that our identities are indeed constituted, by our individual projects and commitments, and that our commitments to particular friends and loved ones are among the most important of these.[17] A criticism of impartialist moral theories, linked to the one described earlier, is that they do not seem to allow particular projects and commitments to be justified on their own terms. If we are to take impartialist moral theory to heart, it seems, then we must be prepared to take a step back from our projects and commitments, from our friendships and our loves, and see whether they stand scrutiny from a more general or objective point of view.

---

[17] See Frankfurt, "Autonomy, Necessity and Love"; and Williams, "A Critique of Utilitarianism."

The objection, then, is that impartialist moral theory, taken seriously, demands that we alienate ourselves from the projects and commitments that make us who we are.

Something like this worry, I think, lies behind much of the movement in favor of moralized conceptions of friendship. The concern is that friendship is cheapened, and we are alienated from our friends and from ourselves, when we see a need to justify particular friendships in terms of considerations that arise from outside friendship itself.

Once we accept that there can be good reasons – good epistemic reasons, for example – not to be a good friend, however, we should accept that reasons of good friendship need to be assessed from a perspective at which they can compete with other kinds of reasons. Taking up such a perspective involves wondering whether the friendship, or at least one small part of it, holds up well in light of considerations that have nothing much to do with friendship. And that is to say, if we insist upon putting it in such terms, that we sometimes need to alienate ourselves from the perspectives that we take as devoted friends. So if the motivation behind moralized views of friendship, and behind particularist or partialist or virtue-oriented or communitarian moral theory, is to do with the avoidance of alienation, then – whatever we think of the ideas about individual identity that lie behind it – the motivation is misplaced. The battle against alienation has already been lost.

THE VALUE AND ROLE OF FRIENDSHIP

Annette Baier has coined the term "misamorism" to apply to the thoughts of philosophers whose theoretical commitments lead them to be suspicious of love and friendship.[18] I would like to avoid that label. Let me close by saying why I think that I can.

From the claim that there can be good reason not to be a good friend, or that it is desirable that we sometimes assess our commitments to

---

[18] "Unsafe Loves."

friends in light of other values, it does not follow that friendship is any less valuable than it would otherwise have been. There remains room for the claim that friendship is of intrinsic value, though sometimes in conflict with other things of intrinsic value, and there certainly remains room for all sorts of claims about how friendship gives rise to things of independent value: how, for example, it so greatly improves the quality of our lives. While I will not pursue the point here, I think that friendship looks more valuable when we begin to enumerate the many ways in which it improves lives than when we say that the question of why our friendships are justified is too foreign to contemplate.

More importantly, the approach to friendship supported by this chapter's argument is quite closely connected to our everyday attitudes to friendship. I discussed earlier some cases in which we regard friendships as impediments to accurate belief: cases, for example, under which we are assessing someone's reports about his friend's character and abilities. And I looked at the distinctive attitude that we take towards our beliefs about our friends, attitudes that lead us to second-guess some of our beliefs about our friends before allowing too much to depend on them. Note also that we sometimes make an effort to avoid situations under which we would have to form certain sorts of beliefs about our friends. If a friend of mine is working on a painting or a novel, I might be worried that if I saw it then I would not like it – that I might even be forced to think that my friend is a little foolish. I do not want to force myself into liking it just because it was produced by my friend, I do not want to pretend that I like it when I do not, and I do not want to fail to be a supportive friend, so I try to avoid having to form any opinion at all.

All of this is to suggest that the achieving of distance from our friendships, and the weighing of the requirements of particular friendships against other considerations, are quite familiar phenomena; in particular, we adopt strategies that help us to avoid and manage conflicts between our desires to be good friends and our desires to be good believers. The idea that we allow friendships to lead us wherever they may, that friendship is something that we embrace without hesitation, is a philosophical fantasy. That does not mean that friendship is any less valuable than we might have thought, but it does say something about the kind of value that friendship has, and the point of view from which its value should be understood.

CHAPTER 3

What is patriotism?

THE PHILOSOPHICAL DEBATE ABOUT PATRIOTISM

Most people think that patriotism is a virtue. That, at least, is what is suggested by a quick glance at the political world and the popular media in contemporary western societies. Politicians constitute an extreme case – I think that many of them would rather be called cowardly, selfish or corrupt than unpatriotic – but their case is odd only for its extremeness.[1] In everyday life, it seems as though you are usually offering a compliment when you call someone a patriot, and as though patriotism is usually thought to be something that we should foster in our children and ourselves. Patriotism, in the popular imagination, may not quite rank alongside kindness, justice, honesty and the like, but it is a virtue nonetheless; it is a character trait that the ideal person would possess.

I think that this common view is mistaken. Patriotism is certainly not a virtue, and is probably a vice. In Chapter 2, I tried to show that friendship often involves a certain sort of loyalty in belief, which can bring the standards of good friendship into conflict with other important evaluative standards. The next two chapters argue that patriotism, too, involves loyalty in belief, but of a more pervasive and damaging kind. The kind of loyalty in belief involved in patriotism, I want to argue, is such as to make it inevitable, or almost

---

[1] In 2001, the US Congress passed a bill called the USA PATRIOT Act. Even though USA PATRIOT is an acronym (for Uniting and Strengthening America by Providing Appropriate Tools Required to Intercept and Obstruct Terrorism), it was said that some members of Congress were reluctant to oppose the bill for fear of looking unpatriotic.

inevitable, that a patriotic person will tend to fall into bad faith – to embrace comforting but unjustified beliefs while deceiving herself about their source – and very likely that a patriot's bad faith will have the effect of distorting her thinking about some very serious matters.

When philosophers talk about patriotism, they usually do so within the context of the debate between universalism and communitarianism. I described the rough outlines of the debate in the Preface; in the context of this debate, universalism is often called "cosmopolitanism," though I will not use that label.[2] Universalists say that the fundamental value of an individual does not have anything to do with her connections with particular countries, communities or other individuals. Universalism tends to lead (and can, for our purposes, be assumed to lead) to impartialism, which is the view that many of the most important ethical judgments are ideally made from an impartial, detached perspective, free of particular allegiances. Universalists believe that it is possible and often desirable to form ethical judgments not as a member of a particular community, but rather from the point of view of a neutral and unencumbered observer – simply as one human among many, perhaps, or as a bare rational agent.[3]

Communitarians believe that ethical judgments are properly made from within a tradition, or a community, or a structure of social roles and allegiances.[4] It is a mistake, on this way of looking

---

[2] Within a cosmopolitan ethical outlook, distinctions are not drawn on the basis of nationality or country of origin. See Simmons, "Human Rights and World Citizenship: The Universality of Human Rights in Kant and Locke"; Nussbaum, "Patriotism and Cosmopolitanism"; and Lu, "The One and Many Faces of Cosmopolitanism."

[3] For a classic statement of impartialism, see Part 1 of Rawls, *A Theory of Justice*.

[4] The version of communitarianism sketched here follows that articulated by MacIntyre in "Is Patriotism a Virtue?" (Future page references to this article are to the version published in Primoratz (ed.), *Patriotism*.) See also Sandel, *Liberalism and the Limits of Justice*; Kymlicka, *Contemporary Political Philosophy*, chapter 6; and Mulhall and Swift, *Liberals and Communitarians*. I should note that the label "communitarianism" may be a little problematic. (See Taylor, "Cross-Purposes: The Liberal-Communitarian Debate.") For one thing, it seems to have gone out of fashion. For another, the relevant view that is of interest in debates about patriotism may be a little different from the view regarded as

at things, to expect us to step back from our membership of communities when deciding how we ought to live. A communitarian is likely to regard as perfectly natural and desirable those moral judgments that are essentially made from the point of view of a member of this or that community.

The contemporary philosophical debate about patriotism can be represented by a cast of three. First, there is the *communitarian patriot*, whose view is classically presented in Alasdair MacIntyre's article, "Is Patriotism a Virtue?" and whose answer to that question is "Yes!" Someone who lacks a patriotic commitment to his country, says the communitarian patriot, is alienated from the embedded perspective that makes ethics possible, and is hence ethically deficient; patriotism is not just a virtue, but a central virtue.

At the other extreme is the *hard universalist*, whose view is expressed in articles like Paul Gomberg's "Patriotism is Like Racism" (though Gomberg himself is not committed, in the end, to universalism).[5] The patriot favors one country and one group of people over others, and such favoritism, says the hard universalist, is abhorrent; no one is inherently more valuable than anyone else, just in virtue of being a citizen of one country rather than another. As Martha Nussbaum puts it: "What is it about the national boundary that magically converts people toward whom we are both incurious and indifferent into people to whom we have duties of mutual respect?"[6] In the eyes of the hard universalist, patriotism is therefore a vice.

"communitarian" in other contexts. I am using the term mainly for dialectical purposes. So far as the debate over patriotism is concerned, the communitarian camp can be taken to include not only those explicitly engaged in communitarian political philosophy, but also many others who take local identity and particularity to play an essential role in good ethical thought. See, for example, in Nussbaum, *For Love of Country?*, Robert Pinsky's contribution, "Eros Against Esperanto" (pp. 85–90); and Hilary Putnam's contribution, "Must We Choose Between Patriotism and Universal Reason?" (pp. 91–97).

[5] Gomberg, "Patriotism Is Like Racism." Gomberg gives a thorough presentation of his own view in "Patriotism in Sports and in War."

[6] "Patriotism and Cosmopolitanism," p. 14.

Between the communitarian patriot and the hard universalist lies the *soft universalist*.[7] Soft universalism is perhaps the most popular view among philosophers; it is given very clear expression in Marcia Baron's "Patriotism and 'Liberal' Morality."[8] The soft universalist's claim is that a good universalist can also be a patriot, in some attenuated sense at least. Patriotic loyalty, on this way of seeing things, can be consistent with the ethical judgments that are correctly made from the neutral point of view; perhaps individuals are able, in the right circumstances, to have special loyalties to their own countries while still meeting the broader obligations that are evident from the neutral point of view. While the soft universalist might be reluctant to classify patriotism as a virtue, he at least thinks that it is not a vice. You might not be obliged to be a patriot, says the soft universalist, but it is allowed.[9]

One reason why the debate over patriotism is a site for the debate between universalists and communitarians is that it is taken to be an illuminating case study, displaying the differing approaches taken by universalists and communitarians to loyalty in general. Some think that it is wrong to try to save your mother rather than a stranger from drowning, when the chances of saving the stranger are slightly higher, but most think that a preference for your mother in such a circumstance is justifiable, even required. But if it is wrong to favor someone just because she is your compatriot, is it not also wrong to favor someone just because she is your mother? If we cannot place patriotism on solid philosophical ground, then won't we have to regard loyalties to family, romantic partners and friends as equally problematic? That is certainly what many philosophers seem to think. The hard universalist is thought to face embarrassment, or at

---

[7] My distinction between the communitarian patriot and the soft universalist is similar to McCabe's distinction between the "hard patriot" and the "soft patriot." See "Patriotic Gore, Again."

[8] Future page references to Baron, "Patriotism and 'Liberal' Morality" are to the version published in Primoratz (ed.), *Patriotism*. See also Stephen Nathanson's defense of "moderate patriotism," in *Patriotism, Morality and Peace*.

[9] For a nice statement of this last point, see Primoratz, "Patriotism: Morally Allowed, Required, or Valuable?" See also Primoratz, "Patriotism: Mundane and Ethical"; and the postscript to Baron's "Patriotism and 'Liberal' Morality."

least the need to bite some bullets, when it comes to loyalty in general. The fate of soft universalism is thought to bear heavily upon the question of whether it is possible to be a universalist without disparaging special moral relationships of all sorts.

It is worth giving further emphasis to the closeness of the analogy that philosophers see between patriotism and other loyalties. MacIntyre treats patriotism as "one of a class of loyalty-exhibiting virtues (that is, if it *is* a virtue at all), other members of which are marital fidelity, the love of one's own family and kin, friendship, and loyalty to such institutions as schools and cricket or baseball clubs."[10] Andrew Oldenquist uses the image of the person sitting at the center of a number of concentric circles, each of which represents a domain of individuals to whom the person feels a loyalty; close to her is a circle representing loyalty to family, much further out is a circle representing loyalty to species, and somewhere in between is a circle representing patriotic loyalty to country.[11] Baron's defense of universalist patriotism is embedded in a general theory about how universalism can be squared with a person's favoring her own family and friends.[12] There are many other examples besides.[13] While it is often admitted that there are more and less extreme forms of patriotism, it is generally accepted that patriotism is an attitude of essentially the same type as our loyalties to family, friends and the rest, just with a different object.

I hope to provide an objection to patriotism that stands independently of the debate between universalists and communitarians, and that counts as an objection to patriotism in particular, not to loyalty in general. In order to do this, I need to show that patriotism has features that distinguish it from other familiar forms of loyalty, and that these distinguishing features are what make it

---

[10] "Is Patriotism a Virtue?," p. 44, italics MacIntyre's.

[11] Oldenquist, "Loyalties," pp. 179–180.

[12] Baron, "Patriotism and 'Liberal' Morality," p. 70.

[13] See also, in Nussbaum, *For Love of Country?*, Sisella Bok's contribution, "From Part to Whole" (pp. 38–44); and Michael W. McConnell's contribution, "Don't Neglect the Little Platoons" (pp. 78–84).

objectionable. This chapter disputes the analogy that philosophers often draw between patriotism and other familiar loyalties; I describe some ways in which loyalties differ, and give reasons to think that patriotism is in certain ways unlike other familiar kinds of loyalty. Chapter 4 presents my case against patriotism.

THE QUESTION

A patriot is loyal to his own country. I will claim that patriotic loyalty is different in kind from other forms of loyalty. It cannot be doubted, though, that patriotism can mean different things to people of different times, places and political inclinations.[14] So what is the point, we might ask, in trying to say something about what patriotism *really* is? Well, it is not my intention just to stipulate a meaning for "patriotism," or to fight over the use of a word. I aim rather to articulate a conception of patriotism that most of us recognize and share, one that captures the notion of patriotism that dominates in public discourse nowadays. (And it is worth noting that most of what I say in characterizing our ordinary notion of patriotism would be accepted by most philosophers who have written about it.) While the story I am about to tell reflects ordinary thought closely enough to be regarded as *the* story about patriotism *simpliciter*, I am not ruling out the possibility that there are other ways in which the term can be and has been understood, nor the possibility that it would really be *better* if we started using it in some different way.[15] In any case, I think that disagreements over the exact meaning of "patriotism" will not have much of a bearing on the basic argument to come. I will say more about this later.

---

[14] See Dietz, "Patriotism: A Brief History of the Term"; section I of Kleingeld, "Kantian Patriotism"; and Moland, "Whose Greater Good? Virtue, Cosmopolitanism and Reform in 18th and 19th Century German Patriotism."

[15] So I have no objection to philosophers (like Kleingeld in "Kantian Patriotism" or Oldenquist in section IV of "Loyalties") who, to ethical or political or analytic ends, advocate various ways of refining or clarifying our ordinary notion.

CHOICE

Some kinds of loyalty are such that the loyal agent is able to choose the object of her loyalty. If you are loyal to a political party, for example, then your loyalty probably originated in a choice to favor this party over others, and is probably experienced as an ongoing choice; you could, at least in principle, transfer your loyalty to a different party, if you choose.

Other forms of loyalty are not subject to choice in the same way. An example is loyalty to parents. You may be able to choose whether or not to be loyal to your parents, but you cannot choose who is to be object of your filial loyalty, if anyone is. The only people to whom you can show filial loyalty are your parents (or those who play that institutional role), and you do not, exceptional cases aside, get to decide which people are your parents (or play that role).

In this regard, patriotism is similar to filial loyalty and different from the described loyalty to a political party, because you cannot, in standard cases, decide which country is your own. There might be exceptions. Perhaps when Robert E. Lee was deciding whether to take command of the Union army or the Confederate army, he was deciding whether to be a Northern or a Southern patriot. Such cases, though, are not representative. An individual who asks herself, "Should I be a patriot?" does not typically face the further question, "If so, then of which country?" and does not typically understand her patriotism as an ongoing choice to be loyal to this country rather than some other.[16]

LOYALTIES DERIVED AND NON-DERIVED

Some loyalties are derived from other, more fundamental commitments. Your loyalty to a political candidate might be derived from a

---

[16] Kleingeld distinguishes three types of patriotism. The one that she is most interested in defending is "civic patriotism" – a state's citizens' "love of their shared political freedom and the institutions that sustain it" – and she says that a person could, in principle, transfer his civic patriotism from one state to another. ("Kantian Patriotism," p. 317.) I think that love of this sort falls short of what we would ordinarily regard as patriotic love, in part because it is so easily transferable.

more fundamental commitment to certain political values, or from a more fundamental loyalty to the candidate's party. You might be loyal to a particular brand of toothpaste because of your deeper loyalty to your hometown, which is where the toothpaste is made. You might maintain your loyalty to the Red Sox out of loyalty to your father, with whom you used to go to the games.

Other loyalties are what we might call non-derived or "first-level" loyalties, or loyalties "in the first instance," meaning that there are no deeper commitments of which they can informatively be regarded as manifestations. Sometimes, the loyalties of fans to sports teams are nonderived. My loyalty to the Geelong Football Club is not an expression of my deeper loyalty to something else, and does not depend essentially on any value or principle that the club represents; I just find myself loving and caring about the club for its own sake. And filial loyalty, again, is an obvious case of a loyalty that tends to be non-derived. There is just no answer to the question, "In virtue of which more fundamental loyalty are you loyal to your mother?" So far as a hierarchy of commitments is concerned, this is a place where explanation bottoms out.

Loyalty to country could be derived. You might feel a loyalty to Switzerland – you might support its sports teams and wish for its flourishing, and you may think of it as a country with which you have a special connection – that is grounded in your affection for the Swiss foreign exchange student who once stayed with your family. Your loyalty to Jamaica may be derived from your appreciation of reggae, and your loyalty to America may be derived from your commitment to the values articulated in its Constitution.

As philosophers have often pointed out, however, something important about patriotism is missing from loyalties like these.[17]

---

[17] See, for example, MacIntyre, "Is Patriotism a Virtue?," p. 44; and Primoratz's "Introduction" to *Patriotism*, pp. 10–12. Kleingeld might have a contrasting view. One of the types of patriotism that she discusses, "trait-based patriotism," does appear to be, in the relevant sense, derived ("Kantian Patriotism," pp. 320–322).

What is missing is the importance of the patriot's country being *her* country. Anyone who appreciates reggae, whether a Jamaican native or not, can feel a derived loyalty to Jamaica. And being Jamaican, loving reggae, and recognizing the home of reggae is not enough to make you a Jamaican patriot. It is not as though the patriot has some pre-existing set of commitments – endorsed from a perspective free of allegiances to this country or that – and then determines that these commitments naturally lead, fortunately enough, to an allegiance to her own country. Patriotic loyalty – unlike some other forms of loyalty to country, including some other forms of loyalty to your own country – is not just a manifestation of some deeper commitment or allegiance. To some extent, the patriot's loyalty to her country is grounded in its being *her* country. A patriot is loyal to her country *in the first instance*, not in virtue of a deeper attachment to something else.

SERIOUSNESS

There is a seriousness involved in some loyalties but not others. If a loyalty of yours is *serious*, as I will use the word, then it can demand that you make significant sacrifices for the sake of its object; that you show its object a genuine, non-ironic reverence; and that you allow that loyalty to have some force when making some morally weighty decisions. Some examples, by now familiar, might make the distinction clearer.

I am, as I say, a lover of the Geelong Football Club. My loyalty to the club is passionate, and I allow it to have a significant impact upon my life. The money I spend on club membership and on going to the games, the time I spend following news of the club, the impact that the club's performance has upon my mood, are considerable. But my loyalty to Geelong is not serious, in the sense in question. I am not about to insist upon standing to attention during the playing of the club song, I am not going to compromise friendships for the sake of the club, and I do not think that my loyalty to the club could ever require me to commit acts of violence or enormous self-sacrifice.[18]

Loyalty to a parent, on the other hand, is often serious. You might make enormous sacrifices for your parents, take your obligations to them to have a serious moral dimension (you might tell lies or break the law to keep them out of trouble), and show them a reverence that – without extending to singing an anthem or saluting a flag – is certainly not ironic or self-conscious. And all of this may be true even though your non-serious loyalty to a football club is in a sense more passionate and takes up more of your energy than your filial loyalty. The kind of seriousness of loyalties that I am trying to bring out here does not necessarily go along with intensity.

Patriotism, as it is usually understood, is a serious loyalty. You can show your patriotism by standing during the national anthem, wearing your country's flag on your lapel or your backpack – in general, by showing an unironic reverence for your country. Patriotism is often cited (or appealed to) as a reason why you make (or should make) significant sacrifices for your country. Many people take patriotism to involve being prepared, under extreme circumstances, to kill or die for your country. It is, at any rate, difficult to imagine someone who is a genuine patriot, but takes her loyalty to country to generate no morally weighty reasons at all.[19] Patriotism is a serious matter, in a way in which some other loyalties – my loyalty to Geelong, for example – are not.

JUSTIFICATION

Sometimes, we are asked to justify our loyalties. Whether or not we are good at providing such justifications, for many loyalties we

---

[18] Some loyalties to sports teams *are* serious, in the relevant sense. There are those who do insist on saluting the flags of their teams, and those who kill and die standing up for their football clubs. My own view is that these people are obviously, depressingly, taking things too far.

[19] As Nathanson puts it, patriotic loyalty generates "a willingness to act on the country's behalf, even if this requires some sacrifice ... A person who merely professed these attitudes but was unwilling to act on them would be a hypocrite, not a patriot" (*Patriotism, Morality and Peace*, p. 35).

think it important that justifications be available – at least in principle. Let me sketch three ways in which we might respond to a demand that a loyalty be justified, and say something about the kinds of loyalties with regard to which each kind of response seems appropriate.

First, you might try to justify a loyalty to something by appealing to some of its characteristics, none of which has to do with its particular relationship to you. Asked to justify your allegiance to a presidential candidate, for example, it may be appropriate or required for you to try to cite features of the candidate that make him objectively the *best* candidate: not the best for you or the best from your perspective, but the plain best.[20] That is to say that you take there to be reasons why anyone, aligned or not, should support your candidate. You think that the force of the justification for your loyalty could be felt even from a perspective uninformed of your particular qualities and relations to others – from the neutral point of view.

Second, you might try to list characteristics whose value could be appreciated from the neutral point of view, without going so far as to say that their existence makes it true that everyone should share your loyalty. To hear the full story about why your loyalty is justified, we have to understand that its object has valuable features, but also something about its particular relation to you.

Loyalties to friends are arguably of the type for which this second kind of justification is appropriate.[21] We like to be able to say what it is about our friends that makes them good people to have as friends; I might mention your sense of humor, your brutal honesty and your generosity, presenting these as characteristics that

---

[20] I do not mean to suggest that this is the kind of justification that is always demanded of those who support political candidates. You might well be justified in supporting a candidate because she best represents the interests of your particular community, or because she is your mother.

[21] This is of course a tough and much-discussed philosophical topic, and I do not pretend to add anything to it here. But I think that the idea about explaining friendly loyalties is clear enough for illustrative purposes. A good place to look for more on this topic is in the papers in Badhwar (ed.), *Friendship: A Philosophical Reader*.

are attractive in themselves, not just because you happen to have them. But the suggestion is not that I would be friends with anyone who had those qualities, or that everyone has good reason to be your friend. Part of what justifies my being your friend is the relationship in which we happen to stand. Perhaps we share a certain history, or are similar in certain ways, or just happen to click. Such considerations work perfectly well as components of my justification, even though they would not be compelling from the neutral point of view.

Finally, the best justification for a loyalty may make no mention at all of characteristics that look valuable from the neutral point of view. If I ask you to justify your love for your father, there might be plenty of wonderful things about him that you could mention. Probably, though, none of those things is essential to your caring about him in the way that you do. You can love your father without holding him in high esteem, without believing him to be a particularly worthy person. Even if you think that your father is cruel or hopeless or pitiable, you can still love him, and still be prepared to make enormous sacrifices for his sake. The most accurate justification of your love (or explanation of why there is no need for justification) may be simply, "He's my father."

This explanation should not be taken to imply that you would love your father no matter what. If you discovered that he was not the man you thought he was – that he was a pathological liar or Nazi collaborator or axe-murderer – you might no longer love him. So your love might not be unconditional, exactly. Neither is it the case, however, that your love for your father is explained or justified by, or grounded in, his having characteristics like "not being an axe murderer." When it comes to understanding your loyalty, it is not very informative to cite such properties. "He's my father" is about as informative and phenomenologically accurate as it gets.

To what extent, then, is a patriot's loyalty to country grounded in, or explained by, characteristics of the country that she regards as having value from the neutral point of view? To what extent does loyalty to country have to make reference to such characteristics, in order to count as patriotism?

PATRIOTISM AND THE QUALITIES OF A COUNTRY

There is a conception of patriotism according to which it necessarily involves the belief that your country is, objectively, the best,
or has features that make it superior to all others.[22] Baron
recommends a way of thinking about patriotism that, she says,
"certainly does not accord with the usual ways of thinking about it
in our culture," because it does not require that the patriot sees her
own country as superior.[23] Certainly, some people seem to believe
that the way to show patriotism is to say that yours is the greatest
country of all, and that someone who said that some other country
was a little better would thereby fail to be truly patriotic.

We should step back, though, from the idea that being a patriot
means taking your own country to be the one that everyone has
most reason to admire, or that looks most valuable from the neutral
point of view. Someone who said, for example, "I don't think that
my own country is by any means the best. There are others I could
name that are more beautiful, have greater histories, and stand
more resolutely for what is right. But there are many wonderful
things about my country, and it's certainly on the whole a good
country, so I'm proud to call it my own," could, surely, properly
count himself a patriot.

Even the belief that your country is on the whole a good
country, however, might not be a requirement of patriotism. There
are dissidents who count themselves as patriotic, even while
making broad condemnations of their own countries, and who
indeed see themselves as expressing their patriotism through their
very concern that their countries become better than they are. This
is what we might call patriotic dissent, and it is not the same thing

---

[22] Consider the definition of patriotism commonly attributed to George Bernard
Shaw (and probably intended more to annoy than for analysis): "Patriotism is
your conviction that this country is superior to all other countries because you
were born in it." (This version of the quotation is taken from Brussel (ed.),
Webster's New World Dictionary of Quotable Definitions.)

[23] "Patriotism and 'Liberal' Morality," p. 77.

as just plain dissent. Distinctively patriotic dissent is made such by
its appeal to qualities that the dissenter takes to be central to the
identity of the country, but that she thinks it to be losing or
ignoring or respecting insufficiently.

Where the (just plain) dissident might say, "This policy needs to
be changed, because it does not respect the rule of law, and the rule
of law should be respected," the patriotic dissident might add, "and
what makes it especially important that we change the policy is that
our country represents and is built upon respect for the rule of law.
If we abandon that principle, then we abandon an aspect of our
very identity; we cease to be the country that I recognize and
love." Cicero and the patriotic dissidents of late Roman times, for
example, attacked their country for failing to live up to its glorious
past. Patriotic American dissidents in the sixties complained that
America was not being true to the values of freedom and equal
rights that lie at its heart. In counting patriotic dissidents as
patriots, we are counting those who say things like, "There are
some wonderful things about my country, but those things are
being outweighed or overlooked in ways that make my country, on
the whole, a pretty awful one at present. As one who understands
what is truly valuable about this country, it is my patriotic duty to
speak out against its present state."

While the patriotic dissident might be reluctant to say that her
country is on the whole a good one, her patriotism makes reference to characteristics of her country that she takes to be genuinely, objectively valuable, and to play an important role in
making that country what it is. And this, I want to suggest, is a
necessary condition for patriotism. Truly patriotic loyalty is
entangled with a conception of the beloved country as having
certain valuable characteristics, characteristics that make it, in
some minimal way at least, worthy of patriotic loyalty. Patriotism,
on the common understanding of the notion, always takes itself to
be grounded in the relevant country's possession of certain specified, reasonably determinate qualities that the patriot takes to be

genuinely valuable, and to make a nontrivial contribution to the country's identity.[24]

One way of grasping this point is to think about how a patriot would respond to the invitation, "Describe your country for me. What is it like?" My suggestion is that when a patriot answers this question – when she expresses her characterization of her own country or her beliefs about what are its most central or defining characteristics – she must call upon some properties that she takes to be good properties for a country to possess. When the patriot thinks about what it is that she loves, or what it is that grounds her loyalty, she must have in mind something that she takes to have value from the neutral point of view. In this respect, patriotic love differs from the love that people characteristically have for their parents. It is missing the point to cite your parents' wonderful characteristics in explaining why you love them, because there are no particular features of your parents (of the type that count as having objective value) in which your love for them is essentially grounded. Not so, I claim, for patriotic love.

Let me say what this rules out. First, it rules out statements like this: "I am a true, genuine patriot, but there is nothing much that I like about my country; there is nothing important about my country for which I feel any affection." That would be a very strange thing to say. That is not to say that it is impossible to be loyal to your own country without taking it to have certain kinds of valuable characteristics, just that such loyalty would not count as patriotism. Rian Malan's book *My Traitor's Heart* is an account of the apartheid years in South Africa, told by a white Afrikaner who has come to

---

[24] For a summary and endorsement of this criterion as presented in the philosophical literature, see Primoratz's "Introduction" to *Patriotism*, especially pp. 10–12. Nathanson may disagree with this claim, though I am not sure. His "moderate patriotism" is defined as involving affection, identification, concern and a willingness to make sacrifices; he doesn't specifically say that it must attribute any particular valuable qualities to the country (*Patriotism, Morality and Peace*, chapter 3). He does, however, think that moderate patriotism can be deserved or undeserved by a country, depending upon the country's moral characteristics, and that the moderate patriot takes his country to *deserve* patriotic loyalty (chapter 10).

believe that his country is cruel, paranoid and violent, and that its national project is rotten to the core. While Malan regards South Africa with a distaste that sometimes seems very much like hatred, he displays a deep personal concern for his country – a concern that he does not hold towards any but his own South Africa. Malan might indeed *love* South Africa, but it would be an odd use of language to call him a South African *patriot*. His feelings for his country are not patriotic feelings. His book could not have been called *My Patriotic Heart*.[25]

I want to press this point a little. The classic appeal to Athenian patriotism in Pericles' funeral oration moves seamlessly between claims that Athens is *ours* and claims that Athens is *great*.[26] If I tell you that a children's book called *America: A Patriotic Primer* has recently been published, I have said enough for you to confidently infer that it is not comprised of anguished acknowledgements of the poor treatment of Native Americans, black slaves or Vietnamese villagers.[27] If I tell you that we are about to be treated to a patriotic discourse, or to attend a patriotic event, then you know that what is to come will involve some praise of our country's qualities. The point is not, of course, that this is all that patriotism can be, but rather that patriotism is a kind of love for country that makes reference to, or latches onto, aspects of a country that are taken to merit pride or approval or affection or reverence. Without that, you do not have patriotism.

This characterization of patriotism also rules out the putative patriotism that latches onto features of a country that are, by the

---

[25] Baron thinks it acceptable to have a "patriotism" that is characteristically expressed as "a greater (and qualitatively different) concern for the flourishing of one's own country than for that of any other" ("Patriotism and 'Liberal' Morality," p. 75, italicized in the original). In describing that concern, Baron gives a convincing portrayal of a feeling that many of us – including, I think, Rian Malan – have for our own countries, and which I take to be in many ways analogous to the concern that we have for our parents. But it is not, as Baron herself suggests on pp. 76–77, the feeling that people normally have in mind when they speak of patriotism. See also chapter 15 of Nathanson's *Patriotism, Morality and Peace*.

[26] Thucydides, *History of the Peloponnesian War*, Book II.

[27] Cheney, *America: A Patriotic Primer*.

patriot's own admission, of only peripheral importance when it comes to understanding what the country really is. Someone who says, "When I think of what my country really is and what it really stands for, I feel only contempt or indifference – but it does have some very nice lakes, for which I feel genuine affection," is a lover of his country's lakes, not a patriot.[28]

Also ruled out is the possibility of a patriot who takes his country to have valuable characteristics, but has no particular beliefs about what they are. This is an odd case, but I have in mind someone who says: "I love my country, and I take it to be characterized by qualities that merit my pride and affection. I cannot say what they are, but there must surely be some; at the heart of every country there are *some* valuable characteristics. My patriotism is grounded in the valuable defining features of my country, whatever they are." And my claim rules out the possibility of a patriot whose patriotism is grounded not in his country's having positive characteristics, but in its lacking negative ones. Here, I am thinking of someone who is speaking literally when she says something like, "The things I love about my country are these. It wasn't the aggressor in World War Two, it has never dropped a nuclear bomb and isn't home to any poisonous spiders."

The reason why it is difficult to see the people we just met as patriots is that they betray no determinate conception of their countries as ones that merit loyalty; none betrays a special conception of what his country *is*. Patriotism is tied up with a fairly well articulated picture of the beloved country, one that includes its having specified valuable features.

---

[28] The same is true of someone whose loyalty is not really to a country, but to a city or region. You might think that London is wonderful, but Britain is not; that is not love of country but love of city. *This* case, however, needs to be contrasted in turn with a love of country that is *expressed* through a love of a city or region. Someone who loves London (because she takes it to be wonderful in particular respects), and believes furthermore that London (so characterized) encapsulates all the great things about Britain, or represents the *real* Britain, could thereby be a patriot. She is attributing valuable qualities to Britain, not just to London.

"MY COUNTRY, RIGHT OR WRONG"

I think that my claim about how a patriot must view his own country accords with our ordinary understanding of the notion, and with most of what philosophers have said about it. It may appear, however, to be out of line with one popular expression of patriotism: the slogan, "My country, right or wrong!" From my experience of talking to people about this slogan, there is a good deal less agreement about its meaning than you would initially expect. I will mention quickly some of the ways in which the slogan might be understood, and say how I think they each relate to the attitudes constitutive of patriotism.

Sometimes, the slogan is taken to mean, "I'll support what my country does, whether I think it's right or wrong." Sometimes, it is taken to mean, "Right and wrong are not my concerns, I am just concerned with standing up for my country." Either of these statements is consistent with (though not, of course, required by) patriotism as I have painted it. It is indeed overwhelmingly likely that someone who made either of these statements would be able to say just what it is about his country that makes it merit such devotion; this would involve pointing to certain valuable characteristics of the country, even if not characteristics like "always being right."

Sometimes, the slogan is taken to have the meaning it takes when placed in the context of the famous remark of Carl Schurz: "My country right or wrong; if right, to be kept right; and if wrong, to be set right." (Note that this evidently is not where the shorter slogan originates. Schurz was responding to a senator from Wisconsin, who was apparently taunting him by saying, "My country, right or wrong."[29]) This version of the slogan expresses an intention to support the moral flourishing of a country, regardless of its starting point. If the speaker's reason for making such a commitment is that she sees valuable features of her country that make its flourishing particularly worth striving for, then she could well be expressing her

---

[29] Trefousse, *Carl Schurz: A Biography*, p. 180.

patriotism through the slogan, on my account. And I think it most likely that someone who utters the slogan with this meaning *would* have such considerations in mind; even if the country concerned needs setting right rather than keeping right, there is a feeling of hopefulness and enthusiasm in the slogan that suggests that there is something about the country that makes it capable and worthy of redemption. (The mood of *My Traitor's Heart* is not one in which the slogan would likely be uttered.)

Still, there might be cases in which someone would endorse the slogan simply in light of the country's being *her* country. This is consistent with her being thoroughly disgusted with and ashamed of her country, with her thinking that there is nothing important to recommend it at all. And that, for reasons I have discussed, just doesn't sound like patriotism. So I am happy to accept that some imaginable exclamations of, "My country, right or wrong" might not be expressions of patriotism – though most of them are.

WHAT IS PATRIOTISM?

Patriotism, I have been trying to show, is not just a loyalty like any other. To be a patriot is to have a serious loyalty to country, one that is not characterized by the phenomenology of choice, is essentially grounded in the country's being yours, and involves reference to what are taken to be valuable defining qualities of the country. In one way or another, the features of patriotism just mentioned set it apart from some familiar forms of loyalty to, for example, political candidates, parents and football clubs. Whether patriotism is thereby set apart from *all* familiar forms of loyalty is a question to which I will return in the next chapter. (It isn't.) But we have at least opened up the space for an argument against the desirability of patriotism that cannot be translated into an attack upon loyalty in general.

CHAPTER 4

Against patriotism

CONFESSIONS

When I am watching Geelong play football and the umpire makes a controversial decision, I very quickly form a judgment about whether the decision is right or wrong. If the decision goes the way of the other team, then even though the umpire is right on the scene and I am a long way away in the stands, I will probably believe that it is the wrong decision. Only when the conclusion is absolutely unavoidable will I believe that the opposing team has been the victim of a bad umpiring decision, and in such cases I will probably still point out that it was about time we got one back. When a fight breaks out or a game turns ugly, I am unlikely to think that a Geelong player is to blame. When I am sitting around talking about football with my friends, I will defend the views that you would expect a Geelong supporter to defend. If the discussion is about who is the greatest footballer in history, I will put the case for one of Geelong's great players. I will do my best to marshal facts in favor of my claim, and I will sometimes get them wrong; I might say that my favorite player kicked more goals than anyone else who has played in his position, and my sparring partner might produce evidence that this is not in fact the case. But this won't move me from my claim about which club is home to the greatest footballer. Perhaps I will say that the statistic in question is not so important after all, or perhaps I will dispute the evidence, or perhaps I will quickly decide that it is not really him but some other Geelong footballer who deserves the title of the greatest ever. One way or another, I will do my best to hang onto the beliefs that go along with being a supporter of my team.

Even as I express my disgust at the umpire's decision, and even as I defend the greatness of my own team's players, my companions and I are aware that my expressed opinions are not really what they present themselves to be. The purported facts to which I appeal in support of my opinions are not really what lead me to hold them. Really, I hold those opinions because I am a Geelong supporter. It would spoil the fun for me or anyone else to point this out, but we nevertheless know it to be the case. That is why my football-related opinions are so easy to predict.

I do not know whether this way of behaving will be familiar to other supporters of football teams, but it is the way things are for me. And my belief-forming habits as a football supporter make me guilty of a mild form of bad faith. "The one who practices bad faith," says Sartre, "is hiding a displeasing truth or presenting as truth a pleasing falsehood." "I must know in my capacity as deceiver the truth which is hidden from me in my capacity as the one deceived. Better yet I must know the truth very exactly *in order* to conceal it more carefully – and this not at two different moments, which at a pinch would allow us to re-establish a semblance of duality – but in the unitary structure of a single project."[1] My project is to form and defend Geelong-centric beliefs about the world of football. For these to be the sorts of beliefs that I can defend in conversation, I must take them to be supported by an interpretation of the evidence that is not influenced by the desire to reach one conclusion rather than another; but for them to be the beliefs that I want them to be, I must actively interpret the evidence in a biased manner. I want to have certain beliefs, but to ensure that I have those beliefs I must deceive myself about my motivations, without acknowledging the deceit.

The use of Sartrean machinery to evaluate my attitudes towards the Geelong Football Club is more than a little overblown, and that is because my support of Geelong is not a very serious matter. My being a supporter of Geelong, rather than some other team, does not influence any really important decisions of mine or result in any

---

[1] *Being and Nothingness*, p. 49.

important change in my view of the world. If things do become a little serious – if, for instance, the player I name as the greatest in the game will be rewarded with a brand new car – then I will know that I should try to rise above my biased perspective and take a more reflective point of view. In any event, the point is not to confess to my own bad faith as a football fan (though I feel better), but to suggest that the same brand of bad faith is displayed by those with the much more serious bundle of attitudes that comprise patriotism.

BAD FAITH AND PATRIOTISM

A patriot's loyalty to country, according to the view laid out in Chapter 3, makes reference to fairly determinate characteristics that play a role in her own conception of her country, and that she takes to be the characteristics that contribute to a country being a good country. This amounts to the patriot's having beliefs, tied in with her patriotism, about her country's purely descriptive qualities. Some likely candidates are, "My country is a free country," "My country is beautiful in a special and unusual way," "My country stands for equality," "My country is founded on the principle of equal rights for all," "My country is, compared to others, open and tolerant," "In my country, great individuals are able to flourish," "Mine is a country of rolling green fields and friendly farmers," "My country defends just causes on the international stage," and, "My country is brave and unyielding in conflict." Even a patriot, whose loyalty to country is entangled with a belief that her country has valuable qualities, has a somewhat independent conception of the sorts of descriptions that a country must meet, if it is to have valuable qualities.

Each of the beliefs just mentioned is one that the patriot could have about any country, not just her own, and could conceivably turn out to be false. It is quite possible to encounter evidence that a country is not really so beautiful; does not really defend just causes on the international stage; in fact contains a preponderance of very grumpy farmers; or is not as open and tolerant as it first seemed. When the patriot encounters such evidence with regard to a country that is not her own, she will, depending on what kind of evidence it is, alter her beliefs in certain ways. Perhaps she will change her mind about whether the country is as she imagined, perhaps she will suspend judgment until further evidence emerges – whatever. But I would claim that she is constitutionally unlikely to respond in the same sorts of ways to evidence that *her* country lacks the valuable qualities that she thought it to have, and that it is here that her bad faith is to be found.

If the patriot is guilty of the brand of bad faith that I display as a football fan, then that is because she interprets evidence with the goal of sustaining her conception of her country as bearing particular, valuable characteristics. Out of patriotic loyalty, she is motivated to believe that her country has certain features, and she marshals the evidence in ways that support this belief; but she cannot maintain the belief in its full-blooded form if she admits to herself that it is not grounded in an unbiased assessment of the evidence; so she does not make this admission. A patriot might find herself confronted with evidence that her country is guilty of systematic wartime atrocities, or that the founders of her country were motivated by a racist ideology, where this is evidence that, were it to concern a different country, would lead her to conclude that the country does not merit affection in the way that she had thought. If she responds in such a way as to avoid drawing the same conclusion about her own country – if she denies the evidence, or starts believing that wartime atrocities and racist ideologies are not so bad after all, or immediately turns her efforts to believing that her country has some different qualities that she can convince herself to think valuable – then we have our instance of bad faith.

All of this presupposes not only that the patriot has certain beliefs, but that she is motivated to maintain them, even in the face of countervailing evidence. Must the patriot be so motivated?

She will be if she sees her patriotism as a virtue. To see a character trait as a virtue is to see it as one that the ideal person would possess, and is hence, in standard cases, to desire to cultivate it in yourself. A society in which patriotism is regarded as a virtue will be one in which people, especially children, are given special encouragement to view their country with pride and reverence, and to hold the associated descriptive beliefs, supported by the relevant evidence or not. It indeed seems quite plausible to think that this pressure, and the brand of bad faith to which it gives rise, is present in societies that value patriotism. We have all heard claims to the effect that teachers and leaders should present our country's history and political system in a positive light, for fear that people will otherwise fail to love our country in the ways that they should.

The deep source of patriotic bad faith, however, lies in the tension between patriotism's demanding certain sorts of beliefs and its failing to be grounded in or dependent upon those beliefs.[2] The patriot does not direct her patriotic love at her country *because* she judges it to have particular valuable qualities, but the kind of loyalty that she has to her country, the kind of fidelity that she shows it, involves an acceptance of that judgment. The patriot is motivated to maintain her belief that her country has valuable features of a certain sort because she has a commitment that is grounded in that country's being *her* country. To admit to any such motivation would be to admit that the belief is not formed in response only to the evidence, and hence to undermine the credibility of the belief and the integrity of the loyalty that depends upon it – and so the motivation cannot be admitted.

The patriot's belief that her country has certain attractive features presents itself as having been formed through an unbiased set of opinions about the nature of her own country plus some neutrally endorsed criteria for what properties of countries count as valuable, but this is not really the full story. Driven by her loyalty to country, the patriot will hide from herself the true nature of the procedure through which she responds to evidence that bears upon the question of what her country is really like.

---

[2] Some awareness of this tension is displayed in the evocative final section of MacIntyre's "Is Patriotism a Virtue?" For a more positive view of the way in which patriotism combines particularity and universal judgments, see Benjamin R Barber's contribution, "Constitutional Faith," to Nussbaum, *For Love of Country?*, pp. 30–37.

That is my basic case for the claim that patriotism is connected with bad faith. I need to say much more about the exact content and status of the claim, why it gives reason to think that patriotism is a vice, and where it leaves patriotism as compared to some other kinds of loyalty.

CLARIFYING THE THESIS

My picture of patriotic bad faith relies upon a scenario in which the patriot encounters evidence that challenges her patriotic beliefs, or her picture of her country as being characterized by particular valuable qualities. (I have concentrated upon evidence that the country does not have the qualities at all, but the job might also be done by evidence that those qualities really play no role, or only a peripheral role, in making the country what it is.[3]) There will be cases, however, in which the patriot's conception of her own country is perfectly accurate, and in which she never faces any reason to think otherwise. The patriot might believe that her country is founded upon the values of freedom and equality, and it may indeed be founded upon those values; if so, then she may never need to creatively interpret any evidence to the contrary.

Such a fortunate patriot might never fall into bad faith, because she might never need to hide from herself the truth about how she responds to the evidence about her country that she actually confronts – but she will still be *disposed* to fall into bad faith, under circumstances that (as it happens) never actually arise. She may never need to hide from herself the truth about how she responds to certain types of evidence, but she would, if such evidence were encountered. So while it is overstating things to say that patriotism

---

[3] Example: I think of my country as a defender of human rights on the international stage, but then encounter strong evidence, first, that most other countries put far more energy into that cause than mine does, and, second, that by far the greatest international priority of my country is to maintain access to certain foreign markets. This evidence might be to the effect not that my country does not defend human rights on the international stage – maybe it does – but rather that that fact captures nothing important about my country's nature.

inevitably involves bad faith, it still seems true – and this is my official claim – that patriotism involves the *disposition* to fall into bad faith under some easily imaginable circumstances.

My claim yields what are, I suppose, empirical predictions, like the prediction that patriotic people will be especially resistant to evidence that casts their home countries in a poor light. But I am not positing just a contingent correlation between patriotism and bad faith, of the sort that I would be positing if I said that patriots are disposed to choose country music over folk. I am positing an internal connection between the disposition to bad faith and the structure of patriotic attitudes themselves. That said, I would not go quite so far as to say that the connection is one of absolute conceptual necessity. I do not think that it is *impossible* to be a patriot who is not disposed to fall into bad faith. Let me explain.

I have described a patriot who, when her conception of her own country is challenged, ignores or creatively reinterprets the evidence, or changes her views about what features it is good for a country to have, in ways that allow her to maintain a picture of her country consistent with patriotic loyalty. Can we imagine a genuine patriot with a different pattern of response? What might a patriot be disposed to do in such circumstances, if not to fall into bad faith?

A couple of cases need to be dismissed at the outset. The first is of the putative patriot who, in response to evidence against her country's having the valuable features she believes it to have, happily abandons those beliefs and ceases to love her country. "I loved my country because I took it to stand for freedom and equality," she might say, "but now that I see that it doesn't, I have no reason to love it." This person never was a true patriot. Her loyalty to country has been revealed to be a derived loyalty, dependent upon her regard for freedom and equality plus the judgment, now revised, that those are things for which her own country happens to stand.

The second case to be dismissed is that of the person who changes her beliefs in light of the evidence – who ceases to think of her country as having the relevant valuable characteristics – but finds that this makes no difference to the way that she feels about her country. "It mattered to me that my country stands, or so I thought, for freedom and equality," she says, "but now that I see that it doesn't, I realize that my thinking that it did was never a condition of my loyalty. It's enough that my country is mine." What is uncovered here is a loyalty that never really was grounded in a conception of the country as being, in some central respects, a good one. So it – again – never really was an instance of genuine patriotism.

More relevant, and interesting, is the case of a patriot who seriously and honestly confronts evidence that his country is not as he thought, and takes such evidence as a reason to examine and rethink his patriotism. Rather than avoiding consideration of the possibility that his country lacks the characteristics to which his patriotism makes reference, such a patriot is prompted to wonder whether he really ought to have the kind of first-order loyalty to country that he does.

This kind of response requires that the patriot examine himself, not just his country. Most likely, it will lead to the loss of any distinctively patriotic outlook, through a process that I think might be familiar to many readers. It is a process of moving away from an instinctive attitude to your own country of the form, "This is my great/ beautiful/ free/ ... country," and towards the recognition that your country, like any other, needs to be critically evaluated, and that the patriotic picture of it held by you and others could well be illusory. In coming to this realization, you come to take a perspective upon your country that is too detached to coexist with genuine patriotism. To be a patriot who comes to such a point of view is to throw into question, and revise, what is likely to be a deeply held element of your way of making sense of the world. It is likely to involve a change, to a greater or lesser extent, in your self-conception; you are likely to cease to take your belonging to your country as a part of your identity in the way that you did. It can be difficult, disillusioning and traumatic. As such, it is not a process upon which most patriots are likely to embark, and it is a process of re-evaluation that patriotic loyalty positively discourages. But it is one way in which a patriot might respond to challenges to his patriotic beliefs, and it need not involve bad faith.

Here, then, is my claim about the nature of the connection between bad faith and patriotism. The patriot can encounter circumstances under which she would, were her patriotism not at stake, revise certain of her beliefs, but under which she feels loyal to her country in a way that requires her to keep them. Usually, that loyalty will provide her with a motive to find ways of keeping those beliefs whatever the evidence, and that motive leads to bad faith. It is possible, however, that other elements of a patriot's psychology or circumstances will be such as to outweigh, or prevent the emergence of, that motive – most likely by prompting the kind of change in perspective described in the previous paragraph.[4] Patriotism by its nature makes the patriot likely to have the disposition to fall into bad faith, but there can be exceptions.

My argument is intended to reveal something about a very broad class of loyalties to country, not just about the unthinking, jingoistic forms of patriotism that are so easy to belittle. The claim also applies to patriotic dissidents, and to those whose patriotism is not really political in nature. Among the patriots whom I think likely to be guilty of bad faith are American dissidents who say that flouting international treaties is not just wrong but un-American, American patriots who are viscerally resistant to suggestions that the defenders of the Alamo did not really go down fighting, Australians overseas who tell us that people are friendlier back home, Australian patriots who insist that inner-city Melbourne or outback Queensland is the

---

[4] I have not gone into questions about exactly which components of a patriot's psychology or circumstances might prevent her from falling into bad faith when her patriotic beliefs are challenged. Perhaps the answer will mention her strong concern with believing the truth, or the fact that her patriotic motivations are relatively weak. Depending upon how that question is resolved, it may be that the right thing to say is that *all* patriots, *necessarily*, are disposed to fall into bad faith, but that in some cases the disposition is masked or outweighed or disappears under the conditions of its manifestation. See Lewis, "Finkish Dispositions."

real Australia, and so on and on. I am not, of course, saying that the beliefs mentioned in these examples are false, just that the patriots concerned are unlikely to consider the evidence on its merits.

This might also be a good time to remind you that there are some passionate forms of loyalty to country that do not, in my view, qualify as patriotism, and that hence are not targets of my argument. The toughest and most relevant case is of someone who feels a kind of moral identity with her country – she feels a special pride in the characteristics of it of which she approves, and shame and embarrassment over its perceived failures, she is committed to making the country better, and she would feel a special kind of anguish if she decided to move elsewhere – but whose attachment to her country really is grounded only in its being her country, not in her taking it to have a particular evaluative profile. Hers is not the kind of loyalty that essentially involves her taking her country to *merit* loyalty.

There are reasons to think that if you have this attitude then you *do* deserve the label "patriot." You have a deep loyalty to country, a quality of concern for your country that you have for no other, and you take your identity to be partially tied up with your being of this country rather than somewhere else. But there are also reasons, which I find more impressive, to think that you do not count as a patriot. You may, consistently with your loyalty, feel a thoroughgoing disgust for your country, detesting all that you take it to symbolize. It would then sound very odd to call you a patriot, and this is the main reason, as I have said, why I think that the kind of loyalty under discussion is not enough for patriotism in the ordinary sense.

Really, though, it does not matter whether the label "patriotism" is extended to this kind of loyalty to country, provided the following two points are understood. First, such loyalty is not touched by my argument in this chapter; I do not claim that it involves the disposition to bad faith. Second, it is quite different from the familiar forms of patriotism that *are* grounded in a conception of the beloved country as having particular valuable features. If it is a form of patriotism, then the argument of this chapter does not apply to patriotism in all its forms – but the argument does apply, I would still maintain, to patriotism of a central, recognizable, distinctive type.

I want to consider two cases in which it might be thought that my posited link between patriotism and bad faith fails to be manifested.

First, we might imagine a patriot whose beliefs about what makes for a good country are so intimately related to the characteristics of his own country that his belief that his country measures up to those standards is unfalsifiable. Imagine, for example, the patriotic French peasant marching off to fight Napoleon's wars. His evaluative outlook may be entirely predicated upon the superiority of France and the righteousness of its national ambitions. There may be no space within this outlook for France's failing to be a great country, no possibility of evidence that could threaten the conviction that France is great.

According to one version of communitarianism, people in general are, or should be, in a situation much like that just described. As the products of a particular community, says the communitarian, our evaluative outlook is forged through and inseparable from the conception of the good life around which that community is organized. In separating the patriot's views about what makes for a good country from her views about what her own country is like, then, I might be said to have smuggled in universalist assumptions about the source and structure of our evaluative judgments.

The problem with this train of thought is that it presents the patriot's commitment to country as almost entirely free of content – as though the commitment is to the values and projects for which a particular country stands, regardless of what they turn out to be. But patriotic loyalty is characteristically expressed in more substantive terms. It is not just, "I'm proud to be an American," but, "I'm proud to be an American; at least I know I'm free." Even for our French peasant, patriotism is sustained by attributing particular characteristics to the beloved country, and it is a conceptually open question, one on which evidence either way is easy to imagine, whether or not the country in fact has those characteristics.[5]

Second, it could be completely obvious, to the patriot and everyone else, that the country really does have the qualities that the patriot sees in it. It might be incredibly unlikely that any real evidence against its having such properties will emerge. Do we really learn anything interesting if we find that such a patriot has a disposition to do certain things under circumstances that, we can be almost certain, will never obtain?

I suppose not. But there are reasons to think that such cases – cases of patriots who can be sure that there will never be reason to question their beliefs about their own countries – will be very rare. For one thing, we are talking here about attributing qualities that help to ground a serious loyalty to country, one that makes coherent a genuine reverence for country and a preparedness to make significant sacrifices for its sake. For another, we are talking about taking such properties to be central to the identity of a *country*, not just to parts of or aspects of a country. (Properties of such things would only ground loyalty to such things.) So we are unlikely to find patriots whose loyalty to country is grounded in its having properties like, "containing at least three trees" or "containing the very nice town in which I grew up." We are much more likely to encounter sweeping attributions of properties, seeking to identify something profound about an entire country: its having a history of a certain character, its standing for certain values, its being founded on certain principles, that sort of thing. And claims that a country has particular properties of this sort are very regularly thrown into

---

[5] In any case, if we restrict our attention to the people who presently live in countries like this one, then it just seems obvious that we are dealing with people whose evaluative outlook is such as to allow the possibility that their own countries are not really all that good. If the communitarian's claim is so strong as to imply that we cannot make sense of the thought that our own country is unworthy of our evaluative endorsement, or that there are aspects of our community's conception of the good life that deserve condemnation, then the claim is obviously false. I do not think that the communitarian is under any obligation to make such a claim, but I do think that such a claim is required to underlie the strategy just sketched.

question by new evidence and new perspectives. They can of course be true, and we can sometimes be fairly certain that they are, but they are nevertheless claims towards which someone seeking the truth should keep a reasonably open mind.

It is also worth noting that it would be aberrant, perhaps impossible, for a genuinely patriotic loyalty to be fashioned in response to considerations like this one. We are not in a position to choose, with the conscious goal of avoiding bad faith, exactly which kind of patriotic loyalty we are to manifest. If you want to be a patriot, but do not want to face the danger of falling into bad faith, you cannot just decide to ground your patriotism in some qualities of your country that you could convince yourself to be of value and whose existence you think unlikely to be challenged by evidence. That would be a strange kind of thought process yielding a strange kind of loyalty, and would probably display some bad faith of its own.

WHAT IS SO BAD ABOUT BAD FAITH?

Assuming that I am right in my claim that patriotism involves the disposition to fall into bad faith, where does this leave our assessment of patriotism? Is bad faith necessarily a bad thing?

I think that the link between patriotism and bad faith yields a clear presumptive case against patriotism's being a virtue, and for its being a vice. The structure and role of patriotic attitudes are such that the patriot is likely to have biased, poorly supported beliefs that play an important role in determining her view of the world. Her resistance to certain sorts of belief is likely to lead her to have an inflated view of her own country's value and importance, and to dismiss without adequate consideration those who put forth reasons to doubt that her country is what she takes it to be. Depending upon what sorts of beliefs ground her patriotism, the patriot is likely to be drawn towards unrealistically rosy pictures of her country's people and history, the principles for which it stands, or the ways in which it operates. All of this could well turn out to be influential when it comes to her making morally significant decisions: decisions about whether to support or fight in a war, about who should get her vote, about whether to make certain significant sacrifices, and so on.

There are various ways in which theoretical perspectives might yield additional concerns. Perhaps the patriot, in deceiving herself about the nature of her belief-forming mechanisms, is treating her rational agency as a means, rather than an end. Perhaps true belief is of intrinsic value to the believer, so that someone who is disposed to form false beliefs is disposed to be worse off than she would otherwise be. Perhaps patriotism is in conflict with fundamental virtues like honesty, and with the epistemic virtues associated with good belief-forming, and perhaps there is good reason to think a character trait a vice if it clashes at a deep level with such basic virtues as these.

The claim that patriotism involves a tendency towards bad faith establishes a pretty strong prejudice in favor of the conclusion that patriotism is a vice. If the conclusion is to be resisted, then some work must be done in patriotism's defense.

A VIRTUE OF IGNORANCE?

Some virtues are said essentially to involve a tendency to have false beliefs, and it might be argued, without disagreeing with most of what I have said, that patriotism is one of them. Julia Driver gives the example of modesty, saying that part of what it is to be a modest person is to underestimate, and hence to lack knowledge about, yourself and your achievements.[6] She goes on to say that ignorance is also involved in the virtues of blind charity and the refusal to hold a grudge. Couldn't patriotism be a virtue like this?

I doubt it, because Driver's defense of modesty so construed, and of the other virtues that she mentions, depends heavily upon the impression that the falsity of the beliefs in question is benign and inconsequential. We do not imagine Driver's modest person holding sweeping views about the world, or making important decisions, that would be substantially different if only her beliefs

[6] "The Virtues of Ignorance."

about herself and her achievements were not so misguided. If we could show that modesty (or whatever) involves a systematic tendency to take false beliefs as inputs to processes through which morally significant beliefs are formed and serious decisions are made – that having the beliefs in question is likely to be morally dangerous – then we would have good reason to wonder whether modesty is really a virtue after all.

FINDING "BAD FAITH" EVERYWHERE

I said that I wanted to offer an argument against patriotism that does not automatically translate into an attack upon loyalties of all sorts. One way of responding to my argument is to say that while I might be right about the self-deception that patriotism involves, I am wrong to think that I have uncovered any special problem for patriotism. What I have called "bad faith," the objection would run, is just a familiar form of bias, present in all sorts of loyalty, and perhaps other commitments too. Consider social democrats who believe, for reasons of justice and compassion, that government should provide an extensive welfare safety net; aren't such people especially sympathetic to evidence that their favored policies are good for economic growth, even though that is not a claim on which their commitment depends? Is it not natural and desirable for parents to be biased towards their own children? Aren't friends, as I argued in Chapter 2, inclined to think well of each other? In short, isn't the thing that I have stigmatized as "bad faith" a feature of loyalty in virtually all of its forms? That would not change anything that I have said about patriotism, but it would allow it to benefit from innocence by association. Over the next few sections, I will respond to this objection.

I do not wish to claim that patriotism is absolutely unique in being connected, by its nature, to a vicious disposition towards bad faith. My case against patriotism could be made against any loyalty that has the following three features: first, it is not grounded in, or answerable to, the judgment that its object has certain valuable characteristics; second, it essentially involves the belief that its object *does* have certain valuable characteristics; and third, it plays a role in the making of important, morally weighty decisions.

Another case in which these features are present is that of a certain kind (certainly not the only kind) of loyalty to family, a kind that involves not just a special affection for your family but an endorsement of the values and way of life with which your family is associated. We can all think of cases in which loyalty to family is taken to have a very serious moral dimension, and is taken essentially to involve taking your family to be a good or excellent family – where this attitude is required simply in virtue of this family's being *your* family. Some religious loyalties might be similar. Of such loyalties, and any others like it, I am committed to drawing the conclusion that I have drawn about patriotism (and I think that it is the right conclusion to draw).

Still, most familiar loyalties, I think, lack at least one of the features that are together necessary for bad faith, or at least can lack at least one such feature while still counting as full-blooded instances of the kind of loyalty in question. And when a loyalty really is like patriotism in the relevant respects, there is very good reason to think it undesirable – so any analogy with patriotism is not good news for patriotism. Let me consider some cases.

THE BIASED SOCIAL DEMOCRAT

Our social democrat (and you can fill in your favorite political example here) is especially receptive to evidence that social democratic policies are economically superior, because he would like it to be the case that there exists one more argument in favor of a view that he already holds for independent reasons. He may then get himself to hold certain beliefs about economics, while deceiving himself about their true source.

The social democrat's special openness to only some sorts of empirical evidence is not derived, however, from his political allegiance itself. It is perfectly possible to be committed to social democratic conceptions of justice and compassion while believing that social democracies will not necessarily be the most economically prosperous of societies. So his disposition to interpret evidence creatively is not a matter of the very structure of his commitment.

Further, it is not only possible but desirable for the social democrat to be able to take a more open-minded approach to the relevant evidence without thereby throwing his commitment into question. History provides many examples of the dangers of overreaching ideology: of socialists who insist that their policies must be the key to prosperity as well as social justice; of libertarians who insist that their policies will not only protect property rights but also improve the lot of the worst-off. These are contentious examples, but they make the point. Where there do exist tendencies to creatively interpret empirical evidence for ideological reasons, it is very difficult to see them as virtuous. If there is an analogy with patriotism here, so much the worse for patriotism.

THE BIASED PARENT

Parents are often especially open to evidence that their children have special talents and other valuable characteristics, and especially inclined to give their own children the benefit of the doubt. And this, leaving aside tennis parents and the like, can be a good thing; there certainly does not seem to be anything sinister about it. Why think differently about the patriot's tendency to think well of her own country?

I think that there *is* a difference when countries rather than children are at issue. The thought that citizens should be indulgent in their judgments about their own countries, or give their own countries the benefit of the doubt, is one that I find obviously false and somewhat disturbing. Surely the opposite is true, if anything.

The important point, though, is that a parent's loyalty to a child need not be essentially tied up with a conception of the child as having specified, objectively valuable distinguishing characteristics. One way to see this is to see that a parent who moves to a more objective point of view is not thereby undermining her love for her child. It makes perfect sense to say, "I think that my child has these special qualities that set him apart from others – I think he's so smart and so handsome – but I'll admit that I could easily be wrong. I'm biased, after all. But whether I'm wrong or not makes no difference to my loving my child, and my being prepared to make significant sacrifices for his sake." You would indeed hope that a parent would be capable of carrying out this exercise. Otherwise, it doesn't seem like such a healthy form of loyalty. (Remember the tennis parent.)

Compare this to someone who says, "As a patriot, I think that there are all these good things about my country – I think it's so free and so beautiful – but I'll admit that I could easily be wrong. I'm biased, after all." It is difficult to hear this statement except as involving a step back from the patriotic attitude. It sounds like the speaker is entertaining the possibility that his country does not have the qualities on which his patriotism relies, and wondering whether he should be a patriot after all. Patriotic loyalty discourages you from wondering whether the object of your loyalty really has the valuable qualities you think it to have. A parent's loyalty to a child, insofar as it is healthy, does not.

THE BIASED FRIEND

The case of friendship is more complicated, especially in light of my argument from Chapter 2. Friendship sometimes involves an inclination to believe things about your friend that you would not, given the same evidence, believe about a stranger, or so I claim. But I also think that in a good friendship, that bias – first – need not involve any really profound form of self-deception, and – second – can be set aside when really serious matters are at stake. That is what distinguishes a good friendship from a certain sort of dysfunctional friendship, and from patriotism.

First, the dispositions of belief described in Chapter 2 sit quite comfortably with a general awareness that you are probably biased towards your friends, and that they are probably biased towards you too. Even while giving Rebecca sincere support and encouragement after her poetry reading, Eric can be aware that his beliefs about his friends are often biased. Even while Rebecca enjoys the good of hearing a sympathetic perspective and the knowledge that someone is on her side, she can be aware that Eric is not a dispassionate judge, and that if she wants a fully objective opinion she should go elsewhere. The biased beliefs can do their job, even when their bias is not hidden too far from view.

Second, a friend's biased beliefs can also do their job without affecting his thinking about any really serious matters. Eric, in the example, is not placing himself at any real risk in relying on his biased beliefs; he is just offering Rebecca encouragement when she is feeling anxious after her reading. Things would be different if Rebecca had just asked Eric to invest his life's savings in her self-publishing venture. Similarly, it is one thing to trust your friend when she says that she is innocent of the crime, and another thing to follow through on your belief by acting as her defense lawyer. It is one thing to assure your friend that he would be a fantastic hire for any department, and another thing to offer the same assurance to your colleagues when they are considering your friend as a job applicant.

Imagine that you are in one of these latter situations. You are considering a matter of real consequence – perhaps your money or professional integrity is at stake – and your decision depends on a judgment about a friend. It seems to me, as I suggested in Chapter 2, that a latent awareness of your friendly bias may well step in. Perhaps you will be able to form a more objective judgment, or perhaps you will realize that you just cannot trust your beliefs on this matter, and so you should, in one way or another, recuse yourself. ("Never go into business with a friend.")

Furthermore, if you have a healthy friendship, you will not feel that you are being disloyal in distancing yourself from the judgments you make as a friend, now that the stakes are high. You may feel a little awkward about it, and may be aware that you could do something good for your friend by sticking by your biased beliefs, but you would hope that your friend would understand. A good friend will see that you should be able to deliberate autonomously and transparently about the things that really matter, even when that means regarding him, for a time, not as a friend but as a generic job candidate or aspiring poet, or whatever. I would put it like this: the norms of friendship do not require that you detach yourself from your friendly bias when things get serious – it is not as though that is itself an act of good friendship – but they do not discourage it either. Good friendships are not that intrusive.

Still, not all friendships are good friendships. You might have a friend who expects that you will always believe the best of him, even when things get serious. (Your friend might expect that you will support his application for promotion, because if you do not believe that he deserves the promotion, then you are not really his friend.) And you may feel that you are acting disloyally, and undermining the friendship, if you do not meet his expectation. But this is a sign of a destructive friendship. You have a friendship that seeks to impede your ability to think for yourself, and you probably also have a friend who overestimates his own importance and underestimates yours. To that extent, things are not going well.

An illuminating analogy can be drawn between friendship and patriotism, but it is not one that makes patriotism look better. An overbearing friend can seek to stifle your good judgment by expecting that you will always be inclined to think well of him, even when that involves putting yourself at risk. Patriotic loyalty stifles your good judgment by demanding that you think well of your country, regardless of the evidence, and even when you are making a decision of real consequence.

Put it this way. There is just no such thing as a patriot who is inclined to believe the best of her country, but puts that inclination to one side when making important decisions. When asked to make sacrifices for her country, or otherwise to act on her belief that her country has certain valuable features, a patriot does not try to forget her allegiance to country and interrogate her beliefs from a more neutral perspective. Nor does she recuse herself on the grounds of possible bias. Rather, these are the kinds of circumstances under which patriotic loyalty is likely to march stridently into view; these are the circumstances under which we find out who is really a patriot and who is just pretending. In this regard, patriotism is unlike a good friendship, but much like a dysfunctional friendship. Again, there is no good news here for patriotism.

CAN WE GET BY WITHOUT PATRIOTISM?

Even if all that I have said so far is correct, space remains for a defense of patriotism as an attitude that has instrumental value, and for the claim that patriotism, whatever its faults, is inevitable. Patriots, it could be argued, are more likely to feel a sense of identification and solidarity with those around them, and are hence more likely to be good citizens. Patriots may be more likely to have a sense of belonging and identity, and so more likely to be happy and well adjusted. Stephen Nathanson argues that anti-patriotism is a political liability, and that it is only by embracing patriotism, in some form or other, that we can hope to have any real political influence.[7] MacIntyre says that we will surely want our soldiers, whom we expect to die defending us if need be, to have a patriotic devotion to the country for which they fight, and so a lack of patriotism among the citizenry from which the army is drawn would leave us in danger.[8] And it is often suggested that patriotism is just an inevitable part of human nature, and so the best hope is not to abolish it, but to see that it is used wisely.

Such claims are difficult to assess and less obvious than their defenders seem to think. We should be wary of claims about what is strictly unavoidable in human nature or political life; in any event, where morally dubious phenomena are unavoidable, it can still be worth pointing out that they are morally dubious.[9] As George Kateb

---

[7] *Patriotism, Morality and Peace.* See especially the Introduction and Chapter 2.

[8] "Is Patriotism a Virtue?," p. 56.

[9] In "Whose Greater Good? Virtue, Cosmopolitanism and Reform in 18th and 19th Century German Patriotism," Lydia Moland gives reasons to think that patriotism as it currently exists is, far from being an inevitable part of human nature, a relatively contingent and recent phenomenon.

has argued, there is a certain defeatism, not to say condescension, in the tendency of philosophers to prescribe patriotism for the masses.[10] When I think of the people I know who are closest to being ideal citizens, I do not think of those who are most patriotic; I think that it is far more important to have a general respect for the rule of law and the interests of others, wherever they are from, than to have a patriotic devotion to country.

However these things stand, there are two points that should be clear. First, along with the good things to which patriotism can lead, there are also the bad: patriotism can underlie warmongering, smugness, intolerance, bigotry and stupidity. Its overall usefulness for society is, at the least, contestable. Second, assuming that my claim about patriotism and bad faith is correct, there is something to regret about patriotism; there is reason to wish that we could get by without it, even if we cannot. If we need patriotism, then that is a shame.

CONCLUSION

I have argued that there are reasons to think that patriotism, by virtue of its very nature, is undesirable. Patriotic loyalty is of a kind that requires certain beliefs about its object, without being premised upon an independent judgment that these beliefs are true. As a result, the patriot tends to make judgments about the qualities of her own country in a way quite different from that in which she makes judgments about others, but she is unable within her patriotism to admit to this tendency. That is patriotic bad faith.

Sometimes, the disposition to patriotic bad faith is not something that we need be too concerned about. In some cases, it will never be expressed. In others, the motivations underlying it will be very weak. Given, however, the moral seriousness of patriotism and the importance that patriotism tends to hold for those who have it, there is good reason to think that the disposition to patriotic bad faith will usually be more than just an interesting psychological quirk or

[10] "Is Patriotism a Mistake?"

harmless indulgence. Patriotic bad faith is likely to play a central role in the patriot's construal of the world and of her own moral obligations, and it is likely to lead the patriot to make bad decisions of real consequence. This, I think, constitutes a presumptive case for the conclusion that patriotism is not a virtue and is probably a vice.

More broadly, I have tried to show that there are strong reasons to think of at least one familiar kind of loyalty – patriotism – that it is positively undesirable. Patriotism might be natural, common, and commonly admired, but that does not mean that we should embrace it. Furthermore, it is possible to say that patriotism is undesirable without thereby finding yourself forced to say the same of other familiar loyalties. We should not be bullied into endorsing particular loyalties on pain of being unable to endorse any loyalties at all.

CHAPTER 5

Filial duty: debt, gratitude and friendship

INTRODUCTION

Even once we have become adults, we have special duties to our parents. These are *special* duties because they are not duties that we have to people generally. You might have the duty to keep in touch with your parents, or to take them into your home when they are sick or elderly, but these are not things that you are obliged to do for just anyone.

Duties to parents are, as duties go, important. It is common for people to make large sacrifices in order to provide for their parents, or to be with their parents at crucial times, and to make those sacrifices, in part, because they feel that it is their duty to do so. Those who neglect their filial duties can evoke deep disapproval; think of a rich son who cannot be bothered doing anything to help his parents – his lonely and impoverished but perfectly loving parents, who did all they could to give him the best possible opportunities in life – and try not to disapprove.

When I spoke about friendship and patriotism, I looked at the different ways in which they can involve belief, and can come into conflict with moral or epistemic standards. My discussion of filial loyalty – loyalty to parents – takes a different approach. This chapter and most of the next look at competing theories of filial *duty*; these are theories that concern the explicitly moral dimensions of the parent–child relationship, giving competing accounts of what we as grown children are obliged to do for our parents. At the end of the discussion of filial duty, I will come back to the topic of loyalty. A proper understanding of filial duty yields a reason to think that we can have a duty to be loyal to our parents, in the fully-fledged psychological sense. If I am right, then there is at least one kind of loyalty that is, under certain conditions, obligatory.

Filial duty has not been a prominent topic in the recent literature, but a few contemporary philosophers have addressed it. Their discussions yield three rival accounts of filial duty: the debt theory, the gratitude theory and the friendship theory.[1] According to the debt theory, your filial duties are duties to repay your parents for the goods that they have given you and the sacrifices that they have made for your sake. The gratitude theory says that filial duties are not duties to provide repayment for those goods and sacrifices, but duties to respond to them with appropriate acts of gratitude. On the friendship theory, your filial duties are not the duties of someone who is responding to benefits received, but are rather the duties of a friend.

I will spend this chapter describing the debt, gratitude and friendship theories, and explaining why I do not find any of them satisfactory. Chapter 6 offers an alternative, which I call "the special goods theory." The idea here is that there are certain goods distinctively associated with relations between parents and children, and special duties to parents are duties to produce those goods within the context of a particular parent–child relationship.

Three preliminary points are worth making. First, there are two different questions that can be asked about filial duty. We can ask of particular grown children why they have duties to their particular parents, if they do; or we can ask why society should have laws and customs that assign filial duties to grown children, if it should. Perhaps there are some individuals whose relationships with their parents do not, considered in isolation, produce special duties, but who nevertheless fall under a justified social practice that requires them to give their parents special treatment. Except where stated, my concern is with the former question.

Second, some may be uncomfortable with talk of filial "duty," worrying that it presupposes an overly moralized picture of the parent–child relationship. Within a healthy parent–child relationship,

---

[1] The labeling follows Blustein, *Parents and Children*, p. 166.

it might be said, the child does things for the parent willingly, out
of love, not out of a motive of duty, so if we get to the point at
which we need to think about filial duty, we are already in trouble. I
think this concern is misguided. Even if thoughts of filial duty do not
motivate, in ideal cases, that does not show that filial duties do
not exist or that there is no point asking what they are. Look at it from
the child's point of view: it is quite possible to do things for your
parent because you love and care for her, while at the same time
believing that in acting as you do you are performing your duty, and
that it would unacceptable to do anything else. And it is in any case
reasonable to think, as others have argued, that a conception of filial
duty can play an important role in shaping the concerns of a grown
child whose deepest motive is love for his parent.[2] In any case, in
speaking of filial duties I do not intend to suggest that those performing them should be motivated (only) by thoughts of duty.

   Third, it is worth noting that filial duty is, perhaps more than most
others, a moral issue on which customs and opinions differ greatly
between different times and cultures. It is difficult to know how to
address such differences, though I will say something about the
question later on. For now, I just want to acknowledge that my
starting point is filial duty as it is understood within the cultural circles
in which I tend to move. When, for example, I call upon the intuition
that it is reasonable to think that a grown child has the duty to do what
he can to ensure that his parent's medical needs are met, but does not
have the duty to marry within the family faith, I just mean – at least at
first pass – to identify a strong opinion that tends to be shared around
here; I am not pretending that no other conceptions of filial duty exist.

THE DEBT THEORY

The debt theory explained

Your parents have done an enormous amount for you, and you owe
them something in return: that is the thought behind the debt

---

[2] See Blustein, *Parents and Children*, pp. 103–104; and Sommers, "Filial Morality,"
   pp. 448–449.

theory. As a grown child, runs the idea, you are in a position analogous to that of someone who has taken out a loan but not yet repaid it. You have enjoyed certain benefits, but those benefits were not free. Filial duties identify the things that you have to do to discharge your debt to your parents.

The debt theory resonates with some familiar ways of thinking about filial relationships. A father may tell his daughter that, after all that he has done for her, she owes it to him to work harder at college or come home for Christmas. When you are deciding whether or not to do something for your parents, and you remember all the things that they did for you when you were a child, it is natural to have the thought, "This is the least that I can do in return."

Parents are certainly analogous to creditors in so far as they have conferred benefits – in standard cases, enormous benefits – upon their children. In some traditions, the profoundest of those benefits is held to be life itself, though most contemporary philosophers do not see the very giving of life as a plausible grounding for filial duty.[3] Still, children are nourished, loved, nurtured and educated by their parents. In order to secure in an open market the benefits that we receive from our parents, we would be prepared to take on an enormous debt. To this extent, the debt theory is plausible, and throughout much of the history of philosophy, it has been regarded as unproblematic and transparently true.[4]

From a contemporary point of view, however, the debt theory can look anachronistic, because relationships between parents and children do not seem to fit into familiar conceptions of contract and compulsory reciprocation. The two most prominent objections are that it is unfair to think of the child as accruing debts in virtue of a relationship that he had no choice but to enter, and that because

---

[3] On historical approaches, see Blustein, *Parents and Children*, Part 1; and Ivanhoe, "Filial Piety as a Virtue." For arguments against the claim that giving life can in itself create reciprocal duties, see Jecker, "Are Filial Duties Unfounded?," p. 74; and Ivanhoe, "Filial Piety as a Virtue."

[4] On filial duties as discussed in the western tradition, see Part 1 of Blustein, *Parents and Children*. On filial duties as discussed in Chinese philosophy, see Ivanhoe, "Filial Piety as a Virtue."

parents are just carrying out their own duty in caring for their children, they are not owed anything in return. I will argue that neither of these objections is as compelling as it seems, though there are other reasons to reject the debt theory.

Duties in response to unrequested benefits?

As philosophers and harassed adolescents have emphasized, we do not ask to be born or nurtured. We never enter into any contract with our parents; we just find ourselves in the state of having been benefited. "Merely receiving benefits or help from another," says Jeffrey Blustein, "does not give rise to a duty of indebtedness." If you mow my lawn unasked, he points out, then it might be appropriate for me to make some gesture of thanks, but you do not place me in your debt.[5]

This complaint about the debt theory is less telling that it initially appears. It relies upon the principle that you cannot incur a debt without consenting to the relationship from which it arises. That principle seems correct with regard to everyday dealings between competent autonomous adults, but is not so clearly correct in some other cases. If an accident leaves you unconscious and a stranger takes you to an American hospital, then you will be billed for your treatment; if you are picked up by an ambulance in Australia, then you will be billed for the ride; these are cases in which you are required to repay someone for the provision of benefits that you did not request, and it is not obvious that they are cases of injustice.

Another case is that of debts to the state. If you do not pay your taxes, for example, then you fall into debt, even though you never enter into any explicit agreement from which the debt arises. The task of explaining how such debts arise legitimately is very difficult, and some doubt that it can be accomplished.[6] Still, most people, and

---

[5] Blustein, *Parents and Children*, p. 180. See also Wicclair, "Caring for Frail Elderly Parents," pp. 174–176; English, "What Do Grown Children Owe Their Parents?," p. 354; and Daniels, *Am I My Parents' Keeper?*, p. 29.

[6] See, for example, Nozick, *Anarchy, State, and Utopia*; and Simmons, *Moral Principles and Political Obligations*.

most philosophers, are confident that there must be some way of saying why states, or some states, can legitimately expect contributions from citizens.

When a valued institution (like the state) is at stake, and when issues of consent are difficult to resolve (as when an unconscious person requires medical treatment), the question of how a person can legitimately incur debts becomes much murkier than the "no debt without consent" slogan allows. It is not implausible to think that the parent–child relationship is similarly murky.[7]

Duties in response to the performance of duties?

A second objection to the debt theory arises from the plausible claim that it is the *duty* of parents to provide their children with nutrition, nurturing, education and so on. Seeing as parents are just doing their duty in providing for their children, runs the argument, they are not entitled to any repayment for doing so. It is not as though parents are free to withdraw their care if their children do not promise to reciprocate in later life; parents have to look after their children in any case, and cannot demand anything in return.[8]

There is reason, however, to reject the principle that you cannot become indebted to someone just because she does her duty. Suppose that I am riding my bicycle, and perhaps being a little reckless, and I crash and lose some skin from my arm. Suppose that you are a passer-by, in a good position to give me some much-needed assistance. And suppose that the best way for you to help me out is to use your jacket to bandage my arm and stem the flow of blood. It

---

[7] See also the comments on p. 342 of Hardimon, "Role Obligations."

[8] Wicclair provides a nice discussion of this objection in "Caring for Frail Elderly Parents," and appears to accept it as showing that parental sacrifices do not generate duties of indebtedness; see pp. 168–171 and 174–176. Blustein says that "grown children are not indebted (in the narrow sense) to their parents for having seen to it that they received an adequate education ... for this is something that the parents, as parents, had a duty to do" (*Parents and Children*, p. 182). The objection is also pressed in Daniels, *Am I My Parents' Keeper?*, pp. 30–31.

seems right to say that in helping me out and sacrificing your jacket, you are doing your moral duty; it would be unacceptable for you to think, "This person clearly needs help, but I am not going to provide it because it will mess up my jacket." It also seems right to say, however, that I, having benefited from your help, have a moral duty to replace your jacket, or at least pay for the dry-cleaning, if I possibly can. It was your duty to help me, but now that you have performed it, I find myself with a duty to compensate you for your loss.

So it is not true, or not obviously true, that the performance of a duty cannot generate a debt. There is nothing immediately para-doxical about the thought that parents are required to provide care for their children, but are permitted to demand certain goods in return; or that children can correctly think that they receive care as a matter of parental duty, but nevertheless incur debts towards their parents as a result of its performance.

The duties of children and the duties of debtors

A better reason to doubt the debt theory is that it leads to implausible claims about what filial duties we actually have. If you give me a loan, then my duty is to repay the loan, or to meet whatever con-ditions I agreed to meet in return for the loan, and no more or less. The size of my debt to you does not alter with your needs, my financial situation, or my lifestyle choices. Whether or not you and I come to be friends or enemies, whether or not we enjoy each other's company or value our personal relationship, makes no difference to the size of my debt or my duty to pay it off.

As Jane English points out, filial duties do not fit this pattern.[9] There is no measure of goods such that, once you have provided it to your parents, your filial duties are discharged. Filial duties do not seem to differ in nature or weightiness depending upon the exact amount of effort and energy devoted by parents; you may have been a healthy and angelic child, undemanding and a delight to nurture,

---

[9] English, "What Do Grown Children Owe Their Parents?," pp. 354–356.

but that does not mean that you have any less of an obligation to respect and help your parents than you would have had if you had been sickly and temperamental and very difficult to raise.

In addition, your filial duties do seem to depend upon your situation, in that you are only required to give your parents what is reasonable, given your abilities and lifestyle choices. To use English's example, if you choose the low-paying career of an artist and are struggling for money, then you do not have the duty to contribute as much to your parents' medical care (say) as you would if you had chosen a better-paying career. Your duties to your parents also vary according to the state of your relationship with them. If you and your parents drift apart, or have a serious and permanent falling-out (for which you cannot reasonably be blamed), then you are left with few filial duties, perhaps none at all. The duties of grown children to parents do not look like the duties of debtors to creditors.

THE GRATITUDE THEORY

The gratitude theory explained

Often, when other people do good things for us (or try to), we are obliged to respond in a certain way, but not in order to repay them for what they have done, nor to honor a contract. Rather, we are obliged to respond with acts of gratitude. Duties of gratitude are not duties of strict indebtedness, meaning that they are not duties to repay a benefactor or meet the terms of a contract. But they can reasonably be counted as duties, in so far as they identify acts that we ought to perform – acts that it would be morally remiss of us not to perform – in response to benefits received. The gratitude theory says that we ought to be grateful for the goods that we receive from our parents, and that filial duties are best understood as duties that arise from this gratitude.

As with the debt theory, it is easy to find connections between the basic idea of the gratitude theory and ordinary thoughts about filial duty. Offhand, it seems that whenever someone has made sacrifices and given you benefits, you ought to feel gratitude; when someone has made enormous sacrifices and given you enormous benefits, your gratitude should be enormous. And when someone is taken to have neglected his filial duty, it is customary to describe him as an "ungrateful child."

Duties of gratitude differ from duties of strict indebtedness in ways that allow the gratitude theory to avoid some objections that have been made to the debt theory. For one thing, it is quite appropriate to be grateful for benefits that you did not request; if someone mows your lawn without being asked, you do not incur a duty to repay her, but you should be grateful. For another, it is perfectly appropriate to be grateful for benefits that you receive from someone who was just doing her duty; you should be grateful to a passer-by who helps you out after a bicycle accident, even if she would have been neglecting her duty had she done anything else.[10]

I have argued that the objections to the debt theory thereby avoided are not such strong objections after all, but the gratitude theory also appears to have the potential to avoid some of the objections to the debt theory that I take to be strongest: those concerning the structure of filial duties. This is because the contents of duties of gratitude, like those of duties to parents, can be vaguely specified and heavily dependent upon circumstances. To give one example, what we ought to do out of gratitude depends upon what we reasonably can do. If you do something nice for me, and I am relatively well-off and live nearby, then it may be that I ought to respond by treating you to a nice dinner; but if I have little money or live faraway, a sincere note of thanks might be perfectly sufficient.

Largely for these sorts of reasons, the gratitude theory is by far the most popular account of filial loyalty in the recent philosophical literature.[11] Where philosophers have objected to the gratitude

---

[10] Blustein, *Parents and Children*, pp. 175–186; Simmons, *Moral Principles and Political Obligations*, pp. 179–181; Wicclair, "Caring for Frail Elderly Parents," pp. 174–176.

[11] For sympathetic discussions of the idea that filial duties are duties of gratitude, see Berger, "Gratitude"; Blustein, *Parents and Children*, Part II, Chapter 3; Ivanhoe, "Filial Piety as a Virtue"; Jecker, "Are Filial Duties Unfounded?"; and Wicclair,

theory, they have tended to do so by denying that the bringing up of a child generates duties of gratitude on the child's part.[12] I will offer a different line of criticism. I do not dispute the claim that it is appropriate or obligatory for children to be grateful to their parents, but the gratitude theory is nonetheless wanting. There is no reasonable, familiar conception of gratitude, I shall argue, that allows children's duties of gratitude to their parents to be anything like the filial duties that we ordinarily think to exist.

Duties of gratitude

Gratitude is, in the first instance, a psychological state. It is a cluster of feelings and attitudes held towards someone (or something) that you take to have acted out of concern for you.[13] It includes feelings of thankfulness and appreciation, and an understanding that something valuable has been done on your behalf; in being grateful for another's efforts, you take it not to be something trivial, but to matter, that they have been put towards to your interests, rather than towards something else.

What is a duty of gratitude? As Fred R Berger has argued, the most familiar duties of gratitude are best construed as duties to demonstrate or communicate feelings of gratitude, which is to say that they are duties to show that you feel appropriately grateful (or perhaps to act as you would if you did feel appropriately grateful) for a given benefit.[14] In demonstrating your gratitude, you show

"Caring for Frail Elderly Parents." Sommers argues in "Filial Morality" that there are duties of gratitude towards parents, though the considerations that she offers are quite different from those mentioned here.

[12] See Simmons, *Moral Principles and Political Obligations*, pp. 157–183; and Slote, "Obedience and Illusions."

[13] In "Gratitude and Justice," Fitzgerald explores the idea that gratitude can be appropriately felt towards those who have harmed you, or those whom you have benefited. Gratitude in these cases, however, could surely not be of the sort that grounds *duties* towards the person to whom you are grateful.

[14] "Gratitude." The claim does not imply that the only reason to perform acts of gratitude is to make someone else aware that you are grateful, just that it is this purpose that is the ground of the *duty* to act out of gratitude.

that you are aware and appreciative of your benefactor's efforts, that you regard her time and energy as valuable, that you do not take her or her efforts for granted.

What counts as an effective or appropriate demonstration of gratitude depends on several different factors. Some have to do with conventions. Knowing what you ought to do by way of showing gratitude in a given instance is often a matter of knowing what is generally expected in such cases. You need to know just how grateful you are expected to be for a given benefit, and whether flowers or chocolates or words of thanks – or whatever – are conventionally understood as communicating the appropriate level of gratitude.

Usually, the greater the benefit you receive, or the more its provision has cost your benefactor, the more you should do by way of showing gratitude. You can do too little or too much by way of displaying gratitude. If you just say "thank you" to the people who carried you out of the wilderness after you broke your leg on a hiking trip, then you have not done enough. If you send a bunch of flowers to the person who held the door open for you, then that is a little creepy, betraying a misunderstanding in the opposite direction of what has been done on your behalf. Too small a gesture of gratitude can send the message that you do not really understand or value the efforts that have been made for your sake. Too great a gesture of gratitude can send the message that your benefactor is not one who often does things for others, and that this deed hence calls for special attention; or that she was not really motivated by benevolence, but by the hope of getting something in return; or that the concern for you expressed through her efforts is greater than it really is, and hence that the relationship between the two of you is closer than she would like it to be.

Doing more by way of showing gratitude usually means conferring a greater benefit upon the person to whom you are grateful. (You might buy her chocolates to thank her for something small, but take her out for dinner to thank her for something big.) It does not follow, though, that your primary goal in acting out of gratitude is to grant your benefactor a benefit. In saying a sincere "thank you" or sending a card, you are not setting out to provide your benefactor with a benefit, exactly. (A $20 check may have greater value, in most respects, than a thank-you card, but you would not be doing a better job of showing gratitude by sending the check instead.) There are times when you will try to make sure that your gesture of gratitude confers a real benefit upon your benefactor. You might make an effort to find a bottle of her favorite wine, or, if she has an allergy, to make sure that the chocolates you buy her do not contain nuts. But the main point, so far as gratitude is concerned, is still just to communicate your appreciation, not to make your benefactor better off. It is just that you communicate your appreciation by showing how much attention you are prepared to devote to making sure that she feels appreciated.

Duties to convincingly demonstrate feelings of gratitude are vague in content, and people in different situations can meet them in different ways. There are usually many different things you could do, any one of which would adequately communicate your gratitude for a particular benefit, so there is not usually a particular act that your duty of gratitude requires you to perform. And your feelings are often more clearly revealed by the effort that you put into a display of gratitude, or by the sincerity with which it is expressed, than by the token of gratitude that you actually offer. A thank-you card offered sincerely by someone with little money can count for more than an expensive gift sent by reflex by someone with money to burn. What you are obliged to do out of gratitude depends on what can reasonably be expected of you, given your situation.

Can filial duties be understood as duties to demonstrate gratitude? Not in my view. In making this claim, I do not mean to suggest that we are not duty-bound to demonstrate gratitude to our parents. It seems perfectly appropriate, in standard cases, to feel gratitude in response to the efforts and sacrifices that your parents made, and it is plausible to think that you have a duty to communicate that gratitude, showing your parents that you value the efforts that they have put into your upbringing. Whether filial duties in general can be marshaled under this duty to demonstrate gratitude is, however, another question. I offer three reasons to think that the gratitude theory, so interpreted, is inadequate.

The point of filial duties

To begin with, filial duties appear to be direct duties to help, respect, please or benefit parents, not duties to do these things in order, or in so far as they are required, to demonstrate gratitude.

Suppose that you go out of your way to make sure that you are with your mother while she goes through a difficult medical procedure. What (conceivably) makes your act obligatory is the fact that your mother needs or wants you there, that things will be better for her in certain respects if you are around – not the fact (if it is a fact) that your presence will be understood by your mother as showing that you are grateful for the sacrifices that she has made for you in the past. To drive the point a little further: suppose that your mother is losing her mental powers, and will not be able to link your care for her in the present with her care for you in the past. Then your act will not make clear to her your gratitude, but that does not show that you have no duty to perform it.

As another way of making this clearer, duties to demonstrate gratitude can vary with the expectations of the benefactor in ways different from those in which filial duties vary. Some people are uncomfortable with or uninterested in displays of gratitude. They might do very significant things for you, but they do not want you to show your gratitude by doing anything too big; if you say a sincere "thank you" and tell them that you appreciate their efforts, then they will understand that you are grateful, and that is all that they want. When you know that you are dealing with such people, it can be pointless, counterproductive or even insulting to mark their contributions with the kinds of gestures of gratitude that you might offer to others in comparable cases, and you certainly are not duty-bound to do so.

Parents can be just like this. You might have parents who really do not want to be thanked all the time, who do not need your gratitude to be regularly emphasized, who would prefer that you did not do anything elaborate for them with the intention of communicating your gratitude. If you have such a parent, then your duty to demonstrate your gratitude to her is less demanding than, or at any rate calls for very different actions from, the duty that you would have otherwise. It is surely not the case, though, that you thereby have less demanding or very different filial duties generally. If you choose to play golf instead of visiting your mother after her operation, then it is no excuse to say, "She's not one for constant displays of gratitude. I have already told her how grateful I am for all that she has done for me, and she wouldn't want me canceling my game just to show how much I appreciate my upbringing." This is no excuse, even if true.

Gratitude and parental sacrifice

Second, the appropriateness of feelings of gratitude and the extent of duties to demonstrate them depend upon how much discomfort, exertion and genuine sacrifice have been involved in providing the relevant benefit, and this makes duties to demonstrate gratitude different in a further respect from filial duties.

Suppose that two people each spend a day helping you to move house. The first, "sacrificing" mover is an avid windsurfer, the day of your move is the only day with decent winds in months, he hates moving boxes and furniture, he has a bad back which he knows will be stiff and sore for days afterwards, he lives far away and has to drive for hours to and from home; but he cares about you and wants to make the move easier, so he helps out anyway. The second, "effortless" mover really quite enjoys the organization and companionship of moving house, he has no other plans for the day and is in fact happy to have something to do, he lives nearby and is strong of back and limb; there are frustrations and annoyances involved in any move, but all in all, he is delighted to have the chance to help out and cannot think of anything he would rather be doing.

You should, of course, be grateful to both the sacrificing mover and the effortless mover, and you should make your gratitude apparent. It would make sense, though, to feel differently about the two of them, and in particular to feel a deeper gratitude, and an obligation to do more by way of demonstrating gratitude, towards the sacrificing mover. He may not have been any more helpful on the day, but he had to make a greater effort to be there, and his participation, unlike that of the effortless mover, required of him non-trivial sacrifices and non-trivial soreness. He merits extra thanks and appreciation, and a more significant gesture of gratitude.

Compare the two movers to two parents. The first, "sacrificing" parent loves her child and is happy to give him a good upbringing, but in order to be a good parent she has to make an enormous conscious effort, sacrifice other valued parts of her life and cope with an extra degree of physical suffering. The second, "effortless" parent finds that she is just made to be a parent; there are difficult times, but she loves being someone who is bringing up a child, can think of nothing else that she would want to do with the time and energy involved, and finds the whole process to be an exhilarating breeze. Now, it might make sense for a child of the sacrificing parent to feel an extra kind of gratitude for her upbringing. There are certainly extra things that the sacrificing parent has to do in order to be a good parent, and they could well be the sorts of things that merit gratitude. But the children of effortless-style parents do not have lesser filial duties, speaking more generally, than those of sacrificing-style parents. It would be odd to think that your duty to look after your father in his old age is mitigated by his having found parenting so trouble-free.

An objection to the debt theory is that it seems to lead to the implausible claim that the extent of a child's duties to her parents depends upon exactly how much effort and sacrifice her parents had to make in bringing her up. What I have just tried to show is that a version of this objection also applies to the thesis that filial duties are duties to demonstrate gratitude. Duties to demonstrate gratitude are much more extensive when much more effort and sacrifice have been involved in the provision of the relevant benefit. Filial duties are not.

The demands of gratitude

Third, the kinds of things that children might have to do to fulfill filial duties are very different from the kinds of things that can legitimately be expected in fulfillment of duties to demonstrate gratitude. Filial duties, but not duties to show gratitude, are ongoing and open-ended, and can be very demanding.

Duties to parents, as has been mentioned, are not duties that can be left behind. In most cases, it seems, you have duties to your parents for as long as they are alive. You cannot resolve to dedicate some short period of time to your filial duties and thereby get them out of the way once and for all. And the fulfillment of filial duties can require non-trivial sacrifices; it can involve significant contributions of money, time and effort, it can involve taking your parents into your home, and so on.

Demonstrating gratitude, in so far as it is a duty, does not require ongoing commitments or significant sacrifices – though this claim needs some argument. We can start by noting that everyday gestures of gratitude tend to be discrete, one-off acts like sending a card or flowers or taking someone to dinner, and that understanding what a particular person is required to do by way of demonstrating gratitude involves understanding, in everyday cases, that she cannot be expected to give up anything that would count, given her situation, as a significant loss. (When you do something nice for someone, you cannot expect him to show gratitude by giving you something that he cannot reasonably afford to give you, or by sacrificing something that is of real value to him.)

Further, there is a good independent reason to think that duties to demonstrate gratitude cannot be ongoing or very demanding. Such duties are responses to benevolence, to someone's doing something to benefit you and not in order to receive something in return. The point of demonstrations of gratitude is to acknowledge acts of benevolence, not to provide repayment. All of this is undermined if those who do things for others can thereby place open-ended and demanding duties upon those whom they benefit.

Think of this from the point of view of the benefactor. If you act
benevolently towards someone, then you can, depending on the
circumstances, expect her to acknowledge your benevolence; you can
legitimately feel disappointed and perhaps affronted if she makes no
effort to show that she appreciates what you have done. But it is quite
another matter to feel that you will only be convinced of her gratitude
if she gives up something she values, or if she is still prepared to do
things for you years after the event. That is plainly unreasonable, and
throws your initial alleged benevolence into doubt. Demonstrations
of gratitude are responses to benevolence, and acts of benevolence do
not place, and should not be expected to place, significant burdens
upon those whom they are intended to benefit.

This claim can seem less persuasive once we turn to cases in which
gratitude is being shown for an exceptionally large benefit, one whose
significance approaches that of the benefits received by children from
their parents. What would count as an adequate demonstration of your
gratitude toward someone who has risked his life to save yours, or who
has dedicated eighteen years to nursing you through an illness? In such
a case, you might feel that there is nothing you could do that would
clearly demonstrate an appropriate level of gratitude. This could lead
you to think that you have to do something really significant (even if it
involves considerable sacrifice), or perform grateful acts for the rest of
your life, if your duty to demonstrate gratitude is to come close to
being met. (Note, though, that the question, "How can I ever show
you how grateful I am?," is not the question, "How can I ever repay
you?," to which the right answer, so far as the duty to demonstrate
gratitude is concerned, is that there is no need.)

That thought is natural, but in my view misguided. It can be seen
as a response to two truths. The first is that there is nothing in our
conventional repertoire of gestures of gratitude – not chocolates or
flowers or thank-you cards or anything – that is intended to
represent sufficient and sincere gratitude for something so enormous.
That can mean that you feel at a loss, wanting to communicate your
gratitude but without clear access to a convincing way of doing so.
Perhaps your best option is to make a lesser gesture – send the
flowers or whatever – while making it clear that you do not take it to

represent the depth of the gratitude that you really feel; or perhaps you should just say or write something that says how grateful you are and hope that it gets the message across. Whatever you choose to do, you are likely to feel a little inadequate.

The second relevant truth is that if someone does something very significant for your sake – something like saving your life or nursing you through an illness – then he may well come to give you a special place among his values and priorities, and to hope that the two of you will have an ongoing relationship. He might want to know more about you, to know what you do with your future life, and perhaps to have you as a friend. And you, of course, may well feel the same way about him. One way in which you can show that you value your benefactor and the efforts that he has made is to show that you are open to the possibility of an ongoing friendship, and to do things that might allow such a friendship to develop. You might demonstrate your gratitude by having your benefactor meet your family, by trying to stay in touch, or by doing other things that give the two of you the opportunity to form a relationship that both of you will value – not just because it commemorates a past act of benevolence, but for its own sake.

As someone to whom another has shown immense benevolence, then, you can find yourself wanting but unable to do something weighty enough to communicate the depth of your gratitude, and you can find yourself making an effort to allow your benefactor to be a part of your future life. It is hence natural and perhaps desirable to feel as though your duty to demonstrate gratitude is very demanding, or requires of you ongoing acts of gratitude. But there are ways to explain this feeling without supposing that duties to demonstrate gratitude really are open-ended, ongoing and demanding, and there is, as I say, good independent reason to think that they – unlike filial duties – are not.

Setting examples and sharing experiences

I have tried to show that the duty to demonstrate gratitude to our parents – while we may well have it – cannot account for filial duties in general. If that is the only kind of duty of gratitude there is, then the gratitude theory fails. But many will have the nagging thought that there must be more to gratitude than I have acknowledged. Sometimes, it may seem, gratitude really does make enormous demands, comparable to the demands of filial duty.

Here is an example of the sort of case I have in mind. Suppose that someone does something for you – suppose that he gives you a significant amount of money, without your asking and with no strings attached, at a time when you are in need – and that you respond with a perfectly appropriate and sincere demonstration of gratitude. Then, sometime later, you have the chance to do something similar for your benefactor – perhaps he has fallen on hard times and you are now quite solvent. You have, by hypothesis, done what you ought to do by way of showing gratitude for the initial act of benevolence. But wouldn't you still feel duty-bound to do for your benefactor what he once did for you, to respond to his needs as he once responded to yours? Wouldn't it be rotten of you to ignore his plight? And wouldn't he legitimately feel disappointed or saddened if you did? And doesn't this suggest that you would be failing in your duties of gratitude if you did not take the chance to reciprocate for his past kindness? Perhaps, then, there exists an additional kind of duty of gratitude: the duty to return your bene-factor's kindness if given the opportunity.

Again, there is a point of view from which it would be odd if this were so – odd to think that acts of *benevolence* could give rise to such extensive duties. Still, there is clearly something going on here; it *would* be lousy of you not to repay your benefactor's kindness, and he *could* legitimately feel disappointed if you did not. But this, I want to suggest, does not really have anything to do with gratitude – not in any sense that would help explain filial duties, anyway.

The first reason why it would be lousy of you not to be kind to your benefactor as he was to you is that his benevolence sets an example that you would do well to follow; he shows you how kind people can be. To live up to that example is not necessarily to show the same kindness to him, however. Circumstances might be such that you ought to show it to somebody else.

Suppose that you are at the supermarket, dealing with your crying children, trying to purchase a big load of groceries, when your credit card is rejected, and the stranger who is next in line buys your groceries for you. Some time later, you are at the supermarket, standing behind a new stranger and his crying children, and his credit card is rejected, and you know that you could easily pay for his groceries. It would be rotten of you not to, given the kindness that was done to you by the old stranger in the past. But paying for the new stranger's shopping would not be an act of gratitude. It would instead represent an understanding, stemming from the example set by the old stranger, that such acts of kindness are possible, and of great value.

In further support of the idea that it is not gratitude but the setting of examples that is at work, consider someone who performs an act of truly extreme benevolence: genuinely benevolent, but not one that any reasonable person would emulate. Suppose that you accidentally drop your bus pass into an icy river, and a stranger plunges in to save it before it sinks out of sight. His is an act of extraordinary kindness, and one for which you should be very, very grateful. But if your situations are later reversed, so that he is the one who has dropped his bus pass and you are the one with the opportunity to make the icy plunge, then you would not feel that you owe it to him, out of gratitude or anything else, to reciprocate. That is because it is plain that his act, generous as it is, does not set an example that a reasonable person should emulate. If gratitude for his act of benevolence included a duty to return the favor if given the chance, then you would have a strong reason to risk the freezing waters in order to save his bus pass, but it is obvious that you do not.

For another reason why there is an expectation that beneficiaries of benevolence will reciprocate, if given the chance, think about things from the point of view of the original benefactor: the person who, I have suggested, could legitimately feel disappointed if he finds himself in need of help, but does not receive it, from the one he has helped previously. The disappointment, I suggest, is less to do with a feeling that your beneficiary is insufficiently grateful – she might, after all, have given very sincere and convincing indications of her gratitude – than with a feeling that a shared experience that might have led to an ongoing relationship of a certain sort has not in fact done so.

As evidence for this claim, notice that the generous bestowal of benefits is not the only thing that can raise the possibility of, and generate the reasonable hope for, an ongoing relationship in which each party will act generously towards the other. Suppose you go through an experience with someone – perhaps a hiking trip or some time spent together as colleagues – that is not characterized primarily by your doing benevolent things for her, but that does lead you to think that the two of you have established the grounds for a long-term friendship. If she then declines a chance to do for you something that you would, given your understanding of the relationship, be prepared to do for her, you can feel sad and disappointed in just the way that you would if you felt that she ought to be grateful for some past act of yours. In either case, it is the failure to form a certain kind of ongoing relationship that is being regretted.

All of this is to suggest that feelings that you ought to reciprocate in response to another's benevolence, and feelings of disappointment when another does not reciprocate in response to your own, are to do with things other than gratitude, at least to the extent to which they are justified. When you act benevolently towards somebody else, you can probably expect her to show that she is grateful. But you cannot demand, though you may hope, that she will value your interests in just the same way that you have valued hers; you have to accept that the fact that you have been generous does not impose upon her an obligation to be generous too.

That said, the phenomena discussed in this section are relevant to the parent–child relationship. The care and concern provided by your parents may well stand as an example that shows you what is possible, and that you may be inspired to emulate, in your treatment of them and of others – especially your own children, if you have them. And the experience of being raised and loved by your parents surely does lay the groundwork for a future, mutually loving relationship, from which you and your parents continue to benefit. But this does not have anything much to do with duties of gratitude.

THE FRIENDSHIP THEORY

The friendship theory explained

The debt theory and the gratitude theory take the goods provided by parents during children's upbringings to play a direct role in generating filial duties. The friendship theory departs from this approach, saying that the source of filial duty is to be found not in what parents have done in the past, but in the relationship shared by children and parents in the present. According to the friendship theory, the duties between grown children and their parents are the duties of friends.

Now, the question of what duties exist between friends is not exactly uncontroversial. There is one aspect of moral relations between friends, however, whose existence is difficult to dispute and that proponents of the friendship theory take to be especially significant. It is that exchanges of goods between friends are controlled by a principle of mutuality, not of reciprocity.[15] Within a friendship, it is not important that each person contribute an equal amount, but rather that each person contribute what he reasonably can. If you and I enjoy surfing together, and you own a house near the beach, then I will naturally spend more time at your house than you will at mine. This does not mean that I am failing to do my duty; this is a friendship, not a business arrangement, and there is no duty for me to return your benefits in kind.

The friendship theory has some clear advantages over the debt and gratitude theories. It is well placed to explain why filial duties do not differ depending upon exactly how much parental sacrifice was involved in raising a given child; it can explain why filial duties are not duties that can be discharged once and for all; and it can (like the gratitude theory but not the debt theory) explain why grown children only have duties to do for their parents what they reasonably

---

[15] See English, "What Do Grown Children Owe Their Parents?"

can. It can also tell a plausible story about how changes in the parent–child relationship can affect filial duties. Suppose that your parents cease all communication with you because they disapprove of a lifestyle choice; you then cease to be friends with your parents, and so the friendship theory says, not implausibly, that you do not have the duty, or not to the extent that you would otherwise, to look after your parents in their old age.[16] And the friendship theory can do all of this just by making familiar observations about the duties that exist between friends, not by making contentious claims about how the parent–child relationship introduces special moral considerations.

Another advantage of the friendship theory is that it has the power to say something about what duties parents have towards grown children. Because friendships carry mutual duties, parents' duties do not cease once the benefits involved in a good upbringing have been distributed, but rather continue, in virtue of the ongoing friendship with their adult children. The debt and gratitude theories can leave the impression that parents of grown children have already made their contributions and can happily sit back and reap the rewards. The friendship theory says that parents have duties to act out of regard for their grown children as they would for any friend – to do their bit in maintaining the relationship, to show friendly concern and respect for their children and their choices, not to make unreasonable demands, and so on.

Friendships between parents and children

It is not uncommon for people to say that they have their parent or grown child as a friend, but when they do, they are usually thinking of the friendship as a kind of bonus, or as something that they have in addition to the basic relationship of parent to child. A relationship between a parent and a grown child may well lack the sorts of

---

[16] As Dixon emphasizes, there is no need for the friendship theory to say that all filial duties are extinguished completely when the child and parents cease to be friends; see "The Friendship Model of Filial Obligations," p. 79.

features – like shared interests, openness and equality – that are often thought to be characteristic of friendship.[17] You might love your parent, and deeply value the part she plays in your life, without thinking of her as a friend, exactly; if it was a friend that you were after, you may think, then you would choose someone else. Parent–child relationships do not have to be friendships in order to generate filial duties.[18]

This might not be much of a concern for advocates of the friendship theory. Perhaps they can appeal to a more inclusive notion of friendship that does incorporate familiar sorts of parent–child relationships.[19] Or, their claim could be weakened, so that the friendship theory does not say that parent–child relationships are friendships, but just that between parents and grown children there exist the same duties as those between friends. You do not have to be friends with your parent, the thought would be, in order to have duties towards her, but if you do have such duties then they are the duties that you would have towards a friend.

The real problem for the friendship theory, I want to argue, is not that you can have duties towards your parent without being her friend, but that duties towards friends and duties towards parents are sharply different in kind.

Discretion and weightiness

There are important respects in which friendship is a matter of ongoing choice. Whether you begin or continue a friendship with a particular person can depend, quite properly, on whether this is someone with whom you enjoy spending time, whether she brings out the best or worst in you, and whether you (still) value the shared activities – drinking, perhaps, or snorkeling – in which the friendship is grounded. Of course, friendship is not *all* about choice;

---

[17] Daniels, *Am I My Parents' Keeper?*, p. 32. For an extensive discussion, see Kupfer, "Can Parents and Children be Friends?"

[18] See Blustein, *Parents and Children*, pp. 190–193, and Ivanhoe, "Filial Piety as a Virtue."

[19] See Dixon, "The Friendship Model of Filial Obligations," pp. 80–82.

you do not sit down periodically and reassess each of your friendships from scratch, and friendships do not suddenly end when one of the friends decides to pursue opportunities elsewhere. Still, as people and circumstances change, friends often drift apart, in ways that are entirely natural and unobjectionable.

As friendships change and end, duties to friends change too. It would really be out of order for one of my old university friends to turn up now and expect to live in my flat for a couple of weeks, even though that is something she could quite reasonably have expected in the old days. Since we have drifted apart, my duties to her are not what they were. Our duties to our friends depend heavily upon what choices we make, and what happens to us, as time goes by.

The same is not true of duties to parents. You should not approach your relationship with your parents, as you would a friendship, with an open mind, hoping but certainly not presuming that your evolving interests and lifestyle choices will enable the relationship to stay strong. Correspondingly, there are some perfectly legitimate explanations of why you do not have certain duties to your friends that are not respectable when applied to filial duties. You cannot explain your failure to look after your parents by saying, "Look, they're great people, and I'll always value the times when we were close, but over the years we've taken different paths. I went my way, they went theirs, it seemed like the relationship wasn't taking us where we wanted to go … things just aren't the way they were." You are stuck with your filial duties, in a way that you are not stuck with your duties of friendship.

Filial duties also differ from duties to friends with regard to what they can demand. It is very plausible to think that if your parent is in need of medical care, and you can afford to pay for it, and there is no special reason why you shouldn't, then it is your duty to do so. It would be very odd, however, to think that you ever have a duty to do the same for a friend. You may of course choose to pay for a friend's medical care, but if you did then it would be beyond the call of duty. A child who makes sacrifices to pay for her parent's care is doing something that is praiseworthy, but expected in the circumstances.

Someone who makes sacrifices to pay the medical bills of a friend is doing something that is truly, unusually generous.

In response to these considerations, there is of course the option of rejecting not the friendship theory, but rather the expectations that are commonly attached to the parent–child relationship. Some of this revisionist spirit can be seen in English's defense of the friendship theory, in which she is concerned to show that certain familiar ways of thinking about filial duty are misguided.[20] There are certainly philosophers, often motivated by doubts about the debt theory, who have argued that the idea that grown children have a special kind of duty to their parents, while common, is grounded in a mistake.[21] If there are no distinctively filial duties, then the duties arising from parent–child friendships may be all that remain.

It is difficult to argue against this happily revisionist version of the friendship theory without providing a persuasive story about why grown children do indeed have special duties to their parents. I have argued that the stories considered so far are inadequate, and the goal of the next chapter is to provide something more promising.

[20] "What Do Grown Children Owe Their Parents?"
[21] See especially Slote, "Obedience and Illusions," and also Simmons, *Moral Principles and Political Obligations*, pp. 161–163 and 182–183.

CHAPTER 6

Filial duty: special goods and compulsory loyalty

THE SPECIAL GOODS THEORY

Desiderata

Let me list some of the claims about filial duty on which I drew in arguing against the debt, gratitude and friendship theories. Filial duties are ongoing and open-ended; they are not duties that can be discharged once and for all. The nature and extent of your filial duties do not vary with the exact nature or quantity of parental sacrifice involved in your upbringing; you do not have lesser filial duties for having been easy to raise.

Filial duties are not easily avoidable; the moral relationship from which they arise is not one that you choose to enter, nor one that you can simply choose to end. But they do vary with certain changes in your ongoing relationship with your parents; if your parents unreasonably disown you, for example, then your filial duties may not be what they were.

The demands made by filial duty do not extend so far that meeting them impedes your ability to exercise a reasonable amount of autonomous choice over the shape of your own life; you do not have filial duties to (for example) pursue a particular career, follow a particular religion, or give more financially than you can reasonably afford. That said, filial duties can be, in a different respect, very demanding; if you can afford to pay for your parents' medical care, for example, then filial duty can require you to do so, even if it is very expensive.

When brought together, our intuitions about filial duty suggest that it is, in structure and content, quite unlike other familiar forms of duty. One of the reasons why the prevailing accounts of filial duty fail is that they all try to explain it by analogy, saying that being someone's grown child is just like being in someone's debt, or having been the recipient of someone's benevolence, or being someone's friend. But being someone's child is not really like any of these things. The kind of relationship that you have with your parents, the way you think about them and the place that they have in your life, just does not have much in common with relationships that you are likely to have with anyone else. It should not be surprising that it is difficult to illuminate the moral relationship between a parent and child by grafting it onto our understanding of some other kind of moral relationship.

In trying to say something helpful about the moral relationship between the parent and the child, I want to begin with the idea that it is a singular kind of relationship giving rise to a singular set of duties, and that it needs to be understood on its own terms. Sometimes, to be sure, your duties to someone who is not your parent may be just like the duties that you would have to him if he were. This might be true of a particular teacher, for example, and it is sometimes, though controversially, said that a child's duties to his parents are analogous to the citizen's duty to the state.[1] In such cases, though, it is more informative to take filial duty as explanatorily fundamental, so that we understand the duties to the relevant teacher or state (or whatever) as being like the duties you would have to a parent, rather than trying to understand filial duty by saying that it is just like the duty that you would have to a state or a really important teacher. The most productive path towards better understanding filial duty, I think, starts with thoughts about what is unusual about the parent–child relationship.

---

[1] For some relevant discussion, see Jecker, "Are Filial Duties Unfounded?"; and Simmons, *Moral Principles and Political Obligations*, chapter 6.

The case for the existence of special goods

Consider the benefits, or improvements to the lives of individuals, involved in a healthy parent–child relationship.[2] While the child is young, she obviously receives important goods from her parent. When the parent is old, he is likely to receive important goods from his grown child. But this is not the whole story. It is not the case that the parent–child relationship is to the advantage of the child but not the parent during the child's upbringing, and to the advantage of the parent but not the child once the child becomes an adult. A healthy parent–child relationship adds value to the life of both the parent and the child for as long as it exists.

The point should be fairly obvious in so far as it concerns the parent. Many people strongly desire to have children. The desire to become a parent is not a straightforwardly altruistic desire to provide help to someone who needs it, nor is it just a desire to shore up your future interests by ensuring that you will have a grown child around to provide benefits in your old age, nor is it (usually) a desire to do what you think to be your moral or political duty. If you desire to become a parent, your desire is much more likely to be a desire about the shape of your own life. It is likely to be a desire that your life include the bringing up of a child, and all the experiences that that involves. Wanting to be a parent is, in a way, like wanting to have a boyfriend or girlfriend, even when there is no particular person that you want your boyfriend or girlfriend to be. You can want yours to be the life of someone who loves and cares for a son or daughter, not because there is a particular child whom you would like to care for and love (yet), but because you think that the life of a parent will be a good life.

The goods that parenting adds to a life can, if our ordinary attitudes are to be trusted, be of enormous value. We all know of people who are prepared to make enormous efforts in order to become parents. People often feel that it is very sad when someone who wants to become a parent is unable to do so. And the sadness is

---

[2] See Daniels, *Am I My Parents' Keeper?*, p. 112.

not that the world, or some unactualized child, will be deprived of parenting. It is sadness for the person concerned, sadness for what he is missing.

The goods of parenting are commonly held to be unique in kind. That is to say that there are not other sources, or not many easily accessible other sources, from which these goods can be gained. Someone who enjoys all good health, wealth, professional success and so on may nevertheless feel that if she never has children then something important will be missing from her life. If you desperately want to have children but never do, but you do win the lottery, you are unlikely to come out thinking, "At least I gained more than I lost." To have that thought would be to fail to understand the specialness – the uniqueness – of the goods of parenting.[3]

A similar story can be told about the goods of having a strong relationship with a parent. Even if you have everything else that you could possibly want, you may feel that you are missing out on something if you are estranged from your parents, or if they are no longer alive. Grown children who have lost contact with their parents will often go to great efforts to find them. (This can be true even if the parents were not involved in the child's upbringing. It is often very important to adopted children, and to children who were institutionalized early in life, to form relationships with their birth parents.) The sadness that is felt upon the death of your parent is not just sadness that someone whom you love and care for has died, nor is it just sadness that someone whose company you enjoyed will not be around anymore. It is also a feeling that something of profound value to your life has been lost.

I should make it clear that the goods on which I am trying to focus are goods that contribute to individual welfare, meaning that they are goods that benefit an individual, or that contribute to her

---

[3] None of this is to suggest that the special goods involved in parenting (or, for that matter, in having a healthy relationship with a parent) are essential, nor the most important, elements of a good life, nor that there is a blight on any life in which they are not contained. There are of course many other things that can make a life go well, and there are all sorts of reasons why it can make sense to choose them over the goods of being a parent.

well-being, or her best interests. The operative notion is not the notion of human flourishing, or of being an excellent instantiation of the human type, which may or may not have something important to do with being well off in the more fundamental sense. And I am not talking about what is good for a person in the sense of making him a morally better person; this, again, is a notion that may or may not have much to do with welfare. The point is that the special goods to which I am trying to draw attention are good for individuals independently of any judgment that having children is in itself such as to make you a better human specimen or a morally better person.

The special goods

I will now try to say something about what these goods are, though identifying the goods is more difficult than making the case for their existence. Consider the loose distinction between two goods that arise in the parent–child relationship: generic goods, which could in principle be received from anyone, and special goods, which the parent can receive from no one (or almost no one) but the child, or the child can receive from no one (or almost no one) but the parent.

A grown child may help out her parent by providing medical care, a ride to the shops, or a place to stay whenever he wants to visit; and she may make sure that his basic needs are met if he falls into financial trouble. From her parent, a grown child may receive the goods just mentioned, plus perhaps such things as babysitting grandchildren, instructions on how to cook a favorite meal, and information about what shots she had as a child. These are all examples of generic goods. They are generic goods because there is no reason in principle why it has to be the parent who provides them to the child, or the child who provides them to the parent. They could just as well be provided by others.

There are other goods that a parent might hope to receive from his grown child, but could not receive from anyone else. You might value your child's keeping in touch, but not because you want to be in touch with someone and your child is someone. The good in question is the good of having your child, the one you raised and the one you love and care about, make an effort to keep in touch. Beyond the good of having people around for Christmas, there is the good of having your children around for Christmas. These are goods that your children are uniquely placed to provide.

There are also larger, profounder special goods that may accrue to the parent of a grown child. Having been responsible for the child's upbringing, and especially if he is the birth parent, the parent may have important traits in common with his child, seeing in her a kind of younger version of himself; he is in any case likely to identify with and have a special understanding of his child. In being part of his child's adulthood, a parent may experience a sense of continuity and transcendence, a feeling that he will, in some respect, persist beyond his own death. There is also a kind of joy, and a kind of wisdom, that comes from a close involvement with the development of a person from birth through childhood and beyond.

What special goods might a grown child gain through a healthy relationship with her parents? There is a special value in having a *parent* from whom to seek advice and a fresh perspective, with whom to talk things through, and to whom to give your news. Given your history together, and the bonds that are likely to have formed, there are respects in which your parent may bring you a distinctive, and distinctively valuable, point of view and level of concern. There are not very many people with whom you can share a relationship that begins in your early childhood and lasts for most of your life. An ongoing, healthy relationship with a parent can provide a link between your life's various stages; from your parents' perspective, you can be helped to see how the different parts of your childhood and adulthood are connected, and are all yours.

An understanding of the parents who produced you can enhance your understanding of yourself. This is to do with your parents' great influence over your childhood environment and cultural inheritance, and also to do with the close genetic links between you and your natural parents; it helps explain, I think, why adopted children can feel that there is a level of self-understanding that they will achieve only when they know more about their birth parents, and why such a great loss is felt by children who are taken from their parents at birth.

There is another important good that can arise from your relationship with your parent or grown child, which is the good of having someone who is especially committed to ensuring that your needs and interests will be met, in the particular way in which parents and children can show each other such concern. Suppose that you come to be in need of a place to live, a loan, money for an operation, or something similar. If you are like most of us, there will be only a few people who will be prepared to make significant sacrifices in order to make sure that you get what you need. And it is very likely that those people will be your parents or grown children, perhaps along with other family members or a romantic partner; it is certainly likely that they are the ones that you could approach with full confidence that they will do whatever is needed. It is good to have such people around. In having such a special concern for you, they can add a level of protection against some of the worst possibilities that life might present.

Any two people could stand in a relationship in which each takes a special concern for the needs and well-being of the other. Whether as a result of biological or cultural factors, however, it happens to be between family members and romantic partners that such relationships are most likely to exist. In other relationships, even in very strong friendships, such dedication is hard to find. (And when it is found, it is natural to describe the people in question being like brothers or sisters, or sharing a relationship that is like one between a parent and child.)

In light of this fact, there is an important sense in which having someone who is especially prepared to do what is needed to protect your interests is a good that is special to the parent–child relationship. It very naturally arises within that relationship, is very difficult to find elsewhere, and takes on a particular sort of valuable character when shared between parents and children. Also, the parent and child are likely, at any given time, to have access to very different kinds of resources and expertise, meaning that the goods that they are able to provide for each other are likely to be particularly important. Even though it does not *need* to be instantiated within a parent–child relationship in order to exist, and even though it includes the disposition to produce generic goods, the good of having someone who has a special concern for your needs and interests is a kind of special good that parents and children can provide for each other.

These are some of the distinctive goods to which the parent–child relationship can give rise, but let me register a disclaimer before moving on. It may seem from the discussion in this section that I am committed to a very rosy picture of parent–child relationship. I do not mean to suggest that it, even in its especially healthy versions, is an unmitigated, glowing exchange of goods that leaves everyone feeling happy and loved and enlightened. Parents and children are also well placed to cause each other distinctive forms of frustration, inconvenience and psychological damage. Most parent–child relationships probably contain fair quantities of the good and the bad, and the special goods on which I have tried to focus attention can certainly be present and important even in a parent–child relationship that is quite destructive in some other respects. Sometimes, the special goods may even be entirely lacking, or their significance may be cancelled out or outweighed by the negative aspects of the relationship. We should bear these cases in mind too.

From special goods to special duties

There are important goods that you can only provide to your parents (or at least to very few others), and that your parents can receive from (almost) no one but you. In standard cases, you as a grown child find yourself in the position of being able to provide your parents with these important goods, and you find yourself in a relationship in which your parent has provided, and continues to provide, important goods for you. I suggest that the reason why you have special duties to your parents is that you are uniquely placed to provide them with these goods, and find yourself in a relationship in which they have provided (and perhaps continue to provide) special goods to you. And the duties themselves are duties to provide the special goods to your parents, within the context of the reciprocal relationship that you and your parents share.

When I say that your duty is to provide the special goods "within the context of your relationship with your parents," I mean to include in the view the facts that your parents are well placed, and probably duty-bound, to provide special goods to you too, and that the parent–child relationship is ideally one in which each party, over the relationship's existence, provides the other with important goods that they are very unlikely to receive from elsewhere. As a result, the expectations that fall upon you as a child apply to your parents to some extent too, and the nature of your duties to provide special goods to your parents depends in certain respects upon how your parents conduct themselves towards you, and upon the state of the relationship as whole.

The special goods theory tells a plausible unifying story about the content of special duties to parents. Doing your duty as a grown child is not like paying money to a bank or giving to a charity or hosting a dinner party for friends. When you make sure that you send a present for your parent's birthday, make an effort to keep in touch, or do what is needed for your parent to get the care that he needs, you are almost certainly providing something for your parent that he will not get otherwise; you are providing your parent with something that no one but his child could (or is at all likely to) give him. When I think about what I ought to do for my parents, I think about the special kinds of things that they can only get with my participation. They will not be miserable or impoverished without me, but there will be something special missing from their lives (and something special missing from mine) if I do not make an effort to do certain things for them.

Thinking of filial duties in terms of special goods makes it easy to see why filial duties are ongoing and open-ended, rather than duties that can be discharged once and for all. Many of the special goods that a parent can receive from his grown child, like the central good of being a part of his child's life, depend upon the existence of a continuing relationship. They are not goods that can be secured once and for all by one long holiday together, or one cash payment.

Often, the fact that you are in a position to provide your parents with important special goods is strongly connected to the fact that they have brought you up, and in doing so have made significant sacrifices for your sake. There is no direct connection, however, between the size of that sacrifice and the nature of the goods to which your relationship with your parents can potentially give rise. What matters is the existence of a parent–child relationship within which the special goods can be manifested, not the exact story about where that relationship originates. That is why the content and extent of filial duties are not determined in any straightforward way by what the parents have done for the child during her upbringing.

There is indeed no reason, according to the special goods theory, why a parent need have made any sacrifices for the sake of his child in order to be the object of filial duties. Suppose that a parent has no option but to give up a child for adoption or institutionalization, or that throughout the child's childhood the parent is required to focus his attention and resources on fighting in a war or for a political cause, or that a long and debilitating illness leaves the parent unable to make any contribution to the child's upbringing. It is still possible that the parent and child will, after the child has become an adult, form an ongoing relationship in which they are each provided with many of the special goods that parents and children can receive from one another. Should the relationship develop in the right ways, the child may eventually find herself in the position of being uniquely able to provide certain important goods to her parent, and may have filial duties towards him, of much the same sort that she would have if the parent had contributed more to the child's upbringing. The parent, of course, may come to have duties towards the child too. (This is very plausible. Once a genuine long-term parent–child relationship has been established, we would expect the parent and child to show a special commitment to each other. If the child chooses not to help out the parent when he needs it in his old age, she could not excuse herself by pointing out that the parent did not – because he could not – provide her with anything much during her childhood.)

Another feature of filial duties is their unavoidability; you cannot, just through your own choices, make your filial duties disappear, and you cannot, in any straightforward way, decide to whom they are owed.[4] In this respect, filial duties differ, as I mentioned earlier, from duties between friends. The difference is explained, I suggest, by the nature of the goods special to the parent–child relationship.

It is very rare for these special goods to be produced in any relationship apart from one between a parent and his child. As a child, you find yourself with particular people who are your parents and with respect to whom you are uniquely placed to provide the special goods, and there is nothing you can do that would get you out of this situation. If special duties to parents flow from special goods, as the special goods theory claims, then there is clear reason to think that such duties are not easily renounced.

That observation alone, however, cannot explain why filial duties and duties of friendship differ in this respect. There can be cases in which you are, in virtue of circumstances and perhaps your history together, uniquely placed to provide certain special goods to a particular friend; perhaps there are distinctive goods associated with having a friend with whom you went to school, and you are his only remaining friend from those days. Does this mean that it is your duty to provide him with the relevant goods of friendship, even if you do not want the friendship to continue? Without wanting to get too far into the question of which goods are associated with friendship, and without wanting to suggest that duties of friendship are best explained by something analogous to the special goods theory, I want to suggest that an important aspect of the value of friendship is its being freely entered into and maintained; one thing that is essential to the good of having friends is their being your friends not out of duty, but because that is what they want.

---

[4] Exception: Perhaps you can make the choice over who is to be the object of your filial loyalty, if you have (something like) the choice at an early age of whether to live with your mother or father, or if you are able to decide who will adopt you.

The special goods associated with the parent–child relationship are not like that, or at least, most of them are not. First, many of them are connected to kinds of discovery. The child gains a better understanding of herself and where she comes from, the parent sees aspects of himself reflected in his child, and through having a special, intimate knowledge of each other over a long period of time, they each learn something about life. These are things that are there to be found in the parent–child relationship, whether the parent and child like it or not; they are not there because the parent and child have made any particular choices about or commitments to the relationship.

Second, many of the goods associated with the parent–child relationship, including the special concern that parents and children are able to have for each other's needs and interests, exist in part because the ties between parents and children are so durable. You cannot simply decide to stop caring for your parent or child, and if you have a healthy relationship with your parent or child then you can expect her concern for you to be very reliable, surviving all sorts of fallings-out, differences in temperament and acts of stupidity. One reason why certain goods are distinctively associated with the parent–child relationship is that that relationship is, characteristically, long lasting and dependable; the emotional bonds between a parent and child do not come and go with changes in taste, interests and lifestyle. The ties between you and your parents, and many of the goods that a parent–child relationship can produce, can be there even if you and your parents do not especially like each other, and even if you would choose to have different parents if you could.

If all of this is right, then there is a way for the special goods theory to explain why filial duties are not easily avoidable. If the parent and child had more effective discretion over what kind of moral relationship they share – were it not the case that they are more or less stuck with their duties to each other – then many of the distinctive goods of the parent–child relationship could not be manifested. You cannot choose your family, and that is not such a bad thing.

A final nice explanatory power of the special goods theory is that it could be expanded to account for other duties that arise between family members; I am thinking particularly of duties between grandchildren and grandparents. It is not only your parents whom you are expected to honor and revere, and for whom you are expected to show a heightened level of concern. You are supposed to do the same, if not to quite the same extent, with regard to your grandparents. But that obviously does not depend upon your grandparents having made enormous sacrifices for the sake of your upbringing, for which you are indebted or should be grateful, and it obviously does not depend upon your being their friends. It is very plausible, though, to think that there are special sorts of goods that can be shared between grandparents and grandchildren, and that somewhere in there your duties to your grandparents are to be found.

Restrictions on filial duties

Filial duties to promote special goods need to be understood as arising within the context of a particular parent–child relationship, one that is ideally to the advantage of both parties and one in which the parent has duties too. By seeing the duties through the lens of such a relationship, we can understand them as falling under certain principles which place restrictions upon the reach of filial duty and the circumstances under which it exists.

First, the child's duties to provide special goods to the parent should not seriously impede the child's ability to live a good life. That is a vague statement to be interpreted differently by those who have different opinions about the nature of the good life, but here is how the principle might work.

Among the special goods that a parent may receive from her grown child are those associated with having grandchildren, having her child marry within the family faith, and having her grown child live within walking distance. If the child had the duty to provide these goods to his parents, then he would be greatly restricted in his ability to make autonomous choices about the shape of his own life, and this is, or is regarded in contemporary western culture as being, a central component of the good life and a central entitlement of the individual. A parent–child relationship in which the child's duties seriously interfered with his autonomy would be one in which a very valuable aspect of his life was compromised for the sake of relatively insignificant gains for the parent. The relationship could fairly be characterized as constituting an unreasonable burden upon the child, not one that improves the lives of both parties.

The second principle that can restrict filial duties concerns whether or not the parent makes a fair effort to play her part in the relationship. If your parent chooses not to carry out her duties towards you, makes unreasonable demands, or is otherwise to blame for the deterioration of the relationship – if she unfairly disowns you, for example – then your duty to provide the special goods to her is mitigated or dissolved. This is an instance of a broader principle applying to relationships within which each party has duties to the other. Compare it to a student's duty to obey a teacher. Should the teacher fail to do what she should to advance the student's education, the student does not have the same duty of obedience to the teacher that she would otherwise have – even when she is still capable of obeying, and even when her obedience would still be of benefit to the teacher.

When the child's duty to provide his parents with special goods is construed as existing within the context of a particular relationship, the special goods theory can explain some important truths about the structure of filial duties. It can explain why the child's duties to the parent do not extend beyond what he can do, given his choices about the basic shape of his life; and it can tell (or co-opt) a plausible story about how filial duties can depend upon the conduct of parents and changes in the state of the relationship.

When do grown children have filial duties?

Not all grown children have duties to their parents, and one way to assess an account of filial duty is to see whether it makes a plausible claim about the conditions under which filial duties do not exist. The debt and gratitude theories say that filial duties arise in response to the sizable contributions and sacrifices made by the parent for the child's sake, which is to suggest that children whose parents have not made such contributions and sacrifices do not have filial duties. As I have said, though, there appear to be children – those whose parents are unable to contribute to the child's upbringing but still share with her a recognizable parent–child relationship – who meet this condition but have filial duties nonetheless. The friendship theory says that filial duties arise from ongoing friendships between parents and grown children, suggesting that those who are not friends with their parents do not have duties towards them; that claim, again, seems false.

If filial duties are duties to provide parents with special goods, then the cases (in addition to those mentioned in the previous section) in which there are no filial duties are those in which the child is not well placed to provide the special goods to the parent. Due to their utterly incompatible personalities or world views, their sharing a destructive or dysfunctional relationship, or their respective financial and other circumstances, a parent and grown child may have very little to offer each other. When you spend time with and try to do things for your parent, the result may be not that you each enjoy the profound special goods distinctive of the parent–child relationship, but that you are each left bored or angry or hurt or depressed. The special goods theory says that where children are not able to improve the lives of their parents by providing the special goods, they do not have filial duties.

At a broader level, the special goods theory says that were it not the case that grown children tend to be uniquely able to provide the special goods to their parents, filial duties, in their familiar form at least, would not exist. If children did not inherit many of their distinguishing characteristics from their parents; if having a particular person as a parent made no difference to what sort of upbringing the child receives and how he turns out; if parents did not care so much about, or judge and understand themselves in light of, the adult lives of their children; if parents and children were not inclined to form emotional bonds that make them able to show each other a special level of concern; if institutional arrangements were such that all of a parent's generic needs were adequately addressed regardless of the child's involvement; if things were different in these ways, then the value of the parent–child relationship, and the duties that children have to their parents, would be very different indeed.

Critiques and disagreements

To those who wonder why the fact that someone is your parent should mean that you ought to treat her differently from anyone else, the special goods theory has something to say. Your duties towards your parents are different, because there are things that you can do for your parents that you cannot do for just anyone. The special goods theory also offers attractive ways of framing, without necessarily resolving, more nuanced critiques and disagreements.

If filial duties are construed as the special goods theory construes them, then there are three obvious ways in which a radical critic could doubt the existence of filial duties, or play down their significance. One is to say that the goods distinctive of the parent–child relationship are not nearly as important as we ordinarily presume, in comparison perhaps with competing goods like class emancipation or completely undifferentiated community spirit. Another is to say that most parent–child relationships do not, in real life, tend to produce the special goods, perhaps generating instead a preponderance of guilt, pettiness and mutual psychological agony. Another is to say that fine as the special goods are, the principle of individual autonomy is of such overwhelming importance that it is unfair to expect anything of grown children, by virtue of a relationship that they never choose to enter. This seems a fair representation of the range of radical critiques of the notion of filial duty, or at least the ones that I hear in conversation. To defend the existence of filial duty against such critiques is to defend aspects of the special goods theory.

It is easy to read some degree of cultural relativity into the special goods theory, because the special goods associated with a given parent–child relationship will differ depending upon its cultural context. The list of distinctive ways in which healthy parent–child relationships improve lives in a contemporary western society will differ, obviously, from the list appropriate to a feudal society, and again from the list appropriate to a hunter-gatherer society. Some cultural differences in conceptions of filial duty come down to the dependence of some special goods upon aspects of the social setting; this, the special goods theory predicts.

But that, of course, is only the beginning. Some cultural differences appear to be straightforward ethical disagreements about what children should do for their parents. Second-generation immigrants often find themselves torn between their parents' expectations and the expectations that prevail in the new country; this is a characteristic part of the experience of many people whose parents immigrated from east Asian to western countries, for example. In many cases these differences can be traced to differing views of the importance of certain sorts of autonomy. To contemporary westerners, as compared with those from other societies, the individual's freedom to choose where she lives, and to choose her career, spouse, religion and lifestyle, are regarded as untouchable, regardless of how much good the individual could do for others if they were compromised. According to the special goods theory as presented here, this naturally translates into conflicting views about the demands of filial duty. I do not know whether it is possible to resolve this normative conflict satisfactorily, even in principle, but the special goods theory at least locates it within a broader, and familiar, cultural difference.

Difficulties for the special goods theory

Two major difficulties face an account in the style of the special goods theory, and I want to explain how I would respond to them. My responses involve some bullet biting, and bring out some respects in which the special goods theory, while attempting to capture much of our ordinary thought about filial duty, might challenge some of it too.

The first difficulty concerns the scope of the account. Perhaps the special goods theory does not find filial duty in every place it should. Suppose, for example, that you truly feel no greater inclination to look after your own parents than to look after others, no especially heightened motivation to make sure that your parents' basic needs and interests are fulfilled. You feel just as drawn towards paying for a stranger's medical care as towards paying for the medical care of your parents. Suppose that this is just a deep psychological fact about you, neither one for which you can be blamed, nor one that you are merely feigning. You lack, by hypothesis, the motivation that makes you especially able to play the role of someone who prioritizes your parents' needs and interests over those of others, and lack what it takes, on the special goods theory, to be duty-bound to play that role. (You might still be well placed to provide your parents with other special goods, like the good of having their child keep in touch.) But don't you still have a duty to look after your parents?

You indeed lack the natural attachment of child to parent that is the standard source of the relevant duties; if everybody were like you, the special goods theory must say, then moral relationships between children and their parents would be different from how they actually are. Still, your duty might have a non-standard source. Perhaps your parents have legitimate expectations that their child would feel a special attachment to them, and perhaps that gives you special reason to favor them over strangers. Or perhaps the presence of natural attachments in normal cases justifies a general social rule that children should look after their parents, and this provides a ground for the duty in your abnormal case.

Whatever can be said along those lines, however, the special goods theory that I favor implies that your filial duty in this case really is mitigated or otherwise changed by your failing to have the sense of attachment to your parents that most of us possess. I do not think that this is so dreadfully implausible, however. If you genuinely lacked an instinctive concern for your parents, and lacked it through no fault of your own and not because you are selfish or immoral or uncaring generally, then that would count as an excuse for your failing to prioritize your parents in the ways that we would normally expect.

The second major difficulty for the special goods theory concerns its use of the language of goods. Pointing out that grown children are uniquely placed to provide certain important goods to their parents might not be enough to show that they have weighty duties to provide those goods. For one thing, grown children may be just as well placed to provide (what look like) far more important goods to others; if your choice is between paying for a trip to visit your parents and paying for immunizations for several children in the developing world, then doesn't consideration of the goods involved say that you should choose the latter? For another thing, there does not appear to exist a general principle that those who are uniquely placed to provide certain important goods to others thereby have a strong duty to do so; if you are the one person in the world with the clinical skills to cure some disease, does that give you a duty, analogous in strength to filial duties, to provide the good of a cure to every sufferer?

I will admit that I do not have a good direct answer to the first challenge, partly because I am not convinced that it is *true* that the performance of filial duties should almost always take priority over other moral considerations. I think that it is enough for an account of filial duty to show that our duties to our parents are different from our duties to people generally, or that there are reasons to do things for our parents that do not count as reasons to do things for people generally. It ought not guarantee that those special duties and reasons are always of overwhelming strength. There is at least something to be said for the claim that we ought not prioritize our parents in the ways that we normally do – where the relevant alternative is providing immunizations to children in the developing world, not playing golf.

It is worth making the additional point that the problem identified here – the problem of making duties to parents look like considerations that override almost everything else – is not really unique to the special goods theory. The friendship theory leaves open the question of whether or not doing relatively minor things for friends should take priority over doing relatively vital things for strangers; if they should, then it is not obvious how the justification will go. The gratitude theory does not in itself say anything about the importance of duties of gratitude in the larger scheme of things; it might be clear enough that we owe a special kind of gratitude to our parents, but not that we should always fulfill duties of gratitude before attending to the greater needs of others. Perhaps the debt theory has an advantage here, because it is quite natural to think that if we truly owe someone a debt, then we do not have the option of ignoring it even if to serve some greater good.

As for whether the special goods theory can be brought under a more general moral principle: it should at least be clear that when you are uniquely placed to provide someone with an important good, you have a moral reason, all things being equal, to do so. And it is not implausible to think that that reason is strengthened if the relevant person is someone with whom you find yourself to be in a special relationship, and in particular one that involves her having provided important special goods to you. It seems likely, then, that there is a general moral principle, combining considerations of the provision of special goods with considerations of reciprocity, under which the special goods theory can be drawn. If I am right to think that the theory offers an intuitively appealing story about the content and force of filial duty – a central case – then that perhaps counts as a reason to think that there is a general principle in the offing.

A DUTY TO BE LOYAL

The good of a loyal child

I have suggested that grown children have duties to provide their parents with certain important goods, which arise uniquely, or almost uniquely, within the parent–child relationship. Among the goods I mentioned are those of having a child who cares about you and is strongly motivated to look after your needs and interests, and the joy, wisdom and feelings of continuity, transcendence and self-understanding that can come from having a child with whom you share a close relationship, lasting from birth into adulthood.

It is difficult to see how such goods could exist in a relationship that is not characterized by mutual loyalty, and – of particular interest here – in one in which the child lacks a strong loyalty to the parent. What makes it possible for the child to be moved to action by thoughts of the parent's needs and welfare, and what grounds the enduring parent–child relationship and the goods to which it gives rise, is, almost certainly, the child's deep emotional attachment to the parent. That is certainly the kind of feeling that we imagine existing between child and parent, when we imagine a healthy parent–child relationship; we imagine a child who cares about his parent for her own sake, instinctively thinking of things from the point of view of her interests, and so on.

As well as making possible other important goods, having a loving child who feels loyal towards you is in itself one of the goods of being a parent. It is one of the things you are likely to hope for, when you have a child; you hope that your child will be someone who genuinely loves you, and is genuinely loyal to you.

If I am correct in saying that filial duties are duties to provide special goods, and now that loyalty to parents lies behind many of the special goods as well as standing as one in its own right, then there is reason to think that among the duties of the grown child is the duty to be loyal to his parents, where this means not just acting like a loyal child, but actually being loyal – really having the feelings, emotions and motivations that loyalty involves. That is correct, within certain limits. Within those limits, and bearing in mind all the restrictions and enabling conditions on filial duty that I mentioned earlier, you do have a duty to be loyal to your parents. Let me deal with some obvious worries about this claim.

Is it enough just to seem loyal?

As I said in Chapter 1, whether or not you are loyal is in large part a matter of your feelings and motivations; it depends upon what is going on inside your own head. It could be accepted that you are more likely to provide the special goods to your parents if you have the right feelings and motivations, but doubted whether your feelings and motivations could themselves be objects of duties to provide such goods. Whether your parents enjoy the goods of parenting, it could be said, can only depend upon your outward behavior; how could it depend upon the hidden contents of your mind? How could their enjoying certain goods depend upon mental states of yours that make no outward difference? Your duties to provide special goods, on this view, could go no further than duties to act as you would if you were loyal, whether you really are or not.

The special goods to which I have drawn attention are goods for individuals, meaning things that improve individuals' lives, or advance individuals' welfare. The question of whether it is conceivable that you could provide such goods by being loyal, as opposed to merely seeming loyal, comes down to the question of whether or not an individual's welfare can be affected by the way things really are, as opposed to merely the way things seem to him. This question has been fairly thoroughly explored in the literature, and my own view, defended elsewhere, is that there are aspects of welfare that depend upon how the world is, not just how it seems; two people can live subjectively similar lives, while one has a higher level of welfare than the other.[5] I will not go into all the arguments here, but here is a relevant example, which hopefully will draw out an intuition in support of the claim.

Imagine a mother who is not really loved or cared for by her children, but whose children pretend that she is. Perhaps they want to make sure that they get their inheritances, or avoid others' disapproval, or set good examples for their own children. In any case, their pretense works perfectly. They tell their mother that they love her and do all the other things that she would expect loving children to do, even while discussing among themselves the fact that they do not like her, really, and sharing thoughts about

---

[5] See, for example, Parfit, *Reasons and Persons*, pp. 493–502; Griffin, *Well-Being*, chapters 1–4; Kagan, "The Limits of Well-Being"; Sumner, *Welfare, Happiness and Ethics*; and, for my view, "Welfare and the Achievement of Goals."

how they can prevent this becoming apparent. As far as the mother is concerned, she has loving, loyal children, and she takes a great deal of pride and pleasure in that false belief.

It seems to me obvious that things are not going as well for the mother as they would be if her children's affections were sincere. While she does not know it, there is something sad and unfortunate about her life, something that makes it a worse life, for her, than it would otherwise be. Certainly, if you had the choice, you would not be indifferent between leading her life and leading one that is just the same, but with genuinely loyal children. Think of it this way: suppose the mother were to discover the children's ruse. As well as feeling disappointed, and losing enjoyment of her present and future life, she probably would take a different attitude towards her past life. She would no longer think of it as a happy, satisfying time, but rather as a blighted time, a time during which things were not going well, though she did not then realize it. And that judgment would be based upon the fact that her children were not really loving and loyal, not the fact that they were not loving and loyal and then she found out about it. The mere fact that her children do not feel love and loyalty towards her is enough for it to be the case that the mother is missing out on one of the special goods of parenting.

Duties of feeling

In being loyal to your parents you can give them one of the special goods of parenting, and that, on the special goods theory, opens up space for the claim that in being loyal you are doing your filial duty. There is a further question to be answered about the idea that you could have a duty to be loyal, however. We do not have direct control over our feelings and emotions; we do not have the ability suddenly to become loyal to a specified individual. Our loyalties are not directly subject to choice, and that is a reason to doubt the suggestion that they are the subjects of duties.

While we do not have direct control over our feelings of loyalty, though, we are able to conduct ourselves in ways that affect our loyalties. I spoke of some relevant strategies in Chapter 2, when discussing the question of how we can manage our beliefs so as to take into account the demands of friendship. We can choose whether to embrace, ignore or try to purge our feelings of loyalty, and we can decide whether or not to act in their light. For most of us, feelings of loyal attachment to our parents are not foreign, ungraspable feelings, not feelings that we must struggle to cultivate; they arise naturally, and our decision is just over what to do with them. And we are able to do things that fortify them or keep them alive. If I have not spoken to my parents for a long time, or if we have been irritating each other or disagreeing about something, then my deciding to call, make an effort to be friendly, or organize an enjoyable day out together can not only cheer them up, but remind me of the things I love about them and reinvigorate my feelings of filial loyalty. By deciding not to make the effort to call, or deciding to be surly or let the disagreement fester, I can increase the chances that we will become further distanced from each other, and that my feelings of love and loyalty will begin to fade.

The claim that we have a duty to be loyal to our parents, then, is not inert. It does not come down to a claim that we have a duty to make the case something that is entirely beyond our control. Still, it is correct to say that that duty operates only within the limits of what we can control.

A child who is loyal to her parents is one who does certain things, and does them out of certain feelings and motives. You cannot decide to have the right feelings and motivations. But, if you have the right feelings and motives, you can provide special goods to your parents by acting in their light – by, for example, ensuring that you not only have a concern for their best interests, but that you act upon that concern. And, you can choose, where possible, to embrace and cultivate the right feelings and motives. That is as close as we can get to a duty of loyalty, and I have given reasons to think that it exists between children and their parents.

CHAPTER 7

Is loyalty a value? Is loyalty a virtue?

THE STORY SO FAR

So far, I have been looking at kinds of loyalty: friendship, patriotism and filial loyalty. Yet, when people talk about the ethical significance of loyalty, they often mean to speak not of loyalty of some particular kind, but of loyalty in general. In describing someone's character, for example, you might say that she is loyal. People sometimes speak of loyalty as a value or a guiding principle. Some philosophers are advocates of the "ethics of loyalty," believing that loyalty should be the foundational concept for ethical theory. The focus in all these cases is on loyalty itself, or on what different forms of loyalty have in common, not what sets them apart.

The next three chapters consider some questions about the ethical importance of loyalty, taken as a general proposition. This chapter begins by drawing some generalizations from claims made earlier in the book. Then, I will argue in turn that loyalty is not a value (in a sense to be specified), and that loyalty is not a virtue. In making my case for these claims, I will ignore some well-known arguments, associated with the communitarian program in moral and political philosophy, according to which loyalty is a central value or virtue; those arguments will be considered in Chapter 8. Chapter 9 looks at the prospects of the ethics of loyalty.

Sometimes, loyalty is obligatory; I said in Chapter 6 that there appears to be a duty to be loyal to parents, for example. That is to say that sometimes, when you are able to make choices that will reinforce your feelings of loyalty, or that involve your acting in light of such feelings, you are morally required to do so.

Loyalty, in any case, is responsible for many good things. As I said in Chapter 6, there are important respects in which lives can be improved through the loyalties characteristic of parent–child relationships. The same, I suggested in Chapter 2, is true of friendship. The point can easily be extended to other relationships of loyalty, like those between romantic partners, between workmates, and between teachers and students. We should be very happy that we are loyal to certain others and that they are loyal to us. We should be very happy that we do not live in a world without loyalty. In such a world, many wonderful things would be missing.

One loyalty that is responsible for some of those wonderful things, however, is friendship, and I argued in Chapter 2 that the value of friendship can conflict with another important value: epistemic integrity. What this suggests – and this generalized claim is probably more obvious than the narrower claim about friendship and belief – is that the values distinctively associated with various loyalties are not the only values, and values of the different kinds sometimes conflict. Sometimes, even though there is value in your being loyal, you can only be loyal by sacrificing other things that are also of value. Even when there are good reasons to be loyal, there can also be good reasons not to be loyal – and sometimes, I would add, the reasons not to be loyal are more compelling.

As well as having the potential to conflict with various external values, an instance of loyalty may have troubles within. Some natural and familiar kinds of loyalty involve by their nature certain dangers, confusions or mistakes. My example here is patriotism, which, I have argued, involves a disposition to fall into bad faith. It does not follow that patriotism and other such internally problematic loyalties are on balance undesirable wherever they are found; perhaps they are necessary if we are to achieve certain other valuable things. But it does follow that there is always something unfortunate about such loyalties. If we need them in order to have some goods that we just cannot do without, then that is something to be regretted.

IS LOYALTY A VALUE?

The question

There are several different things that could be meant by the question, "Is loyalty a value?" Loyalty can obviously be *valuable*, in at least the following sense: a particular relationship of loyalty, or loyalty as manifested within a particular relationship, can be valuable. Relationships of loyalty between friends, parents and children, and so on, can make lives much better, and are the sorts of things towards which it makes sense to have attitudes of valuing; it makes sense to value not just your friends, but your friendships, which is to say that it makes sense to value particular loyalties, and to value loyalty as it is manifested within particular relationships.

It is doubtful, however, whether loyalty could carry *intrinsic value*, on at least some ways of understanding that notion. Loyalty does not add value to a world independently of its effect upon the interests of individuals; and it is difficult to know what to make of – and just as difficult to get interested in – the question of whether a world would be valuable if it contained nothing apart from loyalty. The phenomenon of loyalty is tied in with the contingent psychologies, needs and interests of humans (and some non-humans), and there does not appear to be anything much to be gained from trying to consider it in isolation from that context.[1]

The interesting question, I think, is about how considerations of loyalty should figure in our decision-making, and, more broadly, in our thinking about what there is reason to do. Is loyalty something that we should care about, just for its own sake? If it is, then it is a value. Something that is plausibly a value in this sense is health. The fact that your doing something would be good for your health or the health of others plausibly counts as a reason to do it; it makes perfect sense to do something just for the sake of your health.

---

[1] For a more precise taxonomy of ways of thinking about intrinsic value, see McShane, "Why Environmental Ethics Shouldn't Give Up on Intrinsic Value."

Other values, in this sense, might be happiness, equality, respect, justice, integrity, beauty and truth.[2]

The question of whether or not loyalty is a value is, for my purposes, the question of whether or not we should think about loyalty in the way that we think about things like health and happiness. If loyalty is a value, then the mere fact that something falls under the concept "loyalty" should sometimes influence our decisions about what to do, and our views about what there is good reason to do.

Many people think about loyalty, or at least say that they think about loyalty, as though it were a value in the sense in question. You will sometimes hear people say that loyalty – or perhaps the principle or ideal of loyalty – is a value by which they try to live. "For me," someone might say, "loyalty always comes first"; or he might say that he tries to live his life according to the values of truth, loyalty and respect for others. What people mean when they say such things is that loyalty, considered just in itself, can make demands upon us, and we should take those demands seriously. They mean that loyalty has a place alongside, and potentially competing with, values like health and happiness.

Being loyal and valuing loyalty

There are, as I say, many valuable things about loyalty, and whether or not loyalty is a value depends in part upon whether or not those valuable things can be explained without appeal to a claim that loyalty itself is valuable. It will be helpful to approach that question in a roundabout way, via the evaluative perspective of the person who acts loyally. Can we be loyal, and enjoy and participate

---

[2] Of course, it is difficult to get much agreement over such a list; I just mean to name some things that are roughly in the ballpark. Also, I hope that it is clear that in listing all of these as separate values I am not claiming that none of them is reducible to any of the others. That is a separate question. Even if the value of (say) health is reducible to the value of (say) happiness, it still makes perfect sense to do something for the sake of your health.

in the important goods associated with loyalty, if loyalty is not
something that we value?

Suppose that a friend calls you in the middle of the night. She is
out at a bar, has had too much to drink, and wants you to pick her
up and drive her home. This is a serious inconvenience – you have
an early start the next morning and are getting little enough sleep as
it is – but you agree to do as she asks.

Consider two stories that could be told about your motivations.
First, you could be moved by direct regard for your friend. You do
not want her driving home drunk, you want to make sure that she
is safe, and you do not like the thought of her making telephone
calls from a bar and finding no one prepared to help her out.
Second, you could be moved by regard for the value of loyalty. In
thinking about what to do, you notice that loyalty calls upon you to
go out and collect your friend, and as someone who values loyalty,
that motivates you to do so. (Of course, these two motives are not
the only ones you could have, and they are not mutually exclusive.)

If you have the second sort of motive, then you treat loyalty as a
value. If you have the first sort of motive, then you needn't treat
loyalty as a value; you act for the sake of your friend, not for the sake
of loyalty. That does not mean, though, that if you have the first sort
of motive then you fail to act loyally; you are loyal to your friend,
even if you are not moved by thoughts of loyalty itself. There is a
difference between acting loyally and acting out of regard for loyalty.

Or at least, there appears to be such a difference. There is a line
of thinking that might suggest that even if your immediate motive
in acting loyally is to do with your friend herself, you must
still value loyalty on some level, on pain of falling into a kind
of evaluative dissonance or inconsistency. Suppose that you really
do not value loyalty: then you act out of loyalty to your friend,
and you presumably value your acting out of loyalty to your
friend – it is not as though you find your act of loyalty valueless or
mystifying – yet loyalty is not something that you value. Are you
not then estranged from your own motives, treating something as
valuable when you make practical decisions, but failing to value it
when you reflect?

It is possible to avoid the posited inconsistency, and two ways of doing so are particularly instructive. You could value your friend, and admit that responding to the value of your friend as you do involves showing her loyalty, but deny that it is valuable to act just for loyalty's sake. Loyalty, you could say, can be appropriate as a way of responding to things that are independently valuable, but it is not valuable considered just in itself. That is no more inconsistent than thinking that it can be appropriate to organize a campaign for justice, without thinking that there is value to campaign organizing in its own right.

Or, you could value not just your friend in particular but friendship in general. You could admit that valuing friendship means valuing a kind of loyalty, without admitting that valuing this kind of loyalty means valuing loyalty considered just in itself. You could say that there is a kind of loyalty that is valuable, even though loyalty in general is not. That is no more inconsistent than valuing the perfectionism of gourmet chefs, without valuing perfectionism in general.

Valuing loyalty and the value of loyalty

We do not need to treat loyalty as a value in order to be loyal. Nor do we need to treat loyalty as a value, I now want to suggest, in order to enjoy what is valuable about loyalty.

If I share with you a friendship, and I mean a good friendship that improves our lives in the distinctive ways in which a friendship can, then we will value each other; I will be moved to do things for you, because it is you. We will also, probably, value our friendship; in making an effort to keep in touch, or in making sure that I do not do anything to undermine our shared trust, I might be acting out of concern for the friendship and a desire that it be maintained – I may be moved by thoughts of our friendship, not just of you.

In addition to valuing each other and our friendship, we may naturally value friendship itself. In being a friend, a person can become aware of the goods that friendship can involve, and come to appreciate the importance of friendship in general, not just this friendship. As a friend of yours who values friendship, I might sometimes be moved to act by thoughts of the form, "you are my friend, and this is what friends do." And as a person who values friendship, I might make sure that I am open to making new friends, and I might see the value in friendships apart from those in which I am involved.

Friends may well value friendship for its own sake, and it may be a good thing that they do. As I said earlier, however, valuing friendship is not the same as valuing loyalty, even though friendship essentially involves a kind of loyalty. So we are yet to see whether good friends will or should treat loyalty as a value in its own right.

Loyalty, I have insisted, is a very thin concept. There are many different kinds of loyalty, and their differences are significant. The loyalty that we have to each other as friends is different in kind from the loyalty of a citizen to a country, a fan to a sports team, or a grown child to a parent; yet these are all instances of loyalty. To value loyalty, then, is surely to value loyalty as it appears in all or most of these cases. It would be odd to say that loyalty is a value, but that considerations of loyalty do not constitute good reasons to act when the loyalty in question is to a country, sports team or parent.

This in mind, I can see no reason why our having a good friendship, with all the goods to which friendship can lead, must involve our valuing loyalty. Whether or not you are able to be a good friend does not appear to depend in any way upon your feelings about loyalty as a general proposition, incorporating as it does all kinds of attitudes with which friendship does not have all that much in common. There is no reason why someone who sees nothing of value in loyalty to country, sports teams or philosophy departments should thereby be a less desirable friend.

The argument that I have offered with regard to friendship could be adapted to all sorts of valuable relationships of loyalty. When I think of those who are loyal to me, and for whose loyalty I am grateful, my gratitude has to do with the fact that they value me and our respective shared relationships, not the fact that they value loyalty itself. Within the valuable relationships of loyalty that can exist between friends, romantic partners, parents and their children, and so on, the ground of the value has principally to do with the fact that the parties to the relationships value each other (perhaps as well as valuing their relationship, and valuing more generally the kind of relationship of which theirs is an instance). When someone is loyal to you, what is most important is her being moved by thoughts of you, not her being moved by thoughts of loyalty.

None of this is to suggest that there is no value to be found in the valuing of loyalty. There are obvious attractions to the thought of a teammate, employee or romantic partner who values loyalty for its own sake. What I have been trying to show is just that it is not the case that the things that are valuable about loyalty can exist *only* among people who value loyalty; a friend, child or romantic partner who truly values you, and the relationship that the two of you share, would be just as good as the one who values loyalty.

Against loyalty as a value

The perspective of the loyal person who does not value loyalty, but who can nevertheless participate in relationships that give rise to all the valuable things about loyalty, can be translated into a view about whether or not loyalty really is a value. This loyal person who does not value loyalty nevertheless understands and appreciates all of the valuable things about the loyal relationships of which he is part. He values the individuals to whom he is loyal, he values the relationships that he shares with them, taken as particulars and taken as kinds. In the same way, I suggest, if we accept that many objects of loyalty are valuable, if we grant that loyalty can be an appropriate way of responding to their value, and if we posit as values certain sorts of things – like friendship and healthy parent–child relationships – that necessarily involve loyalty, then we can give an adequate account of the ways in which loyalty can be valuable, and do so without saying that loyalty itself is, in the relevant sense, a value. This approach appears to be available, and there are reasons, at least if what I have said in previous chapters is correct, to think that it is attractive.

There are genuine loyalties, and acts of genuine loyalty, that are, by virtue of their very nature, objectionable. A patriot is truly loyal, but patriotism is not desirable. A person who is loyal to the Nazi Party is truly loyal, but it would be better if he were not. The bare fact that some act is the loyal thing to do, or that some attitude is the loyal attitude to have, does not guarantee that there is any reason to do or have it. Someone who is influenced by considerations of loyalty, just for their own sake, will sometimes be influenced by considerations that are not good considerations; sometimes, he will get it wrong. These are reasons to think that loyalty is not a value; they are reasons to think that it is a mistake to take loyalty seriously, or to listen to its demands, just because it is loyalty.

The evaluative role that I have carved out for the notion of loyalty can be informatively compared with the evaluative role that plausibly suits the notion of belief – though the analogy is not perfect. We ought to be pleased that we have beliefs, because our lives would be worse in all sorts of ways if we did not. It is a good thing that we do not live in a belief-free world. Some of our beliefs play a direct role in our motivations; we act out of regard for what we believe, and if our beliefs were different then we would be motivated to do different things. It would be very odd, however, to think that there is such a value as belief. You can be motivated by the contents of your particular beliefs, but things would be going awry if you were motivated by thoughts of belief itself. In the same way, it is a good thing that we have loyalties, our particular loyalties properly serve as sources of motivation, we often treat the things towards which we are loyal as having value in their own rights, and we would be motivated in different ways if our loyalties were different; but loyalty is not a value.

IS LOYALTY A VIRTUE?

The ethics of character

So far, I have spoken of loyalty as a cluster of attitudes and feelings directed at a particular entity, so that an instance of loyalty involves someone who is loyal and something to which she is loyal. The term "loyalty" also makes an appearance, however, in our thinking about character traits. Thought of in that way, instances of loyalty involve not a relation between a subject and an object, but an individual's being of a certain kind. Sometimes, it seems right to describe a person as "loyal," meaning not that there is some specified thing to which she is loyal, but that she is loyal by nature.

To approach the topic of character from an ethical point of view is to ask about the nature of good character. There is a metaphysical question, about what it means for something to be a good character, which I will not get into here.[3] And there are questions about what traits of character, perhaps in what combinations, help constitute psychological profiles that make for a good person, or a person whom you would like to be, or a way that you would like your child to turn out. A trait of character can be a virtue (like generosity or honesty) or a vice (like cruelty or greed). Or, it can be neither, while perhaps being able to contribute to a good or bad character in combination with other traits (gentleness, single-mindedness); or its status as a virtue or vice can be controversial (tolerance, irreverence); or it can be peripheral to questions of good character, while still being more or less attractive or unattractive (creativity, anxiety); and there are surely many other ways of evaluating a trait besides these. The question for now is where loyalty, conceived as a character trait, fits in. But first we have to say something about what loyalty, conceived as a character trait, is.

Loyalty as a character trait: version one

Often, a person manifests the trait of loyalty within a particular role, or with regard to particular temptations. We might call you a loyal soldier, a loyal employee, a loyal husband or a loyal friend. Usually, it is pretty clear what such attributions mean. Attributions of loyalty unqualified – when we say that someone is just plain

---

[3] For two contrasting treatments of this question, see Hurka's *Virtue, Vice and Value*; and Hursthouse's *On Virtue Ethics*.

loyal – are more opaque. I think that there are two different things, related but distinguishable, that we can be getting at when we describe a person as loyal.

There is a sense of "loyal" that is associated with being dependable, or reliable, or dutiful, or *true* – as in, "straight and true." In telling you that somebody is loyal in this sense, I am telling you that you can trust him; he is not scheming or deceitful or manipulative; he will not sell you out; he takes his promises and commitments seriously; he knows his job and he gets it done. But my describing someone as "loyal" in this sense may also carry less positive connotations, to do with a hint of the unadventurous or unquestioning. The loyal person knows his job and gets it done, but perhaps he is unlikely to challenge his job description when it needs challenging; perhaps he is a little unreflective or a little quick to accept the system; perhaps one thing on which we can depend is that he will not ask awkward questions.

That is the first version of loyalty the character trait, and I am not going to say much more about it, for a couple of reasons. First, "loyal," used in this sense, is not an especially helpful way of describing someone, as compared to some obvious alternatives. The term "true" is more evocative, and leaves less room for equivocation. The terms "trustworthy," "dependable" and "reliable" are sharper and more informative. In contrast, "loyal" sounds like a fudge, perhaps a way of hinting that someone is simple-minded without quite coming out and saying it. When told that someone is loyal, in the sense in question, I think that our first natural response would not be to feel enlightened, but to ask the speaker what, exactly, she means.

The second reason for leaving this sense of "loyal" behind is that it does not have much to do with the broader notion of loyalty under discussion in this book. There is nothing in the content of this version of the trait to guarantee that our loyal person ever acts out of the distinctive kind of motive associated with loyalty. He might be reliable, and so on, not out of a particularized regard for any entity with which he takes himself to have a special relationship, but simply because he values the keeping of commitments, or because that is the way of dealing with the world that he finds easiest. There need not be anything to which he is loyal.

Loyalty as a character trait: version two

Another version of the character trait loyalty does involve a tendency to form particular bonds of loyalty and act in their light. This is the second trait that we might have in mind when we call someone "loyal." Think about what we mean when we characterize a dog, or a breed of dog, as loyal. If I say that golden retrievers are loyal, I obviously do not mean that there is some particular thing to which all golden retrievers are loyal. What I mean is that golden retrievers tend to develop strong loyalties to one thing or another, and to act loyally once those bonds are formed. In the same way, when I talk about a particular dog and say that she is loyal by nature, I am saying something a little different from what I would be saying if I said that she is loyal to her owner. I am saying that she is a loyal creature, meaning not only that she is loyal to her present owner, but that if she had had some different owner then she would have been loyal to him, and perhaps that if somebody else becomes her owner later on then she will probably be loyal to the new owner too. She is the kind of dog in whose life loyalty looms large. If you win her loyalty, you can depend on her forever.

Comparisons with dogs can be unflattering, but I am not, honestly, trying to stack the deck against the trait of loyalty by bringing out this commonality: a person who has loyalty as a character trait, in the sense that I am trying to get at here, is also someone in whose life loyalty looms large. He is inclined to form loyalties and to act in their light. He is often moved by thoughts of particular entities with which he takes himself to have a special connection. If you can win his loyalty, then you can rely on him to be on your side, and to be on your side out of loyalty to you. When you hear that someone is loyal in this sense, you have an insight into his passions, not just his actions. When you hear that someone is in this sense loyal, you might surmise that he will probably have strong feelings of identification with and concern for his friends and his family, and perhaps also his school, employer and country.

Along with dispositions to have feelings and to perform acts of loyalty, the loyal person is likely (but not guaranteed) to value loyalty. Someone for whom loyalty looms large is likely to think that loyalty is important in himself and others, just as an honest person is likely (but not guaranteed) to think that honesty is important in himself and others. I of course think, for reasons mentioned earlier, that you could have feelings of loyalty and perform acts of loyalty without valuing loyalty. But someone who has loyalty as a character trait is someone in whose life loyalty plays a significant role, and so it might be expected of this person that he values loyalty itself.

I have said enough by way of identifying the character trait that I want to discuss. Is it a virtue? It is helpful to approach that question by way of two others.

Usually, virtues are character traits that you would want your child to have, to the extent that you want your child to live a good life and be a good person; parents do their best to teach their children to be honest, wise and courageous, and are pleased when they are told by others that their children have these qualities. First, then, would you want your child to have the character trait of loyalty? If those who described your child tended to use the term "loyal" – if you received a school report in which your child was described as "loyal" – would that be something to be happy about?

And usually, if a character trait is a virtue then at least some traces of the behavior and motives associated with the trait are to be found in anyone who lives a minimally morally decent life. So – and this is the second question – what would we think of someone who was not at all loyal?

Would you want your child to be loyal?

Would you want your child to be loyal? You would certainly want your child to live a life that includes good friendships, romantic relationships, and so on. You would encourage her to seek out such relationships – to be someone who values and cultivates loyal relationships of various sorts. To that extent, you would want your child to live a life marked by loyalty.

It is a separate question, though, whether you would want your child to have loyalty as a character trait. And I doubt that you should, on the whole, hope that the child you raise is loyal, in the sense of being by nature inclined to develop loyalties and act in their light. For one thing, it is difficult to think of such a person except as someone whose character includes the tendency to form familiar kinds of patriotic loyalty, along with other sorts of loyalty that are not, if you accept what I have said earlier in the book, desirable kinds of loyalty to have.

Less contentiously, though, there is reason to worry that a child who has the character trait of loyalty might be inclined to get herself into trouble. She might be too quick to commit herself emotionally to projects or individuals that she would be better to avoid. Someone who has the character trait of loyalty sounds a little too much like someone who is undiscriminating, and whose emotional attachments to particular entities play too much of a role in determining how she will live her life. In sending into the world a child who is correctly characterized as "loyal," I would be concerned about her ability to navigate various moral and personal hazards – manipulative friends, seductive but misguided causes – that any person inevitably will encounter.

This is not just the obvious point that a tendency to form loyalties had better go along with a capacity for good judgment. It is not just to say that the character trait of loyalty needs to exist alongside other important character traits. A useful comparison is with the trait of being opinionated. The opinionated person also sounds like someone who is a little undiscriminating. He forms and voices opinions without adequate reflection, almost as though he holds his opinions not because he has reason to think them true but just because he likes having opinions; his predilections for certainty and assertion race ahead of his measured judgment. Of someone who has opinions but forms them only in the light of careful, open-minded reflection, we do not say that she is deliberate and reflective about her opinions, and also opinionated. If in the forming of her opinions she is careful, open-minded, deliberate and reflective, then she is not informatively described as "opinionated" – even if she does have opinions.

In the same way, if a person forms loyalties and acts in their light, but does so carefully, with an eye for other important values and a clear awareness of the dangers to which loyalty can lead, and without any drive towards loyalty for its own sake, then we would not describe her as someone of judicious judgment, who also has the character trait of loyalty. She is rather someone who is not, by nature, loyal. She is loyal to some things and sometimes acts loyally, but she is not one of those people who are loyal by nature. She is not the person you would imagine when told that you are about to meet someone who is loyal.

Usually, it is a slight insult to call someone opinionated and something of a compliment (though not always an unqualified compliment) to call someone loyal. But I think that the two traits should be regarded in roughly the same way, when it comes to their desirability in our children. I would be dismayed to think that my child might not have any opinions, but I do not want her to be opinionated. I would be dismayed to think that my child might not have any loyalties, but I do not want her to be loyal by nature. To be opinionated is to be inclined to have opinions just for the sake of having opinions. To be loyal by nature is to be inclined to form loyalties just for the sake of having loyalties – not, necessarily, because you have encountered things towards which it would be good for you to be loyal. You should want your child to be honest, courageous and just, but there are reasons to doubt that you should want her to have the trait of loyalty.

On the complete lack of loyalty

Consider now the perhaps bizarre case of a person who has not a trace of loyalty: someone who has no feelings of loyalty, does not value loyalty, is not loyal to anything. This is a person who is never moved to help, respect, revere, or otherwise take the side of something, just out of regard for the thing itself and with a sense that he shares with it some special relationship. He never feels for anything the loyalty that you might feel to your spouse, brother or best friend. What can we say about such a person?

We should, for a start, be sorry for him. There are some important goods, like genuine friendship, in which he will not share. Whether we would have a distinctively *moral* complaint against him, by which I mean a good reason to disapprove of him, as well as pity him, depends upon some particulars about his story.

One way to imagine him is as someone who deliberately stamps out any loyalty to which his natural inclinations give rise, and deliberately prevents himself from acting out of any loyal motivations. This aversion to loyalty might be excusable – it might be the predictable result, for example, of a childhood in which his loved ones took advantage of his loyalties – but assuming that it is not, I think that this character is likely to be a fair target of moral disapproval. He is deliberately conducting himself in a way that inhibits valuable possibilities; and these are possibilities not just for himself, but for those with whom he might reasonably be expected to share valuable relationships, like perhaps his parents and siblings. He might justly be accused of being callous and misanthropic. His might be a truly moral failing.

Another way to imagine our entirely non-loyal character is as someone who does not stamp out his loyal inclinations, but rather finds himself not to have them. He finds the motivations associated with loyalty foreign and inaccessible; he does not feel them and does not wish that he did. Such a person would probably not be capable of forming genuine friendships or romantic relationships, and perhaps could not be a perfectly good parent (he may well have no desire to be a parent). But he could still have a strong sense of right and wrong, could still be honest, well meaning, generous and compassionate, and capable of honoring his commitments. However, his motivations would be grounded in universal or principled considerations, concern for others for what they are inherently, not for their special relationships with him. He would not do something for you because you are *you*, but he might do something for you because you are in need and he recognizes your need.

I do not think that we would have a moral complaint against this character, merely by virtue of the fact that he bears no trace of loyalty. We would, again, be pleased that we are not like him, but we would not have automatic reason to disapprove of him. He need not be someone who commits wrongful acts, or who is a threatening or bewildering creature to have around. He could be a conscientious and upright member of the moral community, a person with whom you can deal – if not a person with whom you can be friends. The fact that someone is not at all loyal need not mean that he is morally compromised.

Compare this person who is not at all loyal with a person who is not at all honest. The person who has no trace of honesty is someone who cannot be relied upon to act honestly, is never driven by motives of honesty, never does something because it is the honest thing to do. Even if the entirely non-honest character were so because of something that is out of her control – because she has some constitutive inability to be honest – we would rightly regard her as morally challenged. She would be a disturbingly, even if pathologically, immoral or non-moral creature. The same would be true of someone in whose life there was no trace at all of courage, generosity or compassion. Some character traits are such that someone who entirely lacks any one of them is thereby compromised in a distinctively moral kind of a way. Loyalty, I am suggesting, is not such a trait.

Two signs that a character trait is a reasonably fundamental virtue are that it is something that we would certainly want to cultivate in our children, and that it is something of which at least some trace is required if a person is to meet minimal standards of moral decency. The character trait of loyalty, I have argued, does not meet either of these tests. Hence, I suggest, it should not be placed among the fundamental virtues. Nor is it one of those traits, like wittiness or creativity, that while not fundamental virtues are nevertheless good traits to have. It is rather like, if I can push the analogy a step further, the trait of being opinionated. There are much worse things than being opinionated by nature, and much worse things than being loyal by nature; neither is of a piece with cruelty or greed. Still, these are traits that it is better, on the whole, to be without.

That concludes my presumptive case for the claim that the general notion of loyalty does not mark out a value or a virtue; loyalty, considered in itself, is not an essentially moral concept, nor one that should be of fundamental importance for our thinking about the good or the good person. My case is presumptive, because I have not yet considered the major arguments pressed by those who do see loyalty as a fundamental moral concept. I will turn to those arguments in the next chapter.

CHAPTER 8

Communitarian arguments for the importance of loyalty

COMMUNITARIANISM AND LOYALTY

Loyalty, I have argued, is not a value or a virtue. But there are arguments that seem to many to speak powerfully against that conclusion, and that I have so far ignored. People are not isolated, self-causing moral atoms. We emerge from complex social contexts; we learn about what matters – we learn who we are – by being brought up within a family, a network of personal relationships, and a wider community. It is by seeing others as essentially connected to us – by seeing them as fellow members of a community – that we are able to take their interests seriously, and care about their interests as we might care about our own. Aren't our allegiances to communities then a vital part of our moral lives? Isn't loyalty a crucial moral virtue?

You do not need to be committed to any particular philosophical theory in order to find these considerations compelling, but there is a broad perspective with which they are closely associated: communitarianism. By the broadly communitarian perspective, I mean the view according to which community memberships are of vital importance in generating genuine moral standards and grounding genuine moral motivation, and according to which that importance is neglected within liberal ethical theory and – it is sometimes added – contemporary political life.[1]

---

[1] Again, I am following the communitarian perspective articulated in MacIntyre, "Is Patriotism a Virtue?" I should note also that there are some philosophers who

I will distinguish between four broadly communitarian arguments for the importance of loyalty, and try to show that each of them is unpersuasive. First is what I will call "the argument from the metaphysical self," which is grounded in a view about what it is to be a particular person. Second is "the argument from the ethical self," which depends upon a view about the source of moral standards and moral motivation. Third is "the empirical argument," according to which loyalty, given some contingent facts about human motivation, tends to lead to good citizenship. Fourth is "the 'morality as loyalty' argument," according to which moral thinking, at the deepest level, is an expression of loyalty.

The goal of these arguments is not just to show that *some* loyalties are ethically important – it is not just to show that friendship, say, or loyalty between romantic partners, is valuable – but nor is it, necessarily, to show that there is deep value to all loyalty wherever it is found. What is being championed in communitarian arguments for the importance of loyalty is rather group loyalty, or community loyalty. To have such a loyalty is to be loyal to a sizable group of people delimited by membership of a specified community, or to be loyal to an entity (like a state) that has associated with it some privileged sizable group (like its citizens) of which the loyal person is a member. The loyalties that a communitarian is likely to think important include patriotism, loyalty to a city, loyalty to a religion, and loyalty to an ethnic group.

THE ARGUMENT FROM THE METAPHYSICAL SELF

When philosophers of broadly communitarian sympathies attack liberalism, they often emphasize a difference that they see between the liberal conception of the self and their own. For the liberal, they say, the self is a thin, unencumbered rational agent, whose

count as broadly communitarian in my sense, but would not call themselves communitarians (or at least would not count themselves opponents of liberalism). Of the philosophers I discuss here, R. Rorty and Oldenquist certainly count as broadly communitarian, but would not describe themselves as critics of liberalism – they think, rather, that liberal justice should be understood as a form of loyalty.

essential properties are shared with every other rational agent. The communitarian view, in contrast, is that the self is a historically and culturally situated entity, one that is essentially of a particular time and place. Part of what it is to be the distinct person you are, on this view, is to be a member of certain groups: your family, your community, your country, and so on. Anything that lacked such memberships, runs the suggestion, could not be you. This anti-liberal conception of the self motivates anti-liberal moral and political views that emphasize the importance of community and the particularity and contingency of moral standards. This is the pattern followed by the first two arguments that I am going to examine.[2]

The argument from the metaphysical self goes like this. You are essentially linked to various communities; you are essentially a native of a particular country, a member of a particular religious group, or whatever. To fail to be loyal to the communities of which you are essentially a member is then to deny essential aspects of your own identity – it is to be alienated from yourself. Group loyalty is a central virtue, because without it a person cannot live a life in which she is fully aware of and comfortable with her own true identity.[3]

There are some familiar concerns with which the argument from the metaphysical self connects. It can feel frightening and alienating to have your group loyalties challenged. When you are asked, say, to take an objective or detached view of your country or your religious community, it can feel as though you are being asked to leave a part of yourself behind. People will sometimes explain their continuing loyalty to a church, tribe or gang on the grounds that "this is who I am."

Still, the argument from the metaphysical self fails. It moves too quickly from the claim that humans are essentially members of

[2] A different argument along similar lines has already been touched upon in Chapter 1, where I considered and rejected the claim that loyalty is by definition an expression of an aspect of the loyal agent's identity. That definitional claim is not required by the arguments to be considered here.

[3] See Fletcher, *Loyalty*, chapter 1, and (especially) the discussion of the death of Socrates on pp. 55–57; and Oldenquist, "Loyalties," Part V.

particular communities to the claim that humans are alienated or self-denying if they are not loyal to those particular communities. There are ways in which a person can be fully aware and accepting of her membership of a community without being loyal to it.

Imagine, for example, an Iowan who decides that he would prefer to live somewhere other than Iowa. He moves elsewhere, but he always identifies himself as an Iowan, maintains some fond memories of his life in Iowa, and understands his ways of making sense of the world as being rooted in his Iowan upbringing. But while knowing that Iowa will always be a part of him, he feels no need to defend Iowa or promote its interests, and does not take it to be any more special than any other state. Thoughts of Iowa do not ignite his passions. He is not someone you would describe as a loyal Iowan, but neither is he alienated from or denying of his true Iowan self. His appreciation of the Iowan aspect of his identity does not demand anything of his loyalties.

Or, imagine a person who grows up Christian, but eventually comes to reject the church and its teachings. She stops going to church and participating in distinctively Christian activities, but she knows herself to be partially constituted by her Christian heritage. She recognizes the influence of her heritage upon her personality and her view of the world; she understands what she has in common with others who share her Christian background; she still hums and enjoys some of the hymns that she was taught in church. Surely it would be stretching things to say either that she is loyal to Christianity and the Christian community, or that she is out of touch with her own deeper self. She is no longer a loyal Christian, but neither is she someone who is alienated from her Christian roots. You can have, and know you have, an essentially Christian identity, without being a loyal Christian.

These cases show that it is a mistake to conflate, "I see this community as my own," with, "I am loyal to this community."[4] But

---

[4] For an example of this conflation, see pp. 187–189 of Oldenquist's "Loyalties," where he moves very quickly between saying of someone that she is not loyal to a community, that she does not see the community as her own, that she is alienated from her community, and that she is alienated simpliciter.

they also show that you face a genuine question about whether or not you should be loyal to a particular community, even once you have acknowledged it as your own. The fact that you are an American, say, neither condemns nor entitles you to be a loyal American.

The communitarian conception of the metaphysical self might yield some claims about what it is to be alienated from yourself; if the conception is correct, then perhaps you are alienated from yourself if you deny or fail to understand your connection with the communities through which your identity is forged. It does not, however, yield the claim that you are alienated from yourself if you are not loyal to those communities.

THE ARGUMENT FROM THE ETHICAL SELF

The next argument I want to consider, the argument from the ethical self, also proceeds in light of an account of the self as essentially connected to particular communities. It takes the subject of that account, though, to be moral agency (in particular), not personal identity (in general). The claim with which the argument begins is this. It is only through the practices and activities of a particular community that a fully-functioning moral consciousness can be acquired and exercised, which is to say that moral beliefs and motivations make sense – find their articulation, justification and reinforcement – only within the context of a particular community and its shared history and form of life. Roughly speaking, the argument moves from there to the claim that loyalty to community is a precondition of healthy moral agency, and from there, reasonably enough, to the claim that loyalty is a virtue.

To fill in the argument, I want to quote a long passage from MacIntyre's "Is Patriotism a Virtue?" It is expressed conditionally, but the line of thought is clear.

If first of all it is the case that I can only apprehend the rules of morality in the version in which they are incarnated in some specific community; and *if* secondly it is the case that the justification of morality must be in terms of particular goods enjoyed within the life of particular communities; and *if* thirdly it is the case that I am characteristically brought into being and maintained as a moral agent only through the particular kinds of sustenance afforded by my moral community, *then* it is clear that deprived of this community, I am unlikely to flourish as a moral agent. Hence my allegiance to the community and what it requires of me – even to the point of requiring me to die to sustain its life – could not meaningfully be contrasted with or counterposed to what morality required of me. Detached from my community, I will be liable to lose my hold upon all genuine standards of judgment. Loyalty to that community, to the hierarchy of particular kinship, particular local community, and particular natural community, is on this view a prerequisite for morality. So patriotism and those loyalties cognate to it are not just virtues but central virtues.[5]

If this argument is sound, then, as well as offering its own reasons why loyalty is a virtue, it undercuts the examples that I used in discussing the argument from the metaphysical self in the previous section. The Iowan who is not loyal to Iowa and the Christian who abandons Christianity, on the view that MacIntyre presents, are separating themselves from the contexts on which their evaluative faculties depend. Outside their ethical identities as an Iowan and as a Christian, where are they to find standards – let alone standards sufficiently culturally embedded and personally internalized to provide complete alternative ethical identities – that could underlie the rejection of their Iowan and Christian moralities?

But the argument is not sound. I will demonstrate this by showing that if the three claims about the ethical self mentioned in MacIntyre's passage (the claims following the *ifs*) are to be understood in ways that make them at all plausible, then his conclusion – that loyalty is a virtue – does not follow. I will begin with a problem case.

Suppose that you are brought up in a certain community, and come to learn and live according to its ethical outlook in just the way that the communitarian expects. And suppose that the content of that ethical outlook – the particular way of making sense of the world that sustains the community's shared life, and is taught and reinforced through the narrative that the community tells about itself – includes the following commitments. All sentient creatures are valuable, and have interests

---

[5] MacIntyre, "Is Patriotism a Virtue?," p. 50 (page references are to the version in Primoratz (ed.), *Patriotism*).

that matter, just because they are sentient; all rational creatures, wherever they are found, are entitled to equal respect; this community is important, but it is one of many, and in the big scheme of things it is your value as a person, not the fact that you are of this community and not another, that gives you dignity and status; you should care for your family and show special concern for your friends, but also remember that there are many other people out there who are valuable too; the way to live an ethical life is to do as little harm as possible, protect the weak and oppressed wherever they are found, promote mutual respect and understanding between people of all communities, and attain an understanding of yourself as one valuable but small part of an enormous and wonderful world.

There are more details to fill in about the life of this lovable community, but we have seen enough to make the point. In the example, the rich and essentially embedded moral code that you learn through your community does not teach loyalty to that community as a central value. In living the life that you have been taught to value, you will not be moved, primarily, by thoughts of your community. There may be things for which you must be prepared to die, but sustaining the existence of this community, just for its own sake, is not among them. You must, of course, remain aware of and in touch with your community, if you are to stay within a context in which your evaluative commitments make sense – but this, as I have stressed, does not mean that you must show it loyalty. What morality requires of you *can* be contrasted with what would be required by allegiance to the community. Perhaps a group of refugees is driven into the lands on which your people have always lived, and allowing the refugees to settle will dilute your community's distinguishing identity; then the interests of the community as an ongoing distinctive entity, which demand that the refugees be sent away, conflict with your community-grounded moral code, which demands that you welcome all those in need.

The argument from the ethical self moves too quickly from a claim about morality's source to a claim about its content. Even if the communitarian is right about the link between having a healthy moral sensibility and being connected to a particular community, it remains an open question – a matter for substantive moral debate – whether that sensibility will or should include loyalty to community as a central virtue. It seems to me that there exist healthy moral traditions that include group loyalty as a virtue, and healthy moral traditions that do not. Some national communities define themselves partially through an ardent devotion to the nation itself, and some define themselves entirely through other values. Some religions take a passionate commitment to the sustenance of the church to be a central requirement of a morally decent life, and some construct their conception of the good life in purely universalist terms. A healthy community's attitude towards group loyalty is not dictated by the communitarian conception of the ethical self – even, as I say, if that conception is correct.

I want to consider two ways of responding to my rejection of the argument from the ethical self. First, I could be accused of failing to give full credit to one aspect of the communitarian's starting point: the one that follows the second *if* in MacIntyre's formulation. The communitarian says not only that any moral sensibility must be grounded in the practices of a particular community, but that moral standards must be directly justified in terms of the goods enjoyed within the life of that community, meaning – perhaps – that they must be justified in terms of what is good for the community. Where in my example is the story about how values like respect for all, a concern for the oppressed, and so on, receive their justification in their contribution to the flourishing of this community in particular?

Well, there are obvious ways in which people who subscribe to the values listed in my example will be better able to get along, construct institutions and deal with those from outside the community, but perhaps that is not really the point. Perhaps the claim is that regard for those values must, on the communitarian view, be underwritten by an understanding of how they make this community prosper: "you should value the interests of all sentient creatures, because, and only to the extent that, doing so contributes to the sustenance of this particular community." But if the communitarian's claim is that the ongoing success of the community must be the one overarching value to which

all others are subservient, then the communitarian's view about
community-grounded morality is obviously false. A community's
moral perspective can transcend the limits of the community's own
best interests; many healthy moral traditions posit non-instrumental
standards for the treatment of those outside the tradition, and appeal to
values whose scope reaches far beyond the confines of this one
community.

Second, it could be said that while it is not conceptually required
that a moral perspective learned through and sustained by a
community include loyalty to the community itself, it is nevertheless the case (and perhaps not surprising) that those moral
communities that have survived and flourished *do* take group
loyalty to be a central virtue, and so we who have been raised in
these communities simply find the value of group loyalty to be an
essential part of our moral sensibility. I doubt that this statement
about the substance of prevailing ethical traditions is true, but in
any case the appeal to it pushes the communitarian too far towards
the uncritical moral conservatism of which she is sometimes
accused and that she should be eager to avoid; she ends up saying
that whatever we find in our moral traditions, we are stuck with.
But of course that is not true, and is not what a plausible-sounding
communitarianism should say.

Communitarianism, if it is to be a going concern, must allow that
community-grounded modes of moral thinking can find within
themselves the capacity for self-criticism and progress.[6] The fact
that some moral commitment is found within a community does not
mean that that commitment is, for that community, sacrosanct. For
a healthily evolving moral community, the community's own moral
standards are up for substantive debate, even if the conflicts that
trigger that debate must come from within the community's moral
tradition itself. The question of whether or not group loyalty is a
virtue is one of the questions that can arise in such debate. Even if

---

[6] On how community-embedded moralities can change and progress, see
MacIntyre's *After Virtue*, especially chapter 15; R. Rorty's *Contingency, irony
and solidarity*, chapter 9; and R. Rorty's "Justice as a Larger Loyalty."

we accept the communitarian stories about the source of morality and the nature of the ethical self, it is still up to us to decide – it is still a matter for substantive moral enquiry – whether or not group loyalty is a virtue.

THE EMPIRICAL ARGUMENT

Most of Andrew Oldenquist's paper "Loyalties" is taken up by some rather theoretical claims about loyalty and morality, which we will come to shortly, but towards the end he comes to the topic of urban malaise:

There are many people who seem not to care at all about their neighborhoods, their cities, or various larger or other wholes. The effects of this attitude can range through indifference, automatic negative votes on tax and bond levies, cynical exploitation of the social services systems, vandalism, and crime. If it is true, as I think it is, that alienation in the sense of absence of group loyalties is a major contributing cause of this, it will be socially useful to investigate the conditions under which people are likely to come to view various social units as their own. For the main problem American society currently faces is not so much the competition of group loyalties as their absence.[7]

And later:

As a matter of historical and sociological fact, moral motives for good citizenship are marginally effective and harder to produce in the first place; it is primarily group loyalties – group egoism and tribal morality – that have produced the caring and commitment that keep our social worlds going.[8]

The view articulated here posits an empirical correlation between group loyalty and good citizenship. It says that people who do not have loyalties to their communities are more likely to be alienated from themselves and their surroundings; they are more likely to be selfish, criminal and nihilistic. If only people felt stronger loyalties to their communities, runs the thought, perhaps we would not have all the problems that we have today.

[7] pp. 189–90.   [8] p. 191.

We should not say that group loyalty is the only thing that can motivate good citizenship. You might refrain from vandalism because you respect others and their property, you might refrain from social security fraud because you know that it is dishonest and exploitative, and you might have a positive and purposive attitude because you believe that there are many worthwhile ways to spend your time. Roughly moral motivations – meaning, here, universalistic motivations – can in principle do the job. But, moral motives are said to be "marginally effective" when compared with the power of motives of loyalty, so that for most people, most of the time, it is loyalty to the community that makes the difference between a good and a bad citizen. Loyalty, if all of this is right, can properly be viewed as an important virtue, and a political value, even if its value is instrumental.

Two things are being suggested. First, in caring about and taking yourself to be a member of a relevant entity, you will find a sense of purpose; you will see yourself as part of something that matters and is greater than yourself. Second, you will have extra motivation to conduct yourself in a way that promotes the interests of the group's members and the reputation of the group as a whole. If you, an Australian, are tempted to commit an act of vandalism, you may be deterred by the thought, "I would not want to hurt a fellow Australian," or by the thought, "My doing this would reflect badly on Australians everywhere."

There are several empirical questions that need to be answered before we can evaluate the argument. Is a human more likely to find a sense of purpose in her membership of and loyalty to groups, or in other things, like seeking to be excellent at some activity, serving a goal or ideal that she takes to be valuable for its own sake, or raising and providing for a family? Is a human's motive in respecting the interests of another more likely to be that she sees the other as a fellow member of a group to which she is loyal, or that she sees the other as one who has interests that matter for their own sake? (Are you more likely to be moved by the thought that this act would cause harm to a fellow American, or by the thought that this act would cause harm?) Does urban malaise, if it exists in the form described, result from a lack of group loyalty, or from a lack of education and other opportunities, or from disillusionment with the particular systems through which our groups are governed, or from a perceived inability to participate in or otherwise meaningfully influence those systems? Does loyalty to a group tend to give rise to respect and concern, or hostility and derision, for those outside the group? More generally, what are the negative social consequences of group loyalty, and how do they measure up against the benefits?

These questions are very difficult to answer, and I do not think that a philosopher's opinion about them ought carry much weight. I am certainly not convinced by assertions, usually offered without empirical support, that once upon a simpler and better time morality was all about group loyalty; or that historically, the most morally admirable societies have always been those in which individuals' behavior towards each other was governed by loyalty to the group.[9]

For my own speculative part, though, it seems to me that good citizenship is much more closely related to a general moral sense, and an understanding of the ways in which a political community can perform a moral function and make its members better off, than to first-level loyalty to the group. When I think of those I know whom I would most like to have as fellow members of a political community, I think of those who value and respect others wherever they are from. As I mentioned in Chapter 3, when I think of people I know who are most patriotic or otherwise loyal to the groups of which they are members, I do not find them to be the better citizens. I worry that those for whom group loyalty is a driving motivation will be more likely to join and stick by groups – political, criminal or religious – that they really ought to avoid, that they will be more likely to mete out poor treatment to those outside the group, and that they will be more likely to support unjust wars and other bad but stirring causes.

Obviously, the consequences of group loyalty are not all bad. If I thought that appealing to his group loyalty was the only way to

---

[9] See Oldenquist, "Loyalties," Part V; and Fletcher, *Loyalty*, p. xi.

get someone to fight for an urgent cause or break out of his urban malaise and become a good citizen, then I would probably do it. I suspect, however, that this is about all the instrumental value that group loyalty has. It can have its uses, but it is not a necessary aspect of a well-functioning state, nor is its lack to blame for contemporary political disillusionment and urban decay; it is not a fundamental political virtue. But that, as I say, is just my opinion, and it is about matters on which I, and my communitarian antagonists, are not the experts. As I have said a number of times already, there exists space for the claim that group loyalty in one form or another has a strong empirical link with various virtues or good consequences – though I think that we should, absent a good empirical argument, be skeptical.

THE "MORALITY AS LOYALTY" ARGUMENT

To return to more solidly theoretical considerations: there is a view according to which morality turns out to be, in one sense or another, all about group loyalty. It is expressed in a well-known article by Richard Rorty, called "Justice as a Larger Loyalty," by Oldenquist in "Loyalties," and perhaps also in passages from Fletcher.[10] The view is elusive, but I will present and criticize it in the form I find most plausible.

You are a member of several different groups, including your immediate family, your extended family, various friendship groups, various clubs and societies, the citizenry of your country, the human species, the class of all sentient beings, and the class of all living things. You have moral relationships with other individuals, in your capacity as fellow members of a community; as members of the same family, you share duties and responsibilities with your brothers and sisters, and as citizens of the same country, you share duties and responsibilities with your fellow citizens. Furthermore,

---

[10] Fletcher, *Loyalty*, pp. 16–21; see especially his comments about the case for sharing wealth with the poor, on p. 18, and his comments on Rawls, on pp. 18–19. See also chapter 9 of Rorty, *Contingency, irony, and solidarity*.

these are the *only* kinds of moral relationships that you have. Any individual that enters your moral consideration must do so in so far as she is fellow member of some group or other. And to take an individual into moral consideration is to express loyalty to a group to which you and she both belong.

A convenient way to represent this idea, Oldenquist says, is to think of the individual as standing at the center of a number of concentric circles of different diameters. Among them will be a small circle that represents loyalty to family, a larger circle that represents loyalty to country, and a very large circle that represents loyalty to species.[11] So, when you worry about the plight of impoverished people in distant parts of the world, for example, you can think of yourself as expressing your loyalty to the human species and your recognition that those people, like you, fall into the circle of concern that that loyalty delineates.

Moral dilemmas, Rorty says, often involve conflicts between loyalties to different groups. Usually, loyalties to the groups "closer" to ourselves are stronger; we may feel loyal to the class of all sentient creatures, including cows and kangaroos, but if "the cows or the kangaroos turn out to be carriers of a newly mutated virus which, harmless to them, is fatal to humans ... we would participate in the necessary massacre. The idea of justice between species would then become irrelevant ... our loyalty to our own species must come first."[12] What we may think of as clashes between loyalty and justice, according to Rorty, are in fact clashes between narrower and wider loyalties. To the extent that we are moved by considerations of justice, he suggests, we are moved by loyalty to groups that are relatively large, like the human species or the class of all sentient creatures.

That is the basic view. Its defenders are not clear about what status it is supposed to have. Sometimes it is put forward as a definitional view, saying that to allow an individual into your moral consideration is, by stipulation, to be loyal to some group to which you and he belong – but then it is hard to see why the stipulation is

[11] pp. 179–180.   [12] "Justice as a Larger Loyalty," p. 139.

interesting.[13] Sometimes it is put forward as a prescriptive view, saying that we *ought* to consider for moral purposes only those to whom we are loyal, and we ought to give greater weight to considerations of those closest to us – but this view would require some positive argument that the relevant texts do not provide.[14] Sometimes it is put forward as a prudent reconstrual of ordinary moral thinking, given certain political sensitivities and doubts about the existence of universal moral standards – but little effort is made to say what needs to be reconstrued and how it could be done.[15] In its most plausible and interesting form, I think, and in the form in which it could ground the other glosses just mentioned, it is intended as a revelatory view, one that lays bare the deep structure of our moral thinking as it really operates.

Rorty says that as much as we may value the interests of animals, it will always be our loyalty to our own species that takes priority; and that as much as westerners may insist that their societies have discovered principles of justice that apply independently of group membership, their real motivation stems from their loyalty to the West.[16] Oldenquist says that while Kantians claim to value rational beings simply because they are rational, they really value them partly because they are ours: "if human space explorers were to discover many rational civilizations, all competing for different resources ... I suspect that a Kantian would come to think in terms of *their* rational beings and *our* rational beings."[17] The suggestion here is that we should acknowledge, if we are honest, that it is group loyalty that really underlies all of our moral motivations. Before being compelled by considerations of the moral claims of others,

---

[13] On p. 145 of "Justice as a Larger Loyalty," Rorty says that "being rational and acquiring a larger loyalty are two descriptions of the same activity."

[14] This is how Fletcher sometimes presents the claim, in the first four chapters (though certainly not in the final chapter) of *Loyalty*. Note that Fletcher does provide arguments that we ought to act loyally (for example, the argument about voice and exit at the beginning of Chapter 1), but not that we should take into consideration *only* those to whom we are loyal.

[15] See chapter 9 of *Contingency, irony, and solidarity*; and the last two pages of "Justice as a Larger Loyalty."

[16] "Justice as a Larger Loyalty," pp. 139, 146–147.   [17] "Loyalties," p. 179.

runs the view, we must first regard those others as members of a group to which we are loyal; we see an individual first as a fellow American or human (or whatever), and only subsequently as someone with rights and interests to which we have reason to respond. Group loyalty is then a virtue, because it is the characteristic source of concern and respect for others, in humans as they actually are.

If I am right in thinking that the "morality as loyalty" picture has its greatest interest and force as a claim about what really motivates us in our moral decision-making, then the way to assess the view is by seeing whether it can account for familiar kinds of moral motivation. I want to suggest that it cannot. To the extent that its concern is with group *loyalty*, the view is inconsistent with some fairly basic aspects of moral phenomenology.

Suppose that your beloved companion and pet dog, Ben, is sick, and will probably die within a few days. His illness is very unpleasant, both for him to suffer and for you to observe. You contact a doctor friend of yours, to ask whether there is anything that can be done. She tells you that there is indeed an experimental life-saving drug, to which she happens to have access, a course of which will most likely save Ben's life and return him to normal. The trouble is that this drug is in very short supply, and several human patients of hers are waiting for their chance to use it. If she diverts the doses of the drug needed to save Ben's life, she will have to delay the beginning of the treatment for many of the humans on her waiting list, and some of them, perhaps two or three, will probably then lose all chance of being saved. Still, she can get you the drug if you like; it is up to you.

It seems obvious what you should do. You should not privilege your dog's life over the lives of two or three humans, even if they are strangers; you should decline your friend's offer and allow Ben to die. (At the very least, there are very strong reasons, given the circumstances, to decline the drug.) But it seems equally obvious that all considerations of loyalty go in the other direction. Ben is your loyal friend, whom you love and value and with whom you share a long and loyal history. These two or three humans, who are likely to die if drugs are diverted for Ben's treatment – you do not even know who they are. You have made them no promises, share with them no relationship; for all you know, if you met them you would not like them. You cannot possibly feel loyal to them, in anything like the way that you feel loyal to Ben. If you feel the force of considerations of loyalty, then surely they will move you to save your beloved dog. Yet, in one way or another, it is the humans' moral claim that wins out.

To say that what we have here is a clash between loyalties is to get the experience of the decision-maker exactly wrong. The one thing that is likely to gnaw at you as you make the right decision is the realization that in doing so you are failing to be loyal, failing to put your loyal companion first. You will not experience the decision as one in which different loyalties pull you in different directions; you will not feel as you would if you were forced to choose which of your two children to save, or if you had to decide whether to support the football team you have always supported or the one for which your brother now plays. In these cases you will feel the presence of two distinct individuals, and feel that whatever you do you will be abandoning one of them. Only Ben has that status in the case in question – yet he loses. There are strong moral considerations, the case suggests, that are not considerations of loyalty.

Defenders of "morality as loyalty" are likely to reply that while the two or three human strangers cannot figure in your motivations in quite the way that Ben does, they are nevertheless the beneficiaries of a loyalty of yours: namely, your loyalty to your species. This is a loyalty, the claim must be, that might not strike you in quite the same way as your loyalty to more immediate and tangible objects, like Ben, but is nevertheless present and powerful enough to overcome your loyalty to your dog.

Some work needs to be done in order to see how this loyalty to species could operate. There is a recognizable kind of concern that people can have for the human species, one that is elicited in science fiction and nuclear war scenarios in which the survival of the race rests upon the shoulders of a few brave individuals. This is a concern for the survival, betterment or flourishing of the species as an ongoing project, and it cannot be what drives you when you choose the human strangers over your dog Ben. The deaths of the strangers would be bad for them and all who love them, but it would be stretching things to say that their deaths would be bad for the human race; the species will still be doing fine. Whether a few of its billions of members die now or a little bit later will make no difference at all to the thriving of the species you love.

Instead, your attachment to the human race must motivate you to look after fellow species members wherever they are found. It must be expressed in the same way as a loyalty that leads you to give extra consideration to a job candidate of whom you know nothing more than that he went to your college; or a loyalty that leads you to offer discounted rates when dealing with people who work in the same trade as you. In each of these cases, your loyalty is expressed not (just) as a concern for the direct object of your loyalty – the college or the trade – but rather through a fellow feeling for those whose links to that object are just like yours. If it is loyalty that leads you to favor the strangers over your dog and decline the drug, then the thought that drives you is not, "The survival of these particular individuals is at stake!," or, "The survival of the human race is at stake!," but, "The survival of fellow humans is at stake!"

The conflict that you face would then be represented like this. On the one hand, there is Ben, your loyalty to whom motivates you to save his life. On the other hand, there is humanity, your loyalty to which motivates you to ensure the survival of fellow humans. There can be little doubt that the first loyalty is immediate and striking in a way that the second is not – Ben, after all, is right there in front of you – but still they are both loyalties; your passions are engaged by thoughts of the human species, as well as by thoughts of Ben. Is this a more compelling representation of your experience?

Suppose that you were wavering in your choice, tempted to take the drug and save your dog, and that you or an advisor were looking for a way to turn you back towards favoring the human strangers. On the picture according to which you are torn between loyalties, the best strategy would be to try to reverse the tide of your passions, reminding you that these are *humans*, just like you, and so re-igniting your emotional attachment to the species. I suppose that might work, if the oratory is rousing enough, but surely it is not the most promising approach. What is likely to work is rather an effort to have you see that, sometimes, you should not allow your emotional attachments to win the day. The mood in which you are most likely to accept that your dog should be allowed to die is one in which you are reflective and sober, one in which you have taken a step back from your particular allegiances and are paying attention to rules or principles instead. That, at least, is how it will feel, and attempts to describe the moral experience as involving a clash between loyalties are bound to go wrong.

The point of all of this, again, is that there are powerful moral considerations that are different in kind from the considerations provided by loyalty, and so the "morality as loyalty" view cannot do justice to the full range of moral motivations that humans experience.

This does not mean that the only option is to embrace the view that sometimes, when we feel the force of others' rights and interests and so on, we feel them as having objective, absolute importance, independently of our community memberships and other special affiliations. (I think that writers like Oldenquist and Rorty tend to assume that that *is* the only alternative to the "morality as loyalty" picture, and that it is one reason why they find "morality as loyalty" so compelling.) Another option is to say that there exist first-order moral principles like, "Your first responsibility is to those closest to you," or, "Pay special regard to the interests of fellow humans," or, "Always look after your own." Such principles link responsibility to others with shared group membership, but would have force whether your loyalties incline you in their direction or not; perhaps they are the sorts of considerations whose force you feel when deciding between your beloved dog and the human strangers. But, of course, such substantive moral principles require substantive moral argument. They cannot be deduced from a claim about the real nature of morality, or of moral motivation.

CONCLUSION

There is a theme to my criticisms of communitarian arguments for the importance of loyalty. Communitarians believe that communities and the moral traditions they carry play a vital role in our moral lives, to the extent that those lives are healthy. Communities are the source of moral standards and moral motivation, and of our identities as people and moral agents. Because of their focus upon various kinds of attachments to communities and groups, communitarians are often regarded, and often regard themselves, as the natural champions of the value of group loyalty. I have argued that this is a mistake. The basic commitments of communitarianism need not, and ought not, include this emphasis upon loyalty. There is a gap between the basic communitarian vision and the claim that loyalty is a central value or virtue, and the gap is difficult to fill. So far as the arguments considered here are concerned, the question of the ethical status of loyalty is still up for grabs – which makes it possible that my arguments in the previous chapter have grabbed it.

CHAPTER 9

Josiah Royce and the ethics of loyalty

THE IDEA OF AN ETHICS OF LOYALTY

There are only two major philosophical books about loyalty, but they both express great ambitions for the concept. Royce, in *The Philosophy of Loyalty*, and Fletcher, in *Loyalty*, both set out to show that loyalty is the foundation of good moral thinking, and they both defend accounts of morality that are built around the notion of loyalty. Royce calls his account "the philosophy of loyalty," and Fletcher calls his "the ethics of loyalty."

While Royce's work on loyalty, especially, has been very influential, the idea of an ethics of loyalty has not really taken hold; no such view stands as a familiar option in debates about ethical theory.[1] Still, the project of grounding morality in loyalty is connected with some prominent recent work in moral and political philosophy, and in particular with certain attacks upon impartial, liberal, or – as I will call it here – universalist morality, and with efforts to find an alternative.

Universalist morality is characterized by two central and related commitments. First, it ascribes value to individuals by virtue of properties that they hold inherently, not by virtue of their relations to particular communities, times or places. Second, it says that many of the most important ethical decisions are made, ideally, from a detached perspective, free of allegiances to some individuals over others.[2] To give some schematic examples: Kant's moral

---

[1] Though see the views of R. Rorty and Oldenquist, described in the previous chapter.

[2] In principle, it is possible to have one of these commitments without the other, but for my purposes here we can assume that they come as a package.

theory counts as an instance of universalist morality, because it seeks to ground moral thinking in universal reason, and posits bare autonomy as the condition of individual value[3]; so does the classical utilitarianism of Bentham and Mill, because it takes bare sentience as the fundamental morally relevant characteristic, and says that agents ought to pay equal attention to the interests of all sentient beings.[4]

Many of the most widely discussed worries about universalist morality have to do with the value of loyalty. Michael Stocker imagines someone who visits you in hospital with the motive of maximizing utility or following a moral rule, and says that such a person could not be acting out of true friendship.[5] Bernard Williams says that if a husband is moved by impartial considerations when he chooses to save his wife, rather than a stranger, from drowning – "This is my wife, and husbands should prioritize the lives of their wives" – then he has a thought too many.[6] There are also more theoretical arguments. One stems from a claim about moral psychology; it is said that moral concern for others is always grounded in some special relationship – being of the same family, say, or the same community.[7] Another stems from skepticism about the existence of universal values and principles, or at least about the possibility that they could by themselves give rise to a full-blooded moral sensibility; an agent who thinks impartially and values everyone equally, runs the thought, is thereby detached from the particular connections to community that are needed to ground both a rich ethical perspective and a robust motivation for caring about it.[8]

For those who find such criticisms compelling, one obvious option is to grant loyalty a fundamental moral role, so that morality

---

[3] Kant, *Groundwork of the Metaphysics of Morals*.
[4] Bentham, *An Introduction to the Principles of Morals and Legislation*; Mill, *Utilitarianism*.
[5] "The Schizophrenia of Modern Ethical Theories."
[6] "Persons, Character and Morality."
[7] See the "morality as loyalty" argument, considered in the previous chapter.
[8] See the argument from the ethical self, considered in the previous chapter.

emerges from loyal relationships, rather than standing over and judging them. This thought often appears within communitarian thinking, as we have seen, and also appears in versions of particularism, republicanism and virtue ethics. The assumption is that the notion of loyalty is the natural friend of the anti-universalist program, and that in so far as an ethical theory gives a central place to loyalty, it will not be a universalist theory.

Fletcher's ethics of loyalty would seem to back up that assumption. He offers his view explicitly as an alternative to universalism (which he calls "impartial morality") and takes himself to be defending special relationships against the pressure placed upon them by the universalist thinking that prevails in our culture today. At the theoretical level, though, Fletcher's view is elusive. He is not exactly clear about what the ethics of loyalty is. The most accurate formulation, I think, is this: a person acts in accordance with the ethics of loyalty to the extent that she acts loyally towards the groups and individuals to which she is attached, by virtue of the contours of her historical self. This does not, however, capture all of his proposals; many of his examples of desirable loyalties, like the loyalty of a student to her classmates, do not seem to have much to do with the *historical* self.[9]

Also, Fletcher is equivocal about the relationship between the ethics of loyalty and impartial morality. In the early chapters of *Loyalty* he takes a hostile attitude towards universalist morality and seems to suggest that we should do away with it altogether, but in the last chapter he envisages universalism working in tension with the ethics of loyalty; he says that their respective demands are "independently binding," and suggests that we need to remain open to the demands of each. Fletcher has a great deal to say about the role of loyalty in dealing with certain issues in the law and public policy, but much of the theoretical work remains to be done.

Royce's work is more revealing. Royce is writing in the first decade of the twentieth century, and his immediate concerns are far

---

[9] Fletcher's notion of the historical self is explained in chapter 7 of *Loyalty*. The example of the student and her classmates is on p. 105.

removed from contemporary debates about universalist morality, but he has something important to say about them.

The bulk of this chapter will consist of an attempt to understand the ethical theory that Royce would have us endorse. I favor an interpretation that leaves the label "philosophy of loyalty" looking a little misleading. Then, I argue that the progression of Royce's thought yields a general lesson about the ethics of loyalty; it suggests that any plausible ethics of loyalty will be, against expectations, an instance of universalist morality. Finally, I say that what Royce teaches us about the ethics of loyalty also carries a message for broadly communitarian positions in ethical theory.

TWO EXPRESSIONS OF LOYALTY

There are two quite different ways in which the notion of loyalty might be placed at the center of an ethical theory, both of which are well represented in *The Philosophy of Loyalty*. Consider this very stylized example.

Alan and Barbara are members of the Community, which has strong historical ties to the Land. The Opposing Community also has strong ties to the Land. The respective claims of the Community and the Opposing Community are incompatible, and raise the threat of a bloody territorial war. A compromise, however, is available. It is proposed that the Land be given to the Opposing Community, in return for ongoing peace. If it accepts the compromise, the Community will give up a cause through which it has for generations defined and understood itself. But it will avert a war.

Alan opposes the compromise. "My loyalty to the cause of the Community," he says, "is what makes me who I am. It tells me why I am here and for what I am good. It is the source of my settled and harmonious plan of life. Of course I recognize and respect the loyalty of those in the Opposing Community, and see that their loyalty has value for them just as my loyalty has value for me. But *my* loyalty is to *my* cause, not theirs, and so I shall stand by the Community. I shall go to war if need be. If I die for the cause then I shall be glad to be the Community's servant and martyr, sure that through my destruction I win the rank of hero."

Barbara supports the compromise. "I value loyalty," she says. "I believe that loyalty is a fundamental human good and the very basis of all morality, and so it is my cause that there be more loyalty in the world rather than less. As a loyal member of the Community, I of course wish that the land could be ours, but my greater commitment is to loyalty itself. A war would destroy the ability of many – within both the Community and the Opposing Community – to display any loyalty at all. To avert war is to show loyalty to loyalty, and that is why I favor the compromise."

These two trains of thought not only lead to opposite decisions, but also represent two very different styles of ethical thinking. Alan is parochial, passionate and unabashedly partial, fully caught up in his loyalty to the Community. Barbara is cosmopolitan, calculating and apparently impartial, able to reflect upon her attachment to the Community and interrogate it in light of other values. Yet they both sound as though they have been reading Royce.[10] Of which decision, and of which way of thinking, would Royce, looking through the lens of his philosophy of loyalty, approve? To answer that question, we need to decide which of two candidate ethical theories is really Royce's. To answer *that* question, we need to decide which parts of *The Philosophy of Loyalty* are those in which Royce is expressing his settled view.

BEING LOYAL

Royce proclaims the benefits of the loyal life, holds up loyal people as models to be emulated, and urges his reader to choose her cause and be loyal to it. He says that loyalty "tends to unify life, to give it center, fixity, stability," that "unless you can find some sort of loyalty, you cannot find unity and peace in your active living."[11]

---

[10] Alan's speech draws on material on pp. 19–20 in Lecture 1. Barbara expresses the view found in Lecture 3.

[11] Lecture 1, pp. 12, 23.

He speaks with admiration of "the loyal captain, steadfastly standing by his sinking ship until his last possible duty for the service to which he belongs has been accomplished," and of "the loyal patriot," and "the loyal religious martyr."[12] "There is only one way to be an ethical individual," Royce tells us. "That is to choose your cause, and then to serve it, as the Samurai his feudal chief, as the ideal knight of romantic story his lady, – in the spirit of all the loyal."[13]

The sentiments expressed in these and similar passages dominate Lectures 1, 2 and 5 of *The Philosophy of Loyalty*, and suggest an ethical view whose central claim is that people ought to be loyal, to one thing or another. The instruction to the individual that emerges from the view is, "Be loyal": choose your cause and serve it loyally.

One problem with the view as it stands is that it does not discriminate between loyalties. It does not tell us how or to what we should be loyal. Until the view is revised so as to answer those questions, it is very implausible; no one could think that acting out of blind loyalty to a tyrannical government, for example, is a way of acting well. Royce, as we will see, is well aware of this problem, and it provides part of the impetus for his development of a second version of the ethics of loyalty.

VALUING LOYALTY

To discriminate between loyalties while seeking to keep the value of loyalty at the heart of his theory, Royce says that the highest and most desirable loyalty is to loyalty itself. What does it mean to be loyal to loyalty? Well, your cause should be one that is essentially "an aid and a furtherance of loyalty in [your] fellows."[14] "So choose your cause and so serve it, that, by reason of your choice and of your service, there shall be more loyalty in the world rather than less."[15] Loyalty is, in Royce's view, contagious, so one way to promote loyalty among

---

[12] Lecture 2, p. 26.   [13] Lecture 2, p. 47.   [14] Lecture 3, p. 56.
[15] Lecture 3, p. 57.

others is just to be loyal, whatever your loyalty's object.[16] Sometimes, however, and especially in cases in which a difficult moral decision must be made, the way to act is out of loyalty not to your particular delimited cause, but to the cause of loyalty in general.[17]

The idea here is that loyalty is a good thing, and should therefore be honored and promoted. There are important differences between this view and the view that people ought simply to be loyal. It can lead to different decisions. Alan, in the example given earlier, is certainly loyal, but Barbara is the one who is most loyal to loyalty. Also, the view that we should be loyal to loyalty requires us to value loyalties, and loyal individuals, wherever they are found. Every human (or almost every human) has the capacity for loyalty, and so every human must enter the considerations of the person who is loyal to loyalty. To this extent, an ethical theory that prizes loyalty to loyalty values people for a characteristic – the capacity for loyalty – that they hold inherently, and recommends a fair measure of impartiality.

There is a problem with attributing this view to Royce, which is that once it is fully developed, it ceases to look like a view whose central notion really is *loyalty*. The person who is loyal to loyalty – someone, like Barbara in the case mentioned earlier, who values all humans and acts so as best to promote the cause of loyalty among them – is not someone whom we ordinarily would describe as "loyal."[18] With her impartial perspective, and her insistence upon evaluating her own local loyalties in light of a universal value, she is more naturally described as "conscientious," or "principled." It is not that she is disloyal, but that her basic commitments are not to particular delimited communities or causes; in that respect, she is unlike the patriot, the religious martyr and the ship's captain. She is loyal only in the sense in which someone who is committed to utilitarianism is thereby "loyal" to the maximization of utility.

The person who is "loyal to loyalty" really has a principled commitment, not a loyalty. But if that is true, then there is reason to

---

[16] Lecture 3, pp. 63–65.   [17] Lecture 4, p. 90.

[18] R. T. Allen says that "loyalty to loyalty" is "a forced and artificial phrase." "When Loyalty No Harm Meant," p. 286.

wonder whether it is really *loyalty* to which she has her principled commitment. After all, *her* attitude is one of the attitudes – indeed the highest and best of the attitudes – that Royce recommends, and would have us honor and promote. So the class of things to which she has a principled commitment must include the attitude of principled commitment. But then her commitment is not to loyalty only; it is to all forms of principled commitment, or, as we might put it, wholehearted devotion. One way to exhibit wholehearted devotion is to be loyal in the style of the patriot, religious martyr and devoted ship's captain, but another is to think carefully about which things in life are most objectively valuable and then devote yourself wholeheartedly to honoring and promoting those valuable things (central among which, if Royce is right, is wholehearted devotion itself).

The person whom Royce describes as being loyal to loyalty is better described as follows. She understands and values the human's capacity to commit himself fully to a higher cause, and thereby give his life structure, unity and certainty. She may be committed to any number of local causes herself, but her greatest commitment is to the nurturing and promotion of this human capacity for wholehearted commitment, wherever it is found. The instruction that emerges from this construal of Royce is, "Devote yourself wholeheartedly to the cause of wholehearted devotion."

INTERPRETING ROYCE

There are two different moral views that Royce might be taken to hold. The first is that people ought to be loyal. The second is that people ought to be loyal to loyalty, where that turns out to mean that people ought to be wholeheartedly devoted to wholehearted devotion. Royce is best read as holding the second view; Barbara is a better Roycean than Alan.

First, it is only if Royce holds the second view that he can coherently claim that his theory of value accounts for "all the commonplace virtues, in so far as they are indeed defensible and effective."[19] Honesty, for example, is said by Royce to derive its value from the fact that "when I speak the truth, my act is directly an act of loyalty to the personal tie which then and there binds me to the man to whom I consent to speak."[20] But if the man to whom I consent to speak is not a member of a community to which I am loyal, then why should I act loyally – honestly – towards him? The answer has to be, as Royce says, that honesty is owed to "mankind at large," because honesty "benefits the community and the general cause of commercial loyalty."[21] For Royce's view to have any chance of accounting for the virtue of honesty, it must be taken to involve a commitment to the promotion of certain sorts of commitment – in this case, commercial loyalty – among humankind in general. The same, for analogous reasons, goes for the virtues of justice and benevolence that Royce considers later.[22]

Second, it is possible to construe Royce's praise of parochial loyalties not as identifying attitudes that he takes to be valuable in themselves, but rather as displaying the kind of passion and self-lessness that he would like us to show in our commitment to a less localized cause. We ought to be as passionate and committed as the patriot and the ship's captain, but ought to direct that passion and commitment towards an ideal that stands above any particular country or ship. Royce gives some indication that he regards parochial loyalties as valuable not for their own sakes, but because they lead to less parochial loyalties. He praises parochialism, but he also speaks of an ascent of loyalties; "if we let our loyalty develop, it tends to turn into the service of the universal cause."[23]

Third, we know from the text that Royce is happy to extend the title "loyalty" to the kind of principled commitment that is involved in a person's devotion to a universal moral principle (as opposed to a more delimited cause or community). When a "very earnest youth" tells Royce that loyalty is the tool of tyrants and needs to be abandoned in favor of enlightenment and independence, Royce's response

[19] Lecture 3, p. 61 (italicized in the original).   [20] Lecture 3, p. 66.
[21] Lecture 3, p. 67.   [22] Lecture 3, pp. 67–69.   [23] Lecture 8, p. 178.

is to say that that youth, with his "passion for the universal triumph of individual freedom" and "hatred of oppression," is showing "loyalty to humanity."[24] The object of the youth's enthusiasm may be a universal value, but it is nevertheless something towards which he can, on Royce's way of speaking, be "loyal." Similarly, Royce speaks of a friend of his who is committed, even when it is against his own interests, to truthfulness, just for its own sake. The friend is committed to a universal, impartial value, but Royce thinks that that commitment constitutes an inspiring instance of loyalty.[25] I of course think that this stretches the meaning of "loyalty," but the important point is that in Royce's mouth "loyalty," and indeed the highest and most admirable form of loyalty, can involve commitment not to a delimited cause or community, but to a universal moral value or humanity in general.

Fourth, Royce tells us that he has no great investment in the ordinary meaning of the term "loyalty." "I have defined my present usage of the popular term 'loyalty,'" he says, "in my own distinctly technical way."[26]

For all these reasons, there is textual license and philosophical reason to interpret Royce as advocating a view whose central value is not loyalty, exactly, but rather something like wholehearted devotion to the cause of wholehearted devotion.

DISCRIMINATING BETWEEN LOYALTIES

If my reading of Royce is correct, then his mature philosophy of loyalty is similar in important respects to the moral theories that we naturally classify as universalist. At the heart of the theory is a value that can be manifested in any person, and the theory tells us to respect and promote that value wherever it is found. It is not what the critics of universalism are looking for.

There are good reasons why Royce ascends from his admiration of loyalty to the universalist theory that he finally defends, and they

---

[24] Lecture 2, pp. 29–30.   [25] Lecture 3, pp. 64–65.   [26] Lecture 6, p. 117.

stem from considerations whose force will be felt in any attempt to articulate an ethics of loyalty.

One reason why Royce's view develops as it does is that he needs to avoid certain obvious worries about the proliferation of undifferentiated loyalty. There is a concern about misguided loyalties, like blind loyalty to a tyrannical regime. And there is a concern about the ways in which clashing loyalties can lead to mutually destructive conflict. We could have a world of constant war and suffering, made up of people who are bigoted and fanatical, yet in which everyone – perhaps because everyone – is loyal; we need to say something, surely, about why such people should resolve their differences and try to live peacefully. The first problem for the ethics of loyalty, then, is that of finding ways to discriminate between loyalties and condemn their excesses. Royce's strategy is to introduce the notion of loyalty to loyalty; this involves a drift away from the ordinary sense of "loyalty," and a drift towards universalism. There are two alternative strategies that might be thought promising.

The first is to peer more deeply into the notion of loyalty itself, hoping to find a guarantee that the truest and purest loyalties will not have undesirable objects and will not be pursued to excess. It is difficult, however, to see how such discriminations could be made without defining loyalty in a way that makes it parasitic upon independent morally loaded notions. (That is what happens when John Ladd, for example, says that true loyalty involves giving something its moral due; this move allows Ladd to achieve his goal of ruling out the possibility of the loyal Nazi, but it also rules out the possibility that the notion of loyalty will be of help in explaining the notion of "moral due."[27])

The second strategy is to make loyalties answerable to independent standards, saying, for example, that the only desirable loyalties are those consistent with the values of freedom and equality. But then we run into two problems. First, once such independent standards are introduced, loyalty's centrality is compromised, and it becomes less likely that the resulting view can accurately be characterized as an

---

[27] *Encyclopedia of Philosophy* entry on loyalty.

ethics of loyalty. Second, we are left with the problem of saying where those independent standards come from. We need to account for them without committing ourselves to universalism, but we no longer have the notion of loyalty to help; any anti-universalist bite must come from elsewhere.

THE PHENOMENOLOGY OF LOYALTY

A second reason why Royce is drawn to speak of universal and absolute values has to do with the phenomenology of loyalty. At the beginning of Lecture 7, he reports that he has received a letter from a friend, complaining that it is very odd to speak of the value of loyalty without ascribing value to the objects of loyalty.[28] The suggestion, in part, is that loyalty is always loyalty to something, and to be loyal to something, in the wholehearted and reflective way of which Royce approves, is to see that thing as valuable, independently of its status as an object of loyalty. Royce is sympathetic to his friend's suggestion, and takes it as his cue to introduce "loyalty's metaphysic."[29] It is difficult to see how loyalty could make sense as the fundamental moral attitude unless there is something that calls for loyalty, meaning something that stands as valuable and worthy and inspiring in its own right, not just because it happens to be something towards which individuals are loyal. As Royce puts it, "morality requires the light of eternal truth."[30] It requires a higher ideal that the loyal person can serve.

For Royce, loyalty is an attitude that posits self-standing value in the world – in the objects of loyalty. If all value is taken to flow from Roycean loyalty, then that loyalty itself looks mistaken. To avoid this consequence, it seems, an ethics of loyalty needs to posit substantive values that exist independently of the value of loyalty. Again, that raises the problem of building such values into the theory without compromising its title as an "ethics of loyalty," as well as – if we are looking for an alternative to universalist theories – the problem

---

[28] *The Philosophy of Loyalty*, Lecture 7, p. 142.
[29] Lecture 7, p. 161.   [30] Lecture 7, p. 146.

of explaining the existence of such values within a non-universalist framework, and without the notion of loyalty to help us out.

THE NEED FOR LOYALTY

The third consideration that pushes Royce towards a universalist theory has to do with the deeper structure of his evaluative commitments. He is interested in loyalty because he believes that it is a fundamental human need, answering to a universal human predicament. A human life is greatly improved, according to Royce, when it has a guiding principle – when it is unified and purposeful. Someone who lives such a life, Royce tells us, is able to be firm in his self-understanding and identity; he knows who he is, why he is here, and what it would mean for his life to be a success.[31] In Royce's view, the best way to achieve such a life is to be loyal.

Royce's line of thought contains a commitment that can be used to assess individuals' loyalties, and their evaluative perspectives more generally. Any loyalty may give meaning to an individual's life, but there is a clear sense in which a loyalty is higher, or wiser, or more in tune with how things are, if it respects the following truth: there is a fundamental human need for loyalty. That is why loyalty to loyalty, for Royce, is the highest form of loyalty; it is a loyalty that, in a sense, gets things right; it embeds an accurate understanding of the human predicament and its solution. Indeed, someone whose life is guided by a delimited loyalty – someone whose life is built around loyalty just to a particular community – is missing something. She may enjoy all the benefits that a loyal life can offer, but her plan of life does not fully incorporate the important moral truth that humans, wherever they are to be found, need loyalty.

Let me try putting this differently. Royce begins with a judgment about what is good for humans by virtue of their humanity. In order to avoid saying that living a good human life must involve failing to

---

[31] These sentiments are expressed at several points in *The Philosophy of Loyalty*; see Lecture 1, p. 12 for one example.

fully understand that judgment – failing to fully understand the truth about why the good life is good – he then finds a way to incorporate it within the perspective of the person who is living the good life. He believes that the good life is a loyal life, and he finds a way to be loyal to the value of the loyal life.[32] But that is a universalist value. To understand it is to see that it can be instantiated in a person regardless of her particular community memberships, and regardless of which special relationships she stands in to others. To honor that value, just for its own sake, is to take an impartial perspective.

The trajectory of Royce's thought makes sense in light of his starting point, and his starting point is not, in relevant respects, idiosyncratic. Arguments for the importance of loyalty, and pleas for an ethics of loyalty, always advance from the suggestion that loyalty answers to certain universal human needs. When Fletcher complains that universalist morality fails to take account of the essentially historical nature of the self, when MacIntyre argues that an individual who lacks loyalty to her community is thereby estranged from her source of moral sustenance, and when Rorty and Oldenquist say that moral motivation is always an expression of group loyalty, they are all talking about the human condition, and making claims about what is needed for a human life to go well.[33] The perspective taken in the making of such judgments is different from the perspective that we take from inside our loyalties. In being loyal, we pay attention to the special relationships that we share with particular individuals; we do not focus upon the needs that humans have just in virtue of being human.

That difference in perspective is all that is required in order to raise the problem that moves Royce towards universalism. If it is good for humans to have loyalty as their basic moral attitude, and if it is impossible to incorporate within that attitude respect

---

[32] Again, I think that that commitment is misdescribed, but that is not the important point here.

[33] Fletcher, *Loyalty*, see especially the Preface and pp. 11–24; MacIntyre, "Is Patriotism a Virtue?"; Rorty, "Justice as a Larger Loyalty"; Oldenquist, "Loyalties."

for the truth about why it is a desirable attitude to have – namely, the truth that loyalty is valuable in all humans, because all humans have certain needs – then we have a difficult choice to make. Either people live in light of what is truly valuable, or they live a life in which their fundamental needs are met. They cannot do both.

There are ways to mitigate the harshness of this dilemma, one of which is Royce's. Royce suggests that the attitude of loyalty is not really inconsistent with an awareness of the source and structure of loyalty's value, because it is possible to be loyal to loyalty; this view stretches the meaning of loyalty, and in any case abandons anti-universalist ambitions.

Another alternative is to endorse a form of two-leveled morality. That would be to recommend that people adopt the two different moral perspectives, and a judicious strategy for moving back and forth between them. In reflective moments, you can think about the value of loyalty as something that answers to characteristic human needs, and value loyalty in yourself and others for the ways that it makes human lives better. But when caught up in your everyday life, you need not pay attention to that universal value, and can live as a partisan, valuing people for their special relationships with you, not the properties that they possess in their own right. By keeping the right balance between the two perspectives, runs the idea, you can both see things as they really are and enjoy the benefits of the loyal life.

The two-leveled approach, however, is the sort of picture that is recommended by universalist philosophers, especially utilitarians, who want to show how their views leave room for partial attitudes, like friendship, and the need for a two-leveled approach is what so often leads the critics of universalist morality to demand an alternative.[34] Critics like Stocker and Williams say that the two-leveled approach is schizophrenic or alienating.[35] Fletcher rejects it out of

---

[34] See, for example, Railton, "Alienation, Consequentialism, and the Demands of Morality"; and Sidgwick, *The Methods of Ethics*, Book IV, chapter 5.

[35] Stocker "The Schizophrenia of Modern Ethical Theories"; Williams, "Persons, Character and Morality."

hand.[36] It is, in any case, impossible to distinguish from universalist moral theories according to which sometimes there are good reasons, in light of universal principles, to fail to pay attention to universal values. If the goal is to come up with an alternative to prevailing forms of universalist morality, then two-leveled moral theory offers no comfort.

ROYCE AND COMMUNITARIANISM

Royce progresses from a commitment to the value of loyalty to a universalist ethical theory. That progression is well motivated, and driven by concerns that will arise in any attempt to build a plausible ethics of loyalty. If we begin from the value of loyalty, we need to find a way to distinguish the good loyalties from the bad, we need to make sense of loyalty by saying how certain things come to merit loyalty, and we need to find a place in our broader theory for the claim about the human condition that (probably) got us interested in loyalty in the first place. It is difficult to see how a fully developed ethics of loyalty could avoid the progression that we see in Royce, if it is to be at all plausible. The assumption that a credible ethics of loyalty will constitute an alternative to universalist morality turns out to be mistaken.

In closing, I want to relate the concerns found in Royce to the broadly communitarian attempt to construct an alternative to universalist morality. The problems for the ethics of loyalty, in so far as it is intended to be an alternative to universalist morality, can be translated into problems for communitarianism.

First, and very obviously, the worry about differentiating good from bad loyalties corresponds to the problem for communitarianism of differentiating good from bad moral communities. It seems conceivable offhand that there could be a healthy, self-sustaining community in which there is embedded a truly appalling conception of the good life; and it seems conceivable that differing community-embedded moral codes could lead to horrible, mutually destructive

[36] *Loyalty*, pp. 11–16, 164–170.

inter-community conflicts. This point is not at all novel and receives a great deal of attention in the literature – communitarians often respond by arguing that certain core values will arise within any well-formed moral community – so let's just leave it as noticed.[37]

Second, the problem of making sense of loyalties, without positing independently valuable things that command loyalty, becomes the problem of making sense of the ways in which community-embedded moral perspectives confer value upon individuals, without positing independently compelling sources of such value. Usually, community-embedded moral codes aspire to latch onto standards that exist beyond the community. The community conceives of itself as, for example, a nation under God, or as serving a divinely given purpose, or as enshrining certain universal self-evident truths, or as upholding the true moral order, or as sustaining the way of life that it is best for humans to live. It is difficult to see how such moral codes can be made to look sensible, if they themselves are what ultimately determine the individual's moral role and status. Just as Roycean loyalty only makes sense, on its own terms, if there are things that are worthy of loyalty; many (if not all) venerable community-embedded moral codes only make sense on their own terms if there exist sturdy sources of value that stand independently of any particular community.

The third worry for communitarianism corresponds to the suggestion that the normative commitment underlying Royce's enthusiasm for loyalty is universalist; it rests on a claim about what is good for humans, by virtue of their being human. Communitarian attacks upon universalist morality almost always proceed in a similar fashion, saying that universalist morality fails to incorporate important truths about the human condition, or about the nature of human morality. Those truths almost always turn out to be evaluative truths; they are truths about what humans need, what lives it is good for humans to live, what it takes for individual humans to flourish, or what allows a human to become a healthy

---

[37] See especially MacIntyre, *After Virtue*, chapter 14, in which it is argued that certain core virtues will be central to any healthy community.

moral agent. There is then a tension between the partial ways of thinking that the critics of universalist morality would like us to adopt, and their own pronouncements about the universal human condition, in the light of which universalist morality is supposed to be found wanting.

The worry is not just that communitarians turn out to be universalists in disguise. It is also that they find themselves recommending moral thinking that has ignorance of the higher evaluative truth as an essential component. Communitarians value commitments to rich, self-sufficient moral communities because they believe that it is only within such a community that a person can have a well-grounded conception of the good life and the motivation to live according to it; but they do not imagine the members of such communities having commitments of the form, "I must be committed to this community because it is only by being committed to some community or other that I can have a well-grounded conception of the good life and the motivation to live according to it." For the communitarian, it seems, to see human needs as they really are is to take a perspective that is incompatible with the one that you need to take, if your human needs are to be met.

These criticisms of communitarianism, needless to say, have been offered quite briefly, and there is clearly more to be said. And they certainly do not resolve the worries about universalist morality that motivate communitarianism and related views. But the development of Royce's philosophy of loyalty, as well as revealing something about what a plausible ethics of loyalty would have to look like, shows that universalist commitments and impartial moral reasoning are very difficult to avoid, whatever the philosophical troubles to which they may lead.

CHAPTER 10

Disloyalty

INTRODUCTION

I have spent much of this book arguing that loyalty is not an important moral category. There are many different forms of loyalty, and their differences tend to be of more ethical interest than their similarities. For the purposes of moral philosophy, it is often important to treat different loyalties separately, and while some are of great value, others are positively undesirable. Loyalty, considered as a general proposition, is not a value or a virtue.

One reason to worry about this set of views is that in playing down the ethical significance of the notion of loyalty, we may also find ourselves playing down the ethical significance of the notion of disloyalty, and that would seem to be a serious mistake. Disloyalty appears to be a distinctive and profound kind of wrong, and the ideas with which it is associated – ideas of letting someone down, betrayal, abandonment, treason and treachery – are highly morally charged.

Suppose that you tell a friend something personal, something that you would not want shared with others, and later she blurts it out in company. It is one thing to express your displeasure by telling her that she was careless, thoughtless or inconsiderate. It is quite another thing to tell her that she was disloyal, that she betrayed or abandoned you, or that she let you down; if you are going to accuse her in those terms, then you had better be sure that it was an important secret that she let slip; you had better be sure that her act was truly egregious.

How are we to account for the gravity of disloyalty and associated sins? One option is to say that loyalty is a fundamental virtue and disloyalty is its opposing vice. This would be a mistake, not just because loyalty is not a virtue, but because disloyalty is a more complicated phenomenon, ethically speaking, than that treatment would suggest. What follows examines the notion of disloyalty and provides a rough account of what it is and when and why it is wrong. If I am right, then the correct treatment of disloyalty can be made to fit with the basic story that I have told about the ethics of loyalty.

IS DISLOYALTY ALWAYS WRONG?

In the recent philosophical literature, the only careful discussion of disloyalty of which I am aware is in the first two pages of a piece about corporate loyalty, written by R. E. Ewin.[1] Ewin says that disloyalty is always a vice, and consists in "the failure of appropriate feelings to move one to do what one should have done anyway on independent grounds."[2] Something only counts as disloyalty, Ewin says, "if it can also be described as *another* vice too."[3] A person who leaves a firm and then hands its secrets over to a new employer, to give one of Ewin's examples, is dishonest, as well as being disloyal, and other cases of disloyalty, says Ewin, may involve such vices as ingratitude and selfishness. For Ewin, the wrongfulness of disloyalty is built into the concept of disloyalty – nothing can be disloyal unless it is wrong – and there is always something that makes an act of disloyalty wrong apart from its being disloyal. It is worth noting that Ewin is able to say all of this without saying that loyalty is a virtue; "loyalty moves one to act, but not necessarily where there are other good grounds for acting."[4]

It is a mistake to say that disloyalty is always wrong, and a mistake to say that disloyalty always involves an independently

---

[1] Ewin, "Corporate Loyalty," pp. 387–388. There are also a few sentences on disloyalty on p. 283 of Allen, "When Loyalty No Harm Meant"; and there is some discussion in chapter 2 of Fletcher's *Loyalty*. Also, Judith Shklar offers an extensive meditation on betrayal in chapter 4 of *Ordinary Vices*.

[2] p. 388.   [3] p. 388, italics Ewin's.

[4] p. 388. For a fuller statement of Ewin's views about loyalty, see his "Loyalty and Virtues" and "Loyalties, and Why Loyalty Should be Ignored."

specifiable vice. Sometimes, people ought to be disloyal, and sometimes, disloyalty involves no vice at all.

Consider the case of the ethical whistle-blower, the employee who publicly exposes the immoral actions of her employer. She might work for a company that is secretly releasing hazardous waste into the water supply, for example, and she might be unable to end this practice without taking the company's secret to the public. It is surely possible that she thereby acts rightly. Could her act at the same time be disloyal?

The whistle-blower releases confidential information that will, once known, cause great damage to her employer. In deciding whether or not to go public with the information, it will be clear to the whistle-blower what company loyalty demands, clear that to give away company secrets is to commit as blatant a betrayal of company as there can be; after all, the company has placed her in a position of trust, and may well have treated *her* very well indeed. Her employer will certainly say that her act is disloyal, and certainly would be right to say so if the employee were releasing secrets that have only strategic importance, like the plans for an upcoming marketing campaign. If it can be disloyal to release damaging information about your employer's next marketing campaign, then why should it not also be disloyal to release damaging information about what your employer does with its hazardous waste? When accused of disloyalty, I think that the whistle-blower's natural response is to say, "Given what the company was doing, it did not deserve my loyalty," meaning not that she is not really disloyal, but that, given the circumstances, her disloyalty is justified.

It seems, then, that the most natural description of the ethical whistle-blower is as someone who does the right thing in being disloyal. Furthermore, in at least some cases, the whistle-blower does not do *anything* ethically questionable. Often, of course, a whistle-blower, even if acting rightly on the whole, will need to do things that would be impermissible under normal circumstances, like telling lies or putting innocent colleagues at risk; in these cases, her act has regrettable aspects that are, in the circumstances, outweighed by the good. But not always: sometimes the whistle-blower will not need to lie, endanger the innocent, or do anything comparably undesirable; sometimes, all the moral considerations will point in the same direction. Given the right specification of the case, the act of the whistle-blower can be clearly, without mitigation, the right thing to do, while still being a disloyal thing to do. Sometimes, disloyalty not only fails to be wrong, but also fails to involve any independently specifiable vice.

The story of the whistle-blower is not all that unusual, in so far as it is a story of justified disloyalty. There are many further cases in which a person, in acting disloyally, does exactly what she should. Think of the soldier who deserts an army that is pointlessly killing innocent people, the bank manager who refuses to follow the company policy of squeezing higher interest rates out of vulnerable borrowers, or the wife who refers her criminal husband to the police.

For a different kind of case, imagine a student who, part way through a dissertation project, realizes that his true interests lie elsewhere, and decides to transfer to a different project with a different advisor. If you are the original advisor, and if you have expended a great deal of time and political capital in funding the student and supervising his work, then you may feel that in choosing to work with someone else, the student lets you down. You can at the same time understand, however, that the student should not continue with the original project just to keep faith with you. He is being disloyal in changing projects, but if that is what he decides is best for him, then that is what he should do.

A disloyal act may be right or wrong. This does not imply, however, that disloyalty never makes a moral difference. Suppose that you tell a friend a personal secret, and are overheard by a stranger who happens to be wandering by. Then, both your friend and the stranger report the secret in public. You would feel more aggrieved at your friend's act than at the stranger's. It does not speak well of the stranger that he acts as he does – his act is inconsiderate and opportunistic – but your friend's act, because it is disloyal, carries a distinctive hurtful quality. Disloyalty may not guarantee wrongness, but neither is it morally inert.

LOYALTY, DISLOYALTY AND MORAL RESPONSIBILITY

You can be loyal, I said in Chapter 1, without knowing it. You may honestly believe that you are regarding your friend the job candidate impartially, when in fact you are influenced by feelings of loyalty; you may honestly believe that you feel no loyalty to your father when it is obvious to everyone else that you do; and a dog or young child can be loyal while having no idea what loyalty is. Disloyalty, by comparison, involves a fairly high level of awareness, or deliberateness, or mental sophistication, though it is not a straightforward matter to say exactly what.

One disloyal thing that you could do is to give your country's secret military plans to the enemy. Suppose, though, that you give the plans to the enemy without really understanding what you are doing. It is not that you do not know that they are plans, or that they are secret, or that this is the enemy. Rather, you just do not understand the significance of the sharing of secret military plans. Perhaps you are a simple soul, or one who is new to the world of international intelligence, and you have no idea how these things work. When the enemy asks for the plans, you simply hand them over without thinking about it, just as you would if the plans were requested by one of your superiors. Plenty of uncomplimentary things could be said about you in such a case, but your act is not disloyal. Something about your situation, something to do with your lack of information or intellect or intent, leaves you without the psychological resources that disloyalty requires.

Some individuals are capable of loyalty but not disloyalty. If you have taken your dog to the park, and he is playing with a large crowd of other dogs and their owners, and when you wander away he notices and runs after you, then he may well be acting out of loyalty; he knows who you are, and he cares about being with you. If, alternatively, he ignores you and trots off after some stranger when the game is finished, then he is not being loyal – but neither is he being disloyal. You can call a dog loyal, but to call a dog disloyal is to attribute to him motives, and a general level of mental sophistication, that dogs do not possess. Again, something that is needed for disloyalty is missing.

It is tempting to think that the only kind of disloyalty is deliberate disloyalty. Then, we would say that disloyalty, as opposed to a simple failure to be loyal, always involves doing something that you know to be disloyal. But that cannot be quite right. As with most kinds of motive, disloyalty is compatible with self-deception, and it is compatible with denial, so that someone who is genuinely disloyal can genuinely believe that she is not.

Also, disloyalty can be a result of simple distraction or lack of effort. You might have a friend who expects and gets of you all the special favors and attention that friends can provide for each other, but goes through a period during which she provides none of the same in return. She never has time to talk when it is you who needs to discuss things, she regularly stands you up, she is careless with your personal information, and so on. Your friend might then be disloyal, even if she would be shocked to hear herself described as such. The reason why she is disloyal may be not that she means to be, but that she is preoccupied or distracted, or is going through a time during which she is forgetful and self-absorbed.

The correct, though still somewhat opaque, thing to say is that for an act of yours to be disloyal, you must be morally responsible for the act. It must make sense to hold you to account – praise, blame, judge you – for what you do. You can be morally responsible for an act because you choose it autonomously, deliberately, and in full awareness of what you are doing. But you can also be morally responsible for an act when you do not know what you are doing, but you should – when you would know what you were doing were it not for your culpable laziness, self-absorption or distraction; and you can be morally responsible for an act when the reason why you do not know what you are doing is that you yourself are denying or suppressing that knowledge. And there may well be other ways in which moral responsibility can arise. Whatever the various conditions sufficient for moral responsibility, though, we can safely presume that none will be met by dogs, and that usually they will not be met by those who act out of non-culpable ignorance. That is why it sounds odd to accuse such individuals of disloyalty. Disloyalty, unlike loyalty, exists only in the realm of moral responsibility.[5]

SUFFERING DISLOYALTY

Disloyalty always has an object, an individual to whom the disloyalty is done. Characteristically, when you are the object of someone's disloyalty you suffer two kinds of harm. First, there is the harm involved in the disloyal person's act, considered independently of the fact that it is disloyal. Second, there is the distinct harm of having that first kind of damage done through an act of disloyalty.

When your friend tells your secret in public, one result is that there are now many people who know what you wanted to conceal; this is a harm that you would suffer even if the secret had been told by a stranger. Then, there is the additional kind of harm that is involved in having the secret broadcast by your friend, someone whom you ought to be able to trust. Similarly, when your spouse spreads a nasty rumor about you, there is, beyond the harm that results from being spoken of in nasty terms, the harm of suffering it at the hands of your spouse, of all people. And when you welcome a guest into your home, and he makes off with some of your treasured pieces of jewelry, you suffer more than merely the harm of being robbed.

To feel like a victim of another's disloyalty is, characteristically, to feel assaulted. To take it as disloyalty is to take it personally. It is to feel that the disloyal person was out to get you, or at least was prepared to take advantage of your vulnerability in order to achieve her nefarious goals. The everyday thief expresses a general lack of regard for others' interests and property, but the house guest who robs you expresses – or so you are likely to feel – a lack of regard for

---

[5] The nature of moral responsibility is a difficult philosophical topic, on which I have nothing to add here. See the papers collected in Fischer and Ravizza (eds.), *Perspectives on Moral Responsibility*.

you specifically. She scorns you and your hospitality; she may as well have made a public declaration of her contempt. This constitutes an additional harm: the harm of being affronted.

The experience of the victim of disloyalty is also, in paradigm cases, an experience of loss. What you lose is, in a sense, the disloyal person herself. You learn that you do not have the special, valuable relationship that you thought you had, or that you might have hoped to have. You would think that a house guest would never exploit your hospitality; you would think that you could trust a friend; and you would think that a spouse would show a special concern for your best interests. Such valuable relationships are the sorts of things that you find yourself to have lost, or to have lacked all along, when you find yourself a victim of disloyalty.

AFFRONTS AND EXPECTATIONS

The next two sections build a rough account of the nature of disloyalty, beginning with the claims suggested in the previous section: that disloyalty involves a kind of affront, and that it involves the compromising of a relationship. To be disloyal, on the view that I will defend, is to fail to meet a certain sort of standard, which can arise within the context of a relationship, and thereby to do someone an affront. I will call these standards "expectations," and the purpose of this section is to try to draw out the notion I intend that label to capture. Let me start with an example of a generic sort of affront, one that does not involve disloyalty.

Suppose that I extend my hand, offering you a handshake, and you fail to take it. Your failure to shake my hand may be an expression of anger, contempt or disdain. In any case, it is likely to constitute a kind of affront or insult or snub. By refusing to shake my hand you are taking a stand against me, so to speak; you are doing the opposite of taking my side.

The reason why you are able to do me an affront by failing to shake my hand is that when I offer you the handshake, I make it the case that your conduct will receive its meaning in light of a certain custom and a certain understanding. I give you the opportunity to acknowledge me and show me respect by shaking my hand, and when you refuse to do so, you communicate an unwillingness to grant me that respect. In offering you a handshake I make it the case that you are subject to an expectation: namely, the expectation that you will show me respect or acknowledgement by shaking my hand. By construing your behavior as a response to that expectation, we can see why your failure to shake my hand is meaningful – why it constitutes an affront.

The existence of the expectation not only enables you to do me an affront by turning down the handshake, but can also make it the case that if you do not shake my hand then you cannot help doing me an affront, whether you want to or not. Suppose that your failure to shake my hand has nothing to do with your attitudes towards me in particular. Perhaps you just do not feel like shaking hands, or perhaps you have decided not to shake anyone's hand because you are fearful of exchanging germs. Then, when you decline my handshake, you really do not mean anything personal by it. But while you do not set out to do me an affront, the circumstances may be such that you nevertheless do. Perhaps our interactions are not sufficiently intimate and relaxed for you to explain to my satisfaction the real reason for your failure to take my hand; or perhaps my offer of a handshake is a very obvious gesture made while the two of us are on stage in front of a large audience. Under those sorts of circumstances, there might be no option available to you, apart from accepting my handshake, that will constitute anything other than an insult.

Even in such restrictive circumstances, however, you are on the moral hook – morally responsible – for doing me an affront. Unless you have a good excuse, like having just arrived from a country in which the custom of shaking hands does not exist, you can be held to account for your conduct, and its meaning. You know what handshakes represent, and you need to take that into account when you decide what to do. We would not be impressed to hear you say, "I just didn't want to shake hands. I didn't mean anything by it. If my actions caused offense, that's nothing to do with me." It may not be your fault that the relevant expectation exists and you are subject to it, but you are nevertheless answerable for your actions, understood in the expectation's light.

To say that you are accountable for doing me an affront by failing to shake my hand is not necessarily to say that you ought to have shaken my hand. You can be morally responsible for good as well as bad acts. It may be that I deserve to be snubbed, or that it is worth doing me a snub in order to avoid the chance of exchanging germs. If so, then perhaps you deserve congratulations for refusing the handshake. The point is just that you are answerable for your behavior, for better or worse, as it appears in light of the operative expectation. Let me try to put this into a slightly more theoretical context.

There are two different ways in which we can speak of expectations. I can tell my class that I expect that everybody's paper will be handed in on the due date, and then tell my colleague that I certainly do not expect that everybody's paper will be handed in on time. In the one case, I am speaking of norms for behavior, or normative expectations; I am telling my students that it ought to be the case, according to relevant standards, that everybody hands in their papers when they are due. In the other case, I am speaking of my predictions about what actually will happen, doubting that the standards referred to in the first case will be met. The expectation that you will shake my extended hand is a normative expectation, not a prediction. Even if everybody predicts that you will refuse my offer of a handshake, you are still subject to an expectation, in the normative sense, that you will shake my hand; the relevant standards still apply. That is why your refusal carries the meaning it does, whether predicted or not. So when I use the term "expectation," I am trying to focus upon the idea of a normative expectation, not a prediction.[6]

An expectation can be a normative expectation without being an expectation that you should meet. The expectation that you will shake my hand, for example, does not flow directly from truths of

---

[6] On p. 141 of *Ordinary Vices*, Shklar seems to suggest that betrayal (though she may just mean treachery – the text is unclear) always involves a disappointed expectation; but she appears to be speaking of predictions, not normative expectations.

morality or practical reason, but rather from a widely accepted social custom. The existence of the custom makes it the case that your conduct carries a certain meaning – it counts as an insult – but even taking this into account, it is an open question whether or not the custom should be followed in any particular instance. Speaking generally, normative expectations are normative only in the following sense: they make claims about what ought to be done. Their claims are not always correct.

I do not have much to say, I am afraid, about where normative expectations come from and how we become subject to them, though I hope that it is clear enough that they come from somewhere and we become subject to them somehow. In the case of the handshake, the relevant expectation appears to be generated, as I say, as a matter of a widely followed custom and habit of interpretation; handshakes and offers of handshakes carry certain sorts of meaning because we take them to do so. Other expectations might arise not through a broad social understanding but through a history of interactions between particular individuals; because I have bought you lunch every day for the last month, I may be subject to an expectation that I will buy you lunch again today, and a refusal to do so might carry a message about how I feel about you today. Or, expectations could flow directly from truths of morality or practical reason, independently of conventions; perhaps we are all subject to the expectation that we will not inflict gratuitous pain upon others, not because we happen to have social institutions that speak against it, but simply because it is wrong. Perhaps it is the case, for example, that whenever you intentionally inflict gratuitous pain, your behavior can be understood in light of the expectation that you will not; in particular, it may be that in inflicting gratuitous pain, you denigrate or insult your victim, as well as hurting him.

Expectations exist. When you are subject to an expectation, it can affect the meaning of your conduct; in particular, it sometimes makes it the case that what you do or fail to do counts as an affront. With the expectation in the background, your conduct can take that meaning – can count as an affront – even if you would prefer that it did not. Absent a good excuse, you can be held morally responsible for your behavior, understood as carrying the meaning that the expectation grants it. None of this suffices to show, however, that you necessarily do the wrong thing if you fail to meet an expectation to which you are subject. That remains an open question.

EXPECTATIONS AND SPECIAL RELATIONSHIPS

Here is my suggested rough treatment of the nature of disloyalty. To be disloyal to something – call it X – is to do X an affront by failing to meet a certain sort of expectation to which you are subject: namely, an expectation that exists by virtue of some special relationship between you and X, and that demands that you, in some sense or other, take X's side.

There are certain things – people, institutions, countries, and so on – with which you share special relationships, meaning relationships that not everyone shares with those things and that you do not share with just anything.[7] Such relationships include being married to a certain person, being a member of a certain club, and being a native of a certain country. Sometimes, as a result of standing in such a relationship, you are subject to expectations. As someone's boyfriend, you are expected to sit next to her at dinner; as a resident of a country, you are expected to follow its laws. And sometimes, the expectation is that you will in one way or another take the thing's side, in the sense explored in Chapter 1. As someone's mother, you are expected to show her a heightened level of concern; as a member of a football club, you are expected to cheer for it and be happy when it wins; as the citizen of a country, you are expected to refrain from sharing its military secrets with its enemies. When you are subject to such an expectation and you fail to meet it, your conduct understood in light of the expectation constitutes an affront, and you are then disloyal. To be disloyal is to fail to take the side of something with which you share a special relationship, when the relationship is such that you are expected to do so. I will try to make

---

[7] On special relationships, see chapter 1.

this suggestion plausible, as well as exploring it a little further, through some examples.

First, a straightforward case. You tell your friend something that you would like to be kept secret, and she spreads the news to everyone. You may, quite reasonably, feel betrayed. She is your friend; the two of you share a special relationship. Friends ought to keep each other's secrets; in virtue of that special relationship, your friend is subject to an expectation that she will be, in a certain respect, on your side. In telling your secret to others, it is as though she is deliberately neglecting your friendship and expressing a lack of regard for you and your privacy; in failing to meet the expectation, she does you an affront.

Second, a case in which you act disloyally, without really meaning to be disloyal. You are out with your elderly mother in winter, and she becomes very cold. You could give her your jacket – you will be fine either way – but you keep it for yourself. An observer might, quite reasonably, think you a disloyal son. He may ask you, "How could you do that to your own mother?" As a son, you are subject to the expectation that you will show a special concern for your mother's wellbeing, and your failure to offer her your jacket seems to amount to a failure to meet that expectation. You might reply, "I'm not doing anything to my mother. I just think that my jacket looks pretty stylish on me. There are many cold people around here who would like my jacket. I wish them nothing but the best, but I choose to keep the jacket for myself. So it is for my mother. It's really nothing personal." But you do not have the option of portraying your act in that way, because, like it or not, your conduct with regard to your own mother receives its meaning as a response to the expectation that you will be especially concerned with her best interests. Your failure to take her side takes the character of a deliberate flouting of that expectation, and hence of an affront to your mother. It is disloyal.

Note, by the way, that this example of disloyalty does not depend upon your mother's *feeling* affronted by your failure to give her your jacket, nor upon its being *predicted*, by your mother or by anyone else, that you will. Even if your mother does not understand that you are able and expected to make sacrifices for the sake of her comfort, and therefore does not register your conduct as an affront, there is still a clear sense in which your behavior *is* an affront. And even if everybody knows that you do not care very much about your mother's comfort, so that nobody expects – meaning "predicts" – that you will prioritize her interests, there is a clear, normative sense in which you are still expected to do so.

Third, a case in which you seem to all outward appearances to be disloyal, but in fact are not. You are at a football game, watching the team that you have supported all your life. The team is being beaten, and you tear off your team colors and start cheering for the opposition. You look like a disloyal fan. In fact, however, your motive in cheering for the opposition is to rile your own players, and thereby goad them into improving their performance. Then, you are not disloyal, though you may be misguided. The reason why you are not disloyal is that you are still on your team's side; once your true motivation is understood, it is clear that your allegiance is still where it is expected to be. This case shows that the expectations that matter for disloyalty really are, in the first instance, expectations that you will take something's side, not necessarily expectations that you will manifest your being on its side through any particular piece of behavior. That is why an insight into your motivations can show that you are meeting the relevant expectation, even though that may not be what your behavior suggests.

COMPARING LOYALTY AND DISLOYALTY

Disloyalty is not the opposite of loyalty, either in the sense of being the same basic kind of thing just oppositely directed, or in the sense of being its absence. Whether or not you are loyal to something can be just a matter of how you feel and think about it, and how you act towards it. Disloyalty is more of a moral, social, public or institutional phenomenon, requiring more in the way of context. Before we can have disloyalty, we need a setting sufficiently rich to give rise to normative expectations.

Feelings of loyalty have more to do with loyalty than feelings of disloyalty have to do with disloyalty. Loyalty is similar, in the relevant respect, to love and hatred. To feel love or hatred towards something is – more or less and leaving aside unusual cases – actually to love or hate it. The same is true of loyalty. It is of course possible to be deceived about whether or not you are loyal to something, but still: if you feel loyal then that usually helps make it the case that you are. Usually, part of what it is to be loyal to America is to feel loyal to America.

Disloyalty is different. You can feel a loyalty to something, but you cannot feel a disloyalty to something, or not in the same way. You can feel disloyal, but to feel disloyal is just to feel that you are disloyal. It is less like feeling love or hatred, and more like feeling attractive or rude. To feel attractive is to feel that you are attractive, and to feel rude is to feel that you are rude; it is a kind of commentary upon yourself and your situation, and it may be mistaken. The fact that you feel rude does not guarantee, or help make it true, that you are rude. In the same way, a feeling of disloyalty is a kind of commentary; it is a judgment about or interpretation of yourself and your situation, as they stand independently of the feeling itself. Feelings of disloyalty do not help constitute disloyalty.

Disloyalty has less to do with motivation and emotional engagement than does loyalty. You cannot be loyal to something without having certain motives directed towards it. If you are loyal to something, then thoughts of the thing itself will play some part in your motivational and emotional life. Disloyalty can involve emotional engagement – disloyalty to something can involve hating it, resenting it or feeling contempt for it, or deliberately setting out to do it damage – but you can also be disloyal because you fail to be emotionally engaged, because you are forgetful or neglectful or because your energy and concerns are directed elsewhere. Whether or not you are disloyal depends upon how you conduct yourself relative to the expectations, of a certain sort, to which you are subject, and whether or not you meet those expectations is not necessarily a matter of how you feel.

WHAT IS WRONG WITH DISLOYALTY?

My rough story about the nature of disloyalty can explain the claims that I made earlier about the ethics of disloyalty. Sometimes, disloyalty is not wrong, and that, I suggest, is because sometimes, people are subject to expectations that they ought not meet. Some expectations do not carry sufficient moral force to override countervailing considerations, and some expectations do not carry any moral force at all.

The actions of the ethical whistle-blower, for example, take place within the context of a public, institutional relationship between employer and employee. That relationship generates expectations. It is expected that the employee will in a certain respect – one that rules out the sharing of company secrets – be on the employer's side. But there are considerations, in the case of the whistle-blower, that count against her following those expectations. These considerations are of two types. First, there are strong reasons for her to take her company's secret to the public, and she cannot do so while meeting the expectations to which she is subject as an employee. Second, given the unethical behavior of the company, the relationship between it and her is not as valuable as it otherwise would be, and the expectations that it generates are, correspondingly, less important. That is not to say that she is not disloyal to the company when she takes its secrets to the public – she is still subject to the expectation, grounded in the employer–employee relationship, that she will keep company secrets – but it is to say that there is really nothing wrong with her disloyalty.

We may take the same attitude towards the relationship between a person and her manipulative friend, a citizen and her totalitarian government, or a student and his abusive fraternity. All of these characters are involved in relationships that demand allegiance, and in some circumstances, to fail to grant the appropriate kind of allegiance would be to do an affront; it would be disloyal. But that does not mean that it would be wrong. These are examples of people who are subject to bad expectations.

Still, disloyalty is a morally loaded notion. Why does disloyalty, even though it is not always wrong, carry such a powerful negative connotation? Why is disloyalty so unloved?

First, in any instance of disloyalty there is a perspective from which it is "against the rules." To see an act as disloyal is to be aware of, without necessarily endorsing, a perspective from which it is undesirable: namely, the perspective constructed from the expectations that are being broken. So while a given instance of disloyalty might not involve wrongdoing, it will take place within some normative context or other, relative to which it will have the status of an infringement.

Second, disloyalty always involves an affront or insult, or at least something that will be interpreted as such. Some individuals deserve to be affronted or insulted, but it is safe to say, as a general rule, that affronts and insults should be avoided. To this extent, there exists a defeasible presumption against disloyalty.

Third, when thinking of ourselves as its potential victims, disloyalty is something that we naturally fear and despise. When someone is disloyal to you, she fails to meet an expectation that she will be on your side, an expectation that arises from the special relationship that the two of you share. We rely to an enormous extent upon our ability to trust that those with whom we share such relationships – friends, spouses, colleagues, fellow citizens, and so on – will be, in particular ways, our allies. Sometimes you do not care about a relationship of which you are a part, or the expectations that it generates, and hence do not care whether or not some particular person is disloyal to you. If you lead a recognizably human life, however, then there will be many others upon whom you depend, and whose allegiance, if it comes, will come through their adherence to a framework of expectations that emerges from your shared relationships. Disloyalty is something to which we all are vulnerable.

Fourth, and related to the previous points, there is a distinctive kind of hurtfulness that disloyalty tends to involve. It is not only that many acts of disloyalty are objectionable, but that they are all the more objectionable for being disloyal. You are disloyal if you fail to support an individual in the way that is expected, given the special relationship that the two of you share. It is therefore likely that the victim of your disloyalty will be counting on you to meet those expectations, so that in being disloyal you take advantage of her good faith or defenselessness. It is likely that your disloyal act will lead to distrust on the part of its victim, and hence undermine a valuable relationship in which the two of you stand, or in which you did or should stand. And it is likely that your disloyal act will threaten the structures of cooperation and shared understanding that allow the operative system of expectations, and the goods to which it may give rise, to emerge and survive. None of these things, as I say, is guaranteed, but they are all associated closely, and for good reason, with disloyalty, and they are all ways of making an act regrettable, in a distinctive kind of a way.

For all of these reasons, disloyalty has, and deserves, a bad reputation, even though an act of disloyalty can, in a given case, be the right thing to do. For the most part, disloyalty is to be discouraged.

Another way to see this is to think of how we would regard someone who has disloyalty as a character trait – someone who has a disloyal nature. If there were such a person, he would be inclined to fail to meet expectations to which he is subject, by virtue of the special relationships in which he stands. He is not the sort of person who is never subject to such expectations, but rather the sort of person who is subject to them and breaks them. He is not a friendless person, so much as a person who makes friends and then lets them down. His inclination is to fail to uphold his side of relationships that proceed on the basis of commonly understood sets of norms. As a character type, he is, obviously, repulsive, and likely to do a great deal of damage to those with whom he interacts. Disloyalty may be desirable in some cases, but as a policy or plan of life, it is loathsome.

If I am on the right track in my story about the nature and moral status of disloyalty, then the correct view of disloyalty is not in tension with the views about loyalty that I have defended in this book. It is possible to say that the character trait of disloyalty is a vice without saying that loyalty is a virtue; and it is possible to say what is wrong with disloyalty, when it is wrong, without making a more fundamental commitment to the value of loyalty.

Conclusion

In its psychological and ethical dimensions, loyalty is complicated and often confusing. It is not morally pure, and it is not morally reliable. It is not the foundation of moral thinking, and it should not be given a fundamental role in ethical theory. Different kinds of loyalty involve different ways of thinking and behaving, and make different demands. There are good loyalties, and obligatory loyalties, but loyalty, and indeed many of the good things about loyalty, can also be intimately linked with mistakes, dangers and delusions. Some forms of loyalty are virtuous, but loyalty is not a virtue.

We need loyalty. We do not need it, though, in order to construct or understand ourselves as individuals, or in order to be moral agents. The source of our need for loyalty is less grand, though no less significant; we need loyalty because it makes our lives better. In all sorts of ways, life is richer, more enjoyable and less frightening when we have loyal relationships. The various reasons why we need loyalty are the various reasons why it is good to have friends, close family ties, a favorite football team, and so on. The value of loyalty is to be understood by way of the value of particular kinds of loyalty, not through the bare notion of loyalty itself.

There exists what we might call "the ethical discourse of loyalty": a way of thinking and judging that treats loyalty as a self-standing value and has a distinctively moralized tone. You can expect to find it within a company, sports team, gang, political party, or university, to give some examples. Good action, within the discourse of loyalty, is identified as loyal action – loyal to whichever entity stands in the background – and disloyalty, betrayal and treachery are regarded as the worst of sins.

It is tempting to try to show that the discourse of loyalty is, properly construed, the discourse of morality – that morality, at its root, is a demand that we be loyal, in some sense or other. But that is a mistake. The moral perspective cannot be fruitfully represented as the perspective of loyalty, and when philosophers try to show that it can, many of the most important aspects of our experience of loyalty are pushed aside and forgotten. Different loyalties require different ethical treatments, and even the most valuable of loyalties – like friendship – exist in tension with other important evaluative standards; our job is to perceive and manage such tensions, not to find some point of view from which they disappear. It always makes sense – and is often a very good idea – to ask, "This is what loyalty demands, but is it right?" and, "This would be disloyal, but does that make it wrong?" To ask those questions is to appeal to a higher, perhaps universal ethical perspective. A proper understanding of the ethics of loyalty leads us towards substantive evaluative truths that stand above and independently of loyalty itself; it does not explain such truths, or show why they are not needed.

Those are the views about loyalty that I have defended in this book. I have also made several claims about particular loyalties. I have argued, among other things, that friendship, even at its best, is not a pure moral phenomenon, that there are good reasons not to be patriotic, and that filial loyalty can, under the right circumstances, be obligatory.

Even if all that I say in the book is convincing, it is clear that I have not said all there is to say about patriotism, friendship and filial loyalty, and certainly not about loyalty in all its other forms. There is much more to be learned from considering loyalties individually and on their own terms, rather than approaching loyalty as a single general phenomenon, and rather than descending to the topic of loyalty from debates in higher-level ethical theory. It is by stepping back from high theoretical ambitions for loyalty – by seeing it as one more complicated and confusing aspect of human psychology – that we can bring the truly important questions into view.

Postscript: Universal morality and the problem of loyalty

In the main body of the book, I have avoided taking a stance on the most well-known ethical question that loyalty raises: the question of whether any impartialist, universalist moral theory can say the right things about how we can and should treat those with whom we share special relationships. I have made some claims that are relevant to the problem, though, and I want to finish by bringing them together.

Here, again, is the problem. Loyalty involves a deeply partial attitude; when you are loyal to something, you favor it because of its special relationship with you, and you (often) care about it for its own sake, not in order to follow some universal principle. But moral theories like utilitarianism and Kantianism seem to demand that we be impartial; they say that how an individual should be treated depends upon how he is inherently, not how he is related to you.

Sometimes, the lesson drawn is that we should reject universalist morality – or at least restrict its scope – and say that loyalties just do not need to be legitimated in external moral terms. The idea is that if you are loyal to something, then you are justified in acting as your loyalty demands (perhaps unless there is some overwhelming reason why you should not); there is no additional question to be asked about whether your loyalty is permissible or desirable. We might say, in the style of Fletcher and other advocates of the ethics of loyalty, that loyalty is a foundational moral attitude, in terms of which other moral phenomena are to be explained and assessed, or we might say that morality is made up of rules that arise within particular contexts and relationships but cannot be generalized, or we might say that there is a sphere of the personal life that morality does not touch.

In light of the views I have presented in the book, this kind of approach is implausible. The fact that something is a loyalty does not in itself grant it any privileged ethical status (and you do not need to presuppose a universalist perspective in order to see this). There are good loyalties, bad loyalties and ethically complicated loyalties. When the husband saves his drowning wife, rather than a stranger, the justification for his act had better be something other than, "It's his wife and so he is loyal to her." We had better add something to the effect that this is a permissible or desirable form of loyalty. (Whether this is how the husband himself should be thinking at the time is, of course, another question.)

Also, loyalties do not always travel under their own ethical steam, so to speak, but rather call upon and interact with external values and standards. I argued for this claim in the discussion of friendship and belief. There is good reason to carry on a friendship while keeping one eye on the epistemic, moral and prudential standards with which the demands of friendship potentially conflict, and there are in fact familiar strategies for doing so. To say that the demands of loyalty stand independently of other important normative stand-ards is to take an overly simplistic view of the ways in which loyalties really function, within a whole, good human life.

Let me address another kind of response to the problem of loyalty, which is sometimes offered as a kind of quick fix on behalf of the universalist. The response is to say that there is no conflict between universal morality and loyalty, because it is possible to construct impartial principles that instruct us to be partial.[1] Nathanson gives the example of "Honor your father and mother"; this rule does not pick out any particular person, and it applies universally, yet it tells each individual to be loyal to those with whom she shares a certain kind of special relationship. Of course, it is not exactly clear how such a rule could be made to follow from utilitarianism or Kantianism, but that is a substantive issue for those theories – it has nothing to do with universalism in general.

[1] For some discussion, see Nathanson, *Patriotism, Morality and Peace*, pp. 70–76; and Baron, "Patriotism and 'Liberal' Morality," pp. 63–65.

For reasons that I brought out in discussing Royce's ascent to "loyalty to loyalty," this response is unsatisfactory. The worry is that in taking on the universalist perspective, we take on a substantive claim about human needs, or more generally the ground of individual value, and it is hard to see how we could then recommend individual conduct that does not proceed in light of this claim.

Put it this way. The principle, "Everyone should promote the interests of those who share their own hair color, and relentlessly hunt down and kill those who do not," is, I suppose, universal in form, but it is clearly inconsistent with the spirit of (enlightened) universalist morality, according to which the color of a person's hair is morally irrelevant. In the same way, I think, for the universalist there just has to be some tension between the conviction that you should favor those with whom you share certain special relationships and the conviction that, in the big scheme of things, how someone happens to be related to you has no bearing at all upon her basic moral importance. There is at least a puzzle to be confronted.

So, there is a need for loyalties and other forms of partiality to be justified in external ethical terms, and there is a genuine question about how the attitude of loyalty can be squared with the perspective of universalist morality. It is obvious that loyalty is often permitted, even required, and I cannot think of how loyal thinking and action could be justified satisfactorily, except by appeal to principles and values that are ultimately impartial and universal. In defending the special goods theory of filial duty and loyalty, I offered one way in which such a justification might go, but certainly fell well short of showing that in being loyal to our parents, we are indirectly maximizing utility, or following the impartial moral law, or anything like that.

If I am on the right track here, then it must be the case that the full justification for loyal thought and conduct cannot always correspond to the motivations of the loyal individual. The full explanation of why it is good to be loyal to your parents, for example, may appeal to impartial principles, but a loyal child is not always moved by impartial considerations. Such a discrepancy between justifying reasons and motives is often seen as involving alienation or schizophrenia.[2] In discussing how the norms of friendship stand with regard to epistemic norms, I suggested that the process of detaching ourselves from the loyal perspective and interrogating it in light of broader considerations is not so unfamiliar, and not so alienating. Perhaps the psychology involved can be described so that it looks sensible and sophisticated, not schizophrenic.

That is how I see the considerations discussed in the main body of the book as bearing upon the problem that loyalty poses for Enlightenment morality. There is obviously much more to be said. In any event, part of the point of the book is to show that loyalty raises many ethical issues beyond this one, and that the problem of how loyalty should figure in foundational ethical theory does not need to be solved before the other issues are confronted.

[2] See especially Stocker, "The Schizophrenia of Modern Ethical Theories."

Bibliography

R. T. Allen, "When Loyalty No Harm Meant," *Review of Metaphysics* 43 (1989): 281–294.

Neera Kapur Badhwar (ed.), *Friendship: A Philosophical Reader* (Ithaca: Cornell University Press, 1993).

Annette Baier, "Unsafe Loves," in Robert C. Solomon and Kathleen M. Higgins (eds.), *The Philosophy of (Erotic) Love* (University Press of Kansas, 1991), pp. 433–450.

Marcia Baron, "Patriotism and 'Liberal' Morality," in D. Weissbord (ed.), *Mind, Value and Culture: Essays in Honor of E. M. Adams* (Atascadero, CA: Ridgeview, 1989), pp. 269–300. Reprinted with modifications in Igor Primoratz (ed.), *Patriotism* (Amherst, NY: Humanity Books, 2002), pp. 59–86.

"Impartiality and Friendship," *Ethics* 101:4 (1991): 836–857.

Jeremy Bentham, *An Introduction to the Principles of Morals and Legislation* (New York: Prometheus Books, 1992 (orig. 1823)).

Fred R. Berger, "Gratitude," *Ethics* 85:4 (1975): 298–309.

Lawrence Blum, *Friendship, Altruism and Morality* (London: Routledge & Kegan Paul, 1980).

Jeffrey Blustein, *Parents and Children* (Oxford University Press, 1982).

Eugene E. Brussel (ed.), *Webster's New World Dictionary of Quotable Definitions* 2nd edn. (Englewood Cliffs, NJ: Prentice Hall, 1988).

Lynne Cheney, *America: A Patriotic Primer* (New York: Simon and Schuster, 2002).

Dean Cocking and Jeanette Kennett, "Friendship and the Self," *Ethics* 108 (1998): 502–527.

"Friendship and Moral Danger," *The Journal of Philosophy* 97:5 (2000): 257–277.

Dean Cocking and Justin Oakley, "Indirect Consequentialism, Friendship, and the Problem of Alienation," *Ethics* 106:1 (1995): 86–111.

Norman Daniels, *Am I My Parents' Keeper?* (Oxford University Press, 1988).

Neil Delaney, "Romantic Love and Loving Commitment: Articulating a Modern Ideal," *American Philosophical Quarterly* 33 (1996): 338–340.

Mary G. Dietz, "Patriotism: A Brief History of the Term," in Igor Primoratz (ed.), *Patriotism* (Amherst, NY: Humanity Books, 2002), pp. 201–215.

Nicholas Dixon, "The Friendship Model of Filial Obligations," *Journal of Applied Philosophy* 12:1 (1995): 77–87.

Julia Driver, "The Virtues of Ignorance," *Journal of Philosophy* 86 (1989): 373–384.

Jane English, "What Do Grown Children Owe Their Parents?," in Onora O'Neill and William Ruddick (eds.), *Having Children* (Oxford University Press, 1979), pp. 351–356.

R. E. Ewin, "Loyalty and Virtues," *The Philosophical Quarterly* 42:169 (1992): 403–419.

"Loyalties, and Why Loyalty Should be Ignored," *Criminal Justice Ethics* 12:1 (1993): 36–43.

"Corporate Loyalty: Its objects and its grounds," *Journal of Business Ethics* 12:5 (1993): 387–396.

John Martin Fischer and Mark Ravizza (eds.), *Perspectives on Moral Responsibility* (Cornell University Press, 1993).

Patrick Fitzgerald, "Gratitude and Justice," *Ethics* 109:1 (1998): 119–153.

George P. Fletcher, *Loyalty* (Oxford University Press, 1993).

Harry G. Frankfurt, "Autonomy, Necessity and Love," in Frankfurt, *Necessity, Volition and Love* (Cambridge University Press, 1999), pp. 129–141.

William Godwin, *An Enquiry Concerning Political Justice* (London: G. G. J. and J. Robinson, 1793).

Paul Gomberg, "Patriotism Is Like Racism," *Ethics* 101 (1990): 144–150.

"Patriotism in Sports and in War," in Claudio Tamburrini and Torbjorn Tannsjo (eds.), *Values in Sport* (New York: Taylor and Francis, 2000), pp. 87–98.

James Griffin, *Well-Being* (Oxford University Press, 1986).

Michael O. Hardimon, "Role Obligations," *The Journal of Philosophy* 91:7 (1994): 333–363.

Thomas Hurka, *Virtue, Vice and Value* (Oxford University Press, 2001).

Rosalind Hursthouse, *On Virtue Ethics* (Oxford University Press, 1999).

Philip J. Ivanhoe, "Filial Piety as a Virtue," forthcoming in Rebecca Walker and Ivanhoe (eds.), *Working Virtue: Virtue Ethics and Contemporary Moral Problems* (Oxford University Press, 2006).

William James, "The Will to Believe," in James, *The Will to Believe and Other Essays in Popular Philosophy* (New York: Longmans, Green and Co., 1927), pp. 1–31.

Nancy S. Jecker, "Are Filial Duties Unfounded?," *American Philosophical Quarterly* 26:1 (1989): 73–80.

Shelly Kagan, "The Limits of Well-Being," in Ellen Frankel Paul, Fred D. Miller Jr. and Jeffrey Paul (eds.), *The Good Life and the Human Good* (Cambridge University Press, 1992), pp. 169–189.

Immanuel Kant, *Groundwork of the Metaphysics of Morals*, trans. Mary Gregor (Cambridge University Press, 1997 (orig. 1785)).

George Kateb, "Is Patriotism a Mistake?," *Social Research* 67:4 (2000): 910–924.

Simon Keller, "How Do I Love Thee? Let Me Count the Properties," *American Philosophical Quarterly* 37 (2000): 163–173.

"Welfare and the Achievement of Goals," *Philosophical Studies* 21 (2004): 27–41.

Pauline Kleingeld, "Kantian Patriotism," *Philosophy and Public Affairs* 29 (2000): 313–341.

Joseph Kupfer, "Can Parents and Children be Friends?," *American Philosophical Quarterly* 27:1 (1990): 15–26.

John Ladd, entry on "Loyalty" in Paul Edwards (editor-in-chief), *The Encyclopedia of Philosophy* (New York: Macmillan and the Free Press, 1967), pp. 97–98.

David Lewis, "Finkish Dispositions," *Philosophical Quarterly* 47 (1997): 143–158.

Catherine Lu, "The One and Many Faces of Cosmopolitanism," *The Journal of Political Philosophy* 8 (2000): 244–267.

David McCabe, "Patriotic Gore, Again," *Southern Journal of Philosophy* 35 (1997): 203–223.

Alasdair MacIntyre, *After Virtue* (University of Notre Dame Press, 1981).

"Is Patriotism a Virtue?," The E. H. Lindley Lecture, University of Kansas, 1984. Reprinted in Igor Primoratz (ed.), *Patriotism* (Amherst, NY: Humanity Books, 2002), pp. 43–58.

Katie McShane, "Why Environmental Ethics Shouldn't Give Up on Intrinsic Value," forthcoming in *Environmental Ethics*.

Rian Malan, *My Traitor's Heart* (New York: The Atlantic Monthly Press, 1990).

John Stuart Mill, *Utilitarianism* (Indianapolis: Hackett, 1979).

Lydia Moland, "Whose Greater Good? Virtue, Cosmopolitanism and Reform in 18th and 19th Century German Patriotism," manuscript, Babson College.

Stephen Mulhall and Adam Swift, *Liberals and Communitarians* (Oxford: Blackwell, 1992).

Stephen Nathanson, *Patriotism, Morality and Peace* (Lanham, MD: Rowman and Littlefield, 1993).

Robert Nozick, *Anarchy, State, and Utopia* (New York: Basic Books, 1974).

The Examined Life (New York: Simon and Schuster, 1989).

Martha C. Nussbaum, "Patriotism and Cosmopolitanism," published along with numerous replies in Nussbaum, *For Love of Country?* (Boston: Beacon Press, 2002).

Andrew Oldenquist, "Loyalties," *Journal of Philosophy* 79 (1982): 173–193.

Derek Parfit, *Reasons and Persons* (Oxford University Press, 1984).

Philip Pettit, "The Paradox of Loyalty," *American Philosophical Quarterly* 25:2 (1988): 163–171.

Igor Primoratz, "Patriotism: Morally Allowed, Required, or Valuable?," in N. Miscevic (ed.), *Nationalism and Ethnic Conflict: Philosophical Perspectives* (Chicago and LaSalle, IL: Open Court, 2000), pp. 101–113. Reprinted in Primoratz (ed.), *Patriotism* (Amherst, NY: Humanity Books, 2002), pp. 187–199.

"Patriotism: Mundane and Ethical," *Croatian Journal of Philosophy* IV (2004): 83–100.

Peter Railton, "Alienation, Consequentialism, and the Demands of Morality," *Philosophy and Public Affairs*, 13:2 (1984): 134–171.

John Rawls, *A Theory of Justice* (Cambridge, MA: Harvard University Press, 1971).

Amélie O. Rorty, "The Historicity of Psychological Attitudes: Love Is Not Love Which Alters Not When It Alteration Finds," *Midwest Studies in Philosophy* 10 (1986): 399–412.

Richard Rorty, *Contingency, Irony, and Solidarity* (Cambridge University Press, 1989).

"Justice as a Larger Loyalty," *Ethical Perspectives* 4:3 (1997): 139–149.

Josiah Royce, *The Philosophy of Loyalty* (Vanderbilt University Press, 1995 (orig. 1908)).

Michael J. Sandel, *Liberalism and the Limits of Justice* (Cambridge University Press, 1982).

Jean-Paul Sartre, *Being and Nothingness* (London: Routledge, 1969).

Judith N. Shklar, *Ordinary Vices* (Harvard University Press, 1984).

Henry Sidgwick, *The Methods of Ethics* 7th edn. (London: Hackett, 1981 (orig. 1907)).

A. John Simmons, *Moral Principles and Political Obligations* (Princeton University Press, 1979).

"Human Rights and World Citizenship: The Universality of Human Rights in Kant and Locke," in Simmons, *Justification and Legitimacy: Essays on Rights and Obligations* (Cambridge: Cambridge University Press, 2001), pp. 179–196.

Michael Slote, "Obedience and Illusions," in Onora O'Neill and William Ruddick (eds.), *Having Children* (Oxford University Press, 1979), pp. 319–326.

Christina Hoff Sommers, "Filial Morality," *The Journal of Philosophy* 83:8 (1986): 439–456.

Michael Stocker, "The Schizophrenia of Modern Ethical Theories," *The Journal of Philosophy*, 73:14 (1976): 453–466.

"How Emotions Reveal Value and Help Cure the Schizophrenia of Modern Ethical Theories," in Roger Crisp (ed.), *How Should One Live? Essays on the Virtues* (Oxford University Press, 1996), pp. 173–190.

Sarah Stroud, "Epistemic Partiality in Friendship," *Ethics*, 116 (2006): 498–524.

L. W. Sumner, *Welfare, Happiness and Ethics* (Oxford University Press, 1996).

Charles Taylor, "Cross-Purposes: The Liberal-Communitarian Debate," in Taylor, *Philosophical Arguments* (Harvard University Press, 1995), pp. 181–203.

Laurence Thomas, *Living Morally: A Psychology of Moral Character* (Temple University Press, 1989).

Thucydides, *History of the Peloponnesian War*, trans. Rex Warner (East Rutherford, NJ: Penguin, 1972).

Hans L. Trefousse, *Carl Schurz: A Biography* (New York: Fordham University Press, 1998).

J. David Velleman, "Love as a Moral Emotion," *Ethics* 109:2 (1999): 338–374.

Mark R. Wicclair, "Caring for Frail Elderly Parents: Past Parental Sacrifices and the Obligations of Adult Children," *Social Theory and Practice* 16:2 (1990): 163–189.

Bernard Williams, "A Critique of Utilitarianism," in J. J. C. Smart and Williams, *Utilitarianism: For and Against* (Cambridge University Press, 1973), pp. 77–150.

"Deciding to Believe," in Williams, *Problems of the Self* (Cambridge University Press, 1973), pp. 136–151.

"Persons, Character and Morality," in Williams, *Moral Luck* (Cambridge University Press, 1981), pp. 1–19.

Ethics and the Limits of Philosophy (Harvard University Press, 1985).

Susan Wolf, "Moral Saints," *The Journal of Philosophy* 79 (1982): 419–439.

Index

229